W9-ATQ-383

ETHNICITY AND AMERICAN SOCIAL THEORY

Toward Critical Pluralism

Gerard A. Postiglione

UNIVERSITY
PRESS OF
AMERICA

LANHAM • NEW YORK • LONDON

4720 Boston Way
Lanham, MD 20706

3 Henrietta Street
London WC2E 8LU England

Printed in the United States of America

ISBN (Perfect): 0-8191-3452-X
ISBN (Cloth): 0-8191-3451-1

TO MY FATHER AND MOTHER

Contents

Preface

This book is primarily designed to be a supplementary text for undergraduate and graduate social science courses variously entitled "ethnic group relations", "American ethnicity", "ethnic and racial studies", and others whose main topic is ethnic intergroup relations in the United States. Related interdisciplinary courses such as "American studies", "urban policy analysis", and "contemporary ethnology" will also find this book to be a useful course supplement. Moreover, general readers having an interest in the concept of ethnicity will find this to be a reasonable introduction to the ideas surrounding this area of study. It will lead both types of readers towards a fuller understanding of where the United States gathered its most sophisticated notions of ethnic intergroup processes.

My main purpose in this book is to provide the student and the general reader with an alternative way of approaching the field of ethnicity. Unlike other textbooks in the field, this one takes a decidedly different approach by focusing on certain major figures in American intellectual history who forged the fundamental unit ideas on this subject. Five individuals were chosen, each of whom represents one of the five major theoretical models of American ethnicity. Their ideas on ethnicity in the United States will be exposed, broken down into parts, and compared. It will be possible to discern a pattern in the historical progression of ideas through the five theorists, especially as seen from the consistent theme of pluralism. At the same time each of these theories will be viewed against the backround of macro-sociological theory to see how each theory aligns itself with functionalism and conflict theory. In this sense, this is a book on the sociology of ethnicity.

In the time since I began putting this work together, I have lived and moved, taught and researched across three continents. There are a multitude of people in between to thank for sharing their society and culture in a way that made me truly appreciate the meaning of being a member of a multi-cultural world and a multi-ethnic society – the United States of America. It is to these people, especially my students among them, that I express thanks for the precious opportunity to understand the subject to which the five theorists in this book dedicated their lives – the processes that occur when people of different ethnic groups come together.

GERARD POSTIGLIONE
MAY 1, 1983
HONG KONG

Acknowledgements

I wish to thank the members of the Foundations of Education Department at SUNY Albany for their time, assistance, patience, and support. I am speaking in particular of Mark Berger, Frank Femminella, Hy Kuritz, Sandra Peterson-Hardt, Jim McClellan, Linda Nicholson, Joe Scimecca, and Paul Vogt. Also, my gratitude goes to Professor Paul Meadows of the Sociology Department for consistently expressing an interest in my work, and to Professor Arnold Foster for his fresh insights during the final stages of the original draft in New York.

I should also like to thank my fellow colleagues Barbara Sjostrom, Richard Leveroni, Tim McLean, Eduardo Suarez, Dennis Reichard, Shari Popen, Jenifer Whittle, Liliana Vogt, Bill Hedberg, Arnold Sherman, Bob Pring, Edith Bjorn, Shirley Sartori, and Michele Kegan for their interest in my work. An extra special thanks goes to Peter Stoll because of his remarkable enthusiasm for all aspects of the study of ethnicity. The earlier draft of this project would not have been completed had it not been for the assistance of Nancy Papish and Cecilia Ormsby. Mrs. Ormsby must be given credit for doing a splendid job in converting my scribblings into neat typewritten pages, right down to the last pages mailed from Adana, Turkey.

Since leaving the United States in 1979 I had the fortune of teaching courses in the sociology of American society to students in Germany, Italy, and Turkey. These students deserve my deep felt acknowledgements for their perseverence and the challenges they offered my teaching. A word of thanks also goes to my colleagues at the University of Maryland's European Division and at the University of Hong Kong who expressed an interest in my work. Also, Herbert Pierson and Norma Holbrook gave their assistance in reading the manuscript. Angela Yan of the University of Hong Kong Library helped with the indexing. Finally, I thank Y.K. Fung of the Hong Kong

University Press for his assistance in the preparation of the manuscript and Jan Scriven for her extremely useful editorial comments. Naturally, I alone am responsible for any errors in the book.

PART ONE

INTRODUCTION

American sociology has never managed to come to grips with the idea of ethnicity.

Harold J. Abramson
1982

I American Ethnicity

With the approach of the 1980's it became more and more apparent that American ethnicity would retain a position as a central element in the increasingly complex equation of culture and social structure in the United States. The ethnic dimension of American life was no longer expected to completely fade away over time. The expectation that it would, has all but disappeared. Even the meaning of the term itself had gone through change. Two notable contemporary theorists who have examined the ethnic element of social life within American society and also throughout other world communities have commented on the centrality of ethnicity in modern society.

> Formally seen as survivals from an earlier age, to be treated variously with annoyance, toleration, and mild celebration, we now have a growing sense that they (ethnic groups) may be *forms* of social life capable of renewing and transforming themselves . . . we are suggesting that a new word reflects a new reality and a new usage reflects a change in that reality. The new word is "ethnicity", and the new usage is the steady expansion of the term "ethnic group" from minority to marginal subgroups at the edge of society – groups expected to assimilate, to disappear, to continue as survivals, exotic or troublesome – to major elements of a society . . . there is something new afoot in the world, and we may label it "ethnicity"[1].

The roots of the sociological study of ethnic groups in the United States can be traced back to the early part of the twentieth century. Ethnic groups began to draw the attention of sociologists not only because the question of immigration had become a great concern to the American public but also because of the appearance of an ascendent current in sociology called the "Chicago School". It was with the sociologists of this school that the area of study known as urban sociology was born. The focus on the dynamic social processes of the vastly growing American cities widened to include more and more phenomena. One of the major pieces of the complex urban scheme was the new pattern of ethnic pluralism that was arising. Well known studies in this era of the sociological study of ethnicity included Robert E. Park's *Race and Culture*[2], W.I. Thomas and Florian Znaniecki's *The Polish Peasant in Europe and America*[3], Harvey Zorbaugh's *The Gold Coast and the Slum*[4], and Louis Wirth's *The Ghetto*[5]. Each of these works touched upon the common problem that concerned all immigrant groups in the United States, that of assimilation and acculturation. While other writers of the period took note that the immigrants had been thrust into a fringe existence within the confines of the ethnic enclaves that dotted the expanding cities of the nation, still others took the view that ethnic communities functioned to protect immigrants from the turbulent forces that were a constant threat to their efforts to adapt and adjust to the new environment of the host society. All seemed to agree, however, that the European immigrations had not resulted in assimilation. Rather, the emphasis was on the resultant pluralism.

During the 1930's and 1940's American sociologists began to study race relations. Before this, the early American sociologists Ward, Small, Ross, Cooley, and Giddings had written occasionally on the topic of race, yet, as E. Franklin Frazer has shown, none had contributed to the analysis of race relations in the United States.[6] This can be accounted for by the fact that some of these men were social Darwinists who, having labored under the biological doctrine of racial superiority, held that the social differences between the races did not represent a sociological problem. To them, it was the unalterable biological fact of race that explained differences among social groups.

As the studies of second generation ethnic groups began to appear, assimilation become the characteristic theme in the work of sociologists of ethnicity – the third volume of Lloyd Warner's "Yankee City Series", which focused on the problem of ethnic communities, was an example of this.[7] Also, Irvin L. Child's *Italian or American?*[8] and P.S. Campisi's study of Italian American family life pointed to evidence of assimilation in the structure of immigrant families.[9] Sociologists in the 1940's began to argue that assimilation was the dominant social process occuring at the time and they used changes in social class position as a key factor in the causal chain.

Marcus Lee Hansen, who wrote the noted study *The Atlantic Migration* suggested that "what the son wishes to forget, the grandson wishes to remember." This proposition, later known as Hansen's Law stated that while assimilations are useful to describe the plight of the second generation, cultural pluralism is the best explanation for the third generation. The third generation, in order to answer the question – What kind of American am I? – is thrown back upon the social identity of their grandfathers in order to avoid suffering a crisis of identity.[10]

By the 1950's religious pluralism became added to the study of American ethnicity. Ruby Jo Reeves Kennedy took the position that ethnic intermarriage was taking place but offered evidence to support the contention that this phenomenon was taking place only within each of the three major religious communities. She concluded that American pluralism was a triple melting pot in which assimilation occurred *within* the Protestant, Catholic, and Jewish groups, but the characteristic relationship between these groups remained one of cultural pluralism.[11] Soon after this, Will Herberg added support to this thesis in his essay *Protestant, Catholic, Jew.*[12] He argued that ethnic differences primarily defined on the basis of national origin were disappearing with the result being that the major American communities of belonging and identity were becoming redefined along the axis of religion.

Sociologists of the 1950's and 1960's began to look toward the suburbs in order to understand American ethnicity. Herbert Gans' *The Urban Villagers* and *The Levittowners,* and Bennett Berger's *Working Class Suburbs* added further support to the previously disputed notion that the suburbs exhibited social class pluralism, but also illustrated that both ethnic and religious difference were significant aspects of suburban life.[13] In short, it began to appear that the ethnic enclaves of the city had not disappeared but were simply being transported to the suburbs.

Beginning in the 1970's, the sociology of ethnicity developed increasing research interest around the pluralisms that existed among Black, Hispanic, Asian and Native American communities. For example, Thomas Sowell noted and traced Black history in the United States according to three groups: free persons of color; emancipated slaves and their dependants; and West Indian immigrants.[14] William Peterson reinforced awareness of the different histories of Chinese and Japanese Americans.[15] The heterogeneity among Americans of Mexican Cuban and Puerto Rican descent became more evident in the use of the term Hispanic-American. And Murray Wax's research on Indian Amerians made clear the diversity that continued to exist among the tribal peoples of Native-American heritage.[16]

Throughout the 1970s American ethnicity became a phrase on the move. It came to represent an essential dimension of American society and an equally important aspect of American culture. American ethnicity had not only shaped the character of American society, but, in structural terms, it had forged a new set of relationships between members of ethnic groups within the major institution of the society. Sociologists of this period such as Nathan Glazer, Andrew Greeley, Milton Gordon, Michael Novak, Michael Parenti, Thomas Pettigrew and F.X. Femminella further defined the notion of ethnic identity until by the end of the decade it became a key concept in the study of ethnic intergroup relations.[17]

As the 1980's unfold, the puzzle of American ethnicity promises to reveal more of its parts in detail. At the same time it will continue to demand a more critical look at both old and new situations. On the one hand, there is a need to trace the path that new immigrant groups are taking as they forge their way into the dynamic American mainstream, and, on the other hand, it remains important to keep abreast of the continued movement of established ethnic formations as they move across the American landscape. Recent works such as Richard Pollenberg's *One Nation Divisible* make clear that the ethnic equation in the United States remains complex.[18]

Almost synonomous with American ethnicity, has always been the notion of pluralism. The relationship between this type of pluralism and the wider context of the "multiple pluralisms" of American society is a central one. Social life in American can be examined in terms of a number of different elemental forces, each one leaving its individual imprint and contributing to larger overlapping patterns of complexity that render a specific character to American society. Pulling these intricate patterns apart is the work of sociologists of American society and focusing the sociological tweezers on the veins of ethnic phenomena is the work of sociologists of American ethnicity. One of the unique aspects of American society is its multiple pluralisms, but *the most* unique pluralism of all is the heritage of its people. This is without a doubt. For this reason, we elevate it to the key variable in our equation, not at the expense of any of the other pluralisms, but rather as a paradigm of that principal character.

Traditionally, American ethnicity has been studied in terms of nationality. However, the evolution of the concept "ethnicity" now allows for inclusion of a diverse number of elements (race, religion, region, nationality, etc.) all tied in some way to the notion of community. *Neighbouring* has been suggested as a term which exemplifies a major process in the formation of American ethnicity.[19] This meaning also allows for the continuing evolution of American ethnicity in which nationality represents only one part of a more complexly ordered system of elements. Future forms of American ethnicity cannot be precisely known to us now, only that they will exist and persist. This is why it is so important to understand each theory of American ethnicity within the historical context out of which it was forged. This is, in part, what this book has done. It has selected five theories of American ethnicity, each representing not only a different historical context in American society, but also a different model of the dynamics of American ethnicity. The second chapter in Part One will describe the basis upon which a critical comparison of selected representative theories of American ethnicity will be made.

Plan of this Book

Up to this point we have discussed some of the major movements in the sociology of American ethnicity with an emphasis placed on the persistence of pluralisms in the study of ethnic intergroup relations. While it is far from being an exhaustive discussion, it is adequate for setting the background from which the rest of this book can be viewed. Chapter II will look at the major questions underlying a study of social theory. An examination of the difference between myths, ideologies, and social theories will be followed by a look at the five main social scientific models most often used to explain ethnic intergroup processes in the United States. The sociological perspective will be introduced in order to help us see the critical relationship between sociological thought in general and the work of five major figures of American ethnicity theory.

Part Two will then take up the task of exposing the more important and essential elements in the writings of the major figures chosen for examination. Throughout Chapters III to VII the procedure will be to present a biographical sketch of each theorist followed by a look at major social and intellectual influences, and principal works. Finally we will focus on the central works of each author which contain his theory of American ethnicity. The intention will be to reduce each theory to its bare bones. In this way it will be possible to see more clearly the line separating theory from ideology.

Part Three will bring together all of the elements carved out in Part Two. This will allow systematic comparisons to be made. In Chapter VIII, different models of comparison are employed to show many of the different types of relationships among theories of American ethnicity. The latter parts of the chapter return to note the evolutionary pattern of the unit ideas of ethnicity and to check how each theory aligns itself with the sociological schools of functionalism and conflict theory. Finally, Chapter IX addresses the question of what direction the study of American ethnicity has taken.

Notes

1. Nathan Glazer and Daniel P. Moynihan, *Ethnicity: Theory and Experience,* Cambridge: Harvard University Press, 1975, pp. 5,6.
2. Robert E. Park, *Race and Culture,* Glencoe, Indiana: The Free Press, 1950
3. W. I. Thomas and Florian Znaniecki, *The Polish Peasant in Europe and America,* Chicago: University of Chicago Press, 1918.
4. Harvey Zorbaugh, *The Gold Coast and the Slum,* Chicago: University of Chicago Press, 1929.
5. Louis Wirth, *The Ghetto,* Chicago: University of Chicago Press, 1928.
6. E. Franklin Frazier, "Sociological Relatives and Race Relatives," in *American Sociological Review,* vol. 12, June, pp.265–271.
7. Lloyd Warner and Leo Srole, *The Social System of American Ethnic Groups,* New Haven: Yale University Press, 1945.
8. Irvin L. Child, *Italian or American?,* New Haven: Yale University Press, 1948.
9. Paul J. Campisi, "Ethnic Family Pattern: The Italian American Family in the United States," *American Journal of Sociology,* vol. 53, May, pp. 443–449.

10. Marcus Lee Hansen, *The Atlantic Migration,* Cambridge, Mass: Harvard University Press, 1942
11. Ruby Jo Reeves Kennedy, "Single or Triple Melting Pot: Intermarriage Trends in New Haven 1870–1940," in *American Journal of Sociology,* vol. 49, 1944, pp. 331–339.
12. Will Herberg, *Protestant, Catholic, Jew,* Garden City, New York: Doubleday, 1955.
13. Bennett Berger, *Working Class Suburbs,* Berkeley: University of California Press, 2nd ed., 1968; Herbert Gans, *The Urban Villagers,* New York: Free Press, 1962; and *The Levittowners,* New York: Pantheon, 1967.
14. Thomas Sowell, "Three Black Histories", in Sowell, ed., *American Ethnic Groups,* The Urban Institute, 1978.
15. William Peterson, "Chinese and Japanese Americans", in Sowell, ed., *American Ethnic Groups,* The Urban Institute, 1978.
16. Murray Wax, *Indian Americans,* Englewood Cliffs, New Jersey: Prentice Hall, 1971.
17. Nathan Glazer, with Daniel Patrick Moynihan, *Beyond The Melting Pot,* Cambridge: MIT Press, 1970; Andrew Greeley, *Ethnicity in The United States,* New York: John Wiley, 1974; Milton Gordon, *Human Nature, Class, and Ethnicity,* New York: Oxford University Press, 1978; Michael Novak, *The Rise of The Unmeltable Ethnics,* New York: MacMillan, 1972; Michael Parenti, "Ethnic Politics and the Persistence of Ethnic Identification," in *American Political Science Review* 61, Sept. 1967: 717–722; Thomas Pettigrew, "Ethnicity in American Life", in Otto Feinstein's *Ethnic Groups In The City,* New York: D.C. Heath, 1971; Francis X. Femminella, "The Immigrant and the Melting Pot", in M. Urofsky (ed), Perspectives on Urban America, New York: Doubleday Publishers, 1973.
18. Richard Pollenberg, *One Nation Divisible: Class, Race and Ethnicity in the United States since 1938,* New York: Viking Press, 1980.
19. Femminella, *Ethnicity in the Suburbs,* op. cit.

II Sociology and the Study of Ethnicity Theory

Myths, Ideologies, and Assumptions

All sociological theory is built on some set of assumptions concerning the nature of man and society. Some of these assumptions are stated explicity, others are tacit and unstated. The former, in a simple sense, refer to the formal postulates of theory, while the latter, although unstated, exert a considerable influence on the formulation of theory because they are closely related to its postulates. Alvin Gouldner, in *The Coming Crisis of Westen Sociology* (1970), refers to both types of assumptions and their relation to each other.

> I call them background assumptions because, on the one hand, they provide the background out of which the postulations emerge and, they remain in the background of the theorist's attention. . . . . Background assumptions are embedded in a theory's postulations. Operating within and alongside of them, they are, as it were, "silent partners" in the theoretical enterprise. Background assumptions provide some of the bases of choice and the invisible cement for linking together postulations. From beginning to end, they influence a theory's formulations and the research to which it leads.[1]

Background assumptions of a more limited type are called domain assumptions. The domain in the case of sociological theory includes those elements concerning the nature of man and society. In short, domain assumptions (as used in this study) are selected background assumptions concerning the nature of man and society. They are also an aspect of the larger culture that is related intimately to the postulations of theory. In this sense, they constitute part of the important connection between the theorist's work and the society within which he works. Gouldner points out how this matter has implications for the work of all sociologists.

> What I am saying, then, is that the work of sociologists, as of others, is influenced by a subtheoretical set of beliefs, for that is what background assumptions are: beliefs about all members of symbolically constituted domains. I am not saying that the work of sociologists should be influenced by background assumptions; this is a problem for methodological moralists. Nor am I saying that sociology logically requires and necessarily rests upon background assumptions; this is a problem for philosophers of science. What I am saying is that sociologists do use and are influenced by background assumptions; this is an empirical matter that sociologists themselves can study and confirm.[2]

What, then, is the connection between domain assumptions and social theory? It is clearly an integral one that can not be discounted in any comparative study of theory since domain assumption influences the formulation of theory. Gouldner again clarifies the relationship by saying that "articulated theories in part derive from, rest on, and are sustained by the usually tacit assumptions that the theorists make about the domains with which they concern themselves. Articulate social theories develop in interaction with the theorists' tacit domain assumptions."[3]

The above, being true of sociological theory in general, is also true of the theories of American ethnicity employed by sociologists to interpret ethnic interaction in the United States. To this extent there are five basic models from which theory has been derived to explain ethnic inter and intra-group dynamics within the pluralism of American society. They may be commonly referred to as Anglo-conformity, melting pot, cultural pluralism, emerging culture, and impact-integration. Before inquiring into the specifics of each theory, it is important at this point to briefly inquire into the distinction between *theory* and *ideology*.

The sometimes fine line between these two can often become clouded, particularly if one does not know how to recognize the difference. When stated, social theories and ideologies may look very similar, but their character can be distinguished in two ways: (1) theories are descriptive statements of what *is,* while ideologies are prescriptive statements of what *ought* to be, and (2) theories are scientifically testable while ideologies are not. In reality, the differences are much more complex than this. By way of definition, ideology may be used to refer to an individual's or group's coherent body of ideas, values, beliefs and ways of perceiving and legitimizing certain social arrangements. A social theory, on the other hand, may be used "to refer to a formal explanation of any social event, social process or of relationships between social phenomena."[4] While the many intricacies involved in the relation between theory and ideology are beyond the scope of this study, we can slightly expand upon this central point by referring to the work of two notable sociologists who were particularly concerned with the nature of social scientific theory.

Max Weber and Karl Mannheim can, in many ways, be considered the founders of the area of sociology that deals with the difference between theory and ideology: the sociology of knowledge. First, they both recognized that complete objectivity in social science is impossible. They reasoned that science is an institution in the society, and, like all others, it is involved with choices and values, elements which make complete objectivity rather difficult. Both, however, offer the necessary adjustments to this inevitability. The ultimate test of science, according to Mannheim, is the degree to which social theory assists men in shaping their social world and solving their social problems.[5] Characteristic of the scientific point of view, contended Weber, is the conscious attempt by the scientist to rid himself of his biases once he has selected his problem.[6]

Concerning the theories of American ethnicity, it is important to note that although used by sociologists to interpret the social processes that emerge in a pluralistic society, these theories did not all originate in the chambers of science. They were, at first, desirable, celebrated, and inherently ideological social doctrines in the United States. They developed out of social philosophies of particular time periods. As such, they have appeared as successive ideological interpretations of the meaning of American history. They were often created and developed to fulfill a hope, dream, or social ideal. As social philosophies, they have bordered on the realm of ideology. Increasingly, however, each became supplanted by the scientific role of functioning as an interpretive device. For instance, they have been used as a basis for describing and interpreting why ethnic group interactions took on certain forms rather than others, and for forecasting the type of forms they might take on in the future. The importance of the difference between the ideological nature of these social philosophies, and the interpretive nature of social scientific theory, should not be underestimated. In referring to some of these social philosophies as myths, Thomas Pettigrew remarks on this important distinction.

> America can never understand herself or achieve full justice until she strips away the intergroup myths that crowd her thinking. And replacing one myth with another is hardly an improvement. We live now in a relatively anomic period of great change and vast disillusionment. Understandably such a period has fashioned a myth of complete pluralism; that we are not only what we have claimed to be but that our nation of immigrants remains a nation of largely separated immigrants. In resisting such views we must avoid swinging the pendulum back to 1908 and the melting pot. Merely rejecting myths is not enough. We need to look at ourselves coldly and boldly, to ply the developing tools of social science to best advantage, and to learn more about the complexity and subtlety of our nation's intergroup relations that cannot be captured in memorable metaphors or dogmatic ideologies.[7]

With this background in mind, we can now specify what we refer to as a theory of American ethnicity simply as a theory employed by sociologists to interpret those processes that occur when people of different ethnic groups come together. Here, the term ethnic group is used to designate an involuntary group of people (within a larger society) having real or putative common ancestral origin and the same cultural traits, who have a sense of peoplehood and a gemeinschaft type of relations, and who are of migrant background.[8]

The Theories of American Ethnicity

We can now begin to approach, specifically, the theoretical models utilized by sociolgists to interpret American ethnicity. To this extent there have been five. Though each of these may contain two or more theoretical strains, they nonetheless represent variations on a common theme. Moreover, each model may in some way intersect at certain points with, or, grow out of another. Based upon the previous discussion concerning the relationship between assumptions, theory, and ideology, each of the five models will be approached in the following way. First, each will be viewed from the social and cultural context out of which it arose. Particular individuals will be identified to the degree that they made a major contribution to the shape and form of a major theory of American ethnicity. Second, we will look at the social scientific refinement and reformulation of these theories.[9]

Anglo-Conformity

The first theory of American ethnicity, "Anglo-conformity" may be represented in the equation $A < - > B = A$. In this case, 'A' represents the dominant status culture of the host population; the double arrow represents the interaction that takes place; and B represents the new immigrant group (the subordinate status culture). It is the contention of this theory that group B will take on the characteristic values, attributes, and ways of life of A because A is a "superior group." The ideological tone of this theory becomes immediately apparent; a scientific theory does not recognize the fact that one culture can be "better" than another.

This social theory originated in 17th century America wherein the English settlers dominated all others and suceeded in establishing their ways as the norm for all. However, it became strengthened and popularized in the late 19th and early 20th century. It asserted that the culture of the Aryan and Nordic races of northern and western Europe was superior to those of the peoples of southern and eastern Europe. It was commonly believed that the inferior cultural groups posed a serious threat to the structure of American society during this historical period. The Anglo-conformity social doctrine was later used as a justification for changes in immigration policies which, in effect, further restricted the entrance of eastern and southern Europeans into the country.

The character of the southern and eastern European groups (among which included Poles, Czechs, Italians, Russians, Greeks and Jews) was thought to include dishonesty, poverty, uncleanliness, and subversive anarchistic political goals. Much support for this Anglo-conformity social doctrine was drawn from Charles Darwin's theory of evolution. In short, the theory stated that human history was to be understood in successive evolutionary phases. Therefore, reasoned many of its supporters, one race must represent the most highly evolved race, and, as the argument went, presumably this was the race of northwestern Europe.

A staunch supporter of the Anglo-conformity doctrine was Madison Grant, a lawyer and leader of the American restrictionists who pressed for immigration legislation in the 1920's. He believed that in order to keep America "pure," it would have to exclude many inferior *races* such as Poles, Italians, Chinese and Blacks. In his book, *The Passing of the Great Race* (1916), Grant interpreted the result of the new immigration.

> The result was the new immigration, while it still included many strong elements from the north of Europe, contained a large and increasing number of the weak, the broken, and the mentally crippled of all races drawn from the lowest stratum of the Mediterranean basin and the Balkans, together with hordes of the wretched, submerged populations of the Polish ghettos.[10]

Other proponents of the Anglo-conformity doctrine included Henry Pratt Fairchild (1926), Howard C. Hill (1919), and Ellwood P. Cubberly (1929).[11] Referring to the immigrants, Cubberly, a prominent educator of the time, observed:

> Everywhere these people tend to settle in groups and settlements, and to set up their national manner, custom, and obvervances. Our task is to break up these groups or settlements, to assimilate and amalgamate these people as a part of our American race, to implant in their children, so far as can be done, the Anglo-conception of righteousness, law and order, and popular government, and to awaken in them a reverence for our democratic institutions and for those things in our national life which we as people hold to be of abiding worth.[12]

The line separating the ideology of Anglo-conformity from the social scientific theory is drawn on the grounds concerning how and why a group becomes the dominant culture. Ideologically, it is simply because it "should" be that way; it is because the culture of one group is "better" than that of another. The social scientific theory of Anglo-conformity recognizes, however, that one culture prevails over another, not due to trait superiority, but rather because of social arrangements of historical circumstance and the power structures which it entails. The direction of assimilation depends, then, on the accessibility to social power actions which each group commands.

Melting Pot

The second theory of American ethnicity, the "melting pot," may be represented by the equation $A < - > B = C$. In this case, A represents the dominant status culture of the host population and B represents the immigrant newcomer, as they interact, C becomes the synthesis of their traits. This synthesis, however, according to the ideological doctrine of melting pot, implies a coming together of the "best" traits of each of the cultures. Clearly, a social scientific theory could not reconcile *this* notion of "best."

This social theory is often viewed as a minority response to the great Atlantic migration. Although the notion of different nationalities "melting" together dates back to the eighteenth century in the writings of Hector St. John de Crevecoeur, it did not become popularized as a minority response until Israel Zangwill's interpretation of it in the early twentieth century. Crevecoeur, a writer and agriculturalist, published his reflections and observations in *Letters from an American Farmer* in 1782: "Who," he asks, "is the American?"

> What then is the American, this new man? He is either a European or a descendent of a European, hence, this strange mixture of blood, which you will find in no other country. I could point out to you a family whose grandfather was an Englishman, whose wife was Dutch, whose son married a French woman, and whose present four sons have now four wives of different nations. *He* is an American, who, leaving behind him all his ancient prejudices and manners, receives new ones from the new mode of life he has embraced, the new government he obeys, and the new rank he holds. He became an American by being received into the broad lap of our great *Alma Mater.* Here all individuals are melted into a new race of men, whose labors and posterity may someday cause great changes in the world.[13]

Another early formulator and adherent of a type of melting pot philosophy was Frederick Jackson Turner. In 1893, as a young historian from Wisconsin, he read a paper entitled "The Significance of the Frontier in American History" before the American Historical Society. The main thesis of the paper was that the shaping of American institutions and American democracy was the experience created by a moving and diverse frontier. The frontier, he believed, and not the European heritage, was the most significant contributor to development of a unified nationality of American people. He states:

> The frontier promoted the formation of a composite nationality for the American people . . . In the crucible of the frontier the immigrants were Americanized, liberated, and fused into a mixed race. English is neither nationality nor characterisitics. The process has gone on from the early days to our own.[14]

The term "melting pot" itself was taken from the title of a play by the Jewish immigrant Israel Zangwill. In his play *The Melting Pot,* first performed in 1908, David, the Russian Jewish immigrant cries out:

> America is God's crucible, the great melting pot where all the races of Europe are melting and reforming. Here you stand, good folk, think I, when I see them at Ellis Island, here you stand in your fifty groups, with your fifty languages and histories, and your fifty blood feuds, hatreds, and rivalries. But you won't be long like that, brother, for there are the fires of God you've come to – these are the fires of God. A fig for your feuds and vendettas, Germans and Frenchmen, Irishmen and Englishmen, Jews and Russians – into the crucible with you all. God is making the American.[15]

Later, Ruby Jo Reeves Kennedy and Will Herberg began to revise the melting pot theory and argued for the notion of multiple melting pots – one for each of the major religious groups.[16]

The line separating the ideological from the scientific aspect of the melting pot theory is drawn on grounds concerning which are the so-called "best" traits that will merge to create the new social order. Again, the sociological theory of melting pot would not reflect the specification of "best" or "worst". It would focus instead on the situational factors which yield association, alliance, or consanguinity between the different cultural groups that are merging.

Cultural Pluralism

The third theory of American ethnicity, "cultural pluralism," may be represented by the equation $A < - > B = A+B$. In this case, A and B are different status cultures which, over time, retain their own unique individual character and traits. Each group retains an identity, while at the same time, the society allows for a peaceful coexistence among the groups. More recent reformulations of this theory of American ethnicity help to emphasize that, although each cultural group retains its own distinct identity, it also interacts with other groups, and to a degree, takes on other traits such as a common language.

Although this notion hinged on John Dewey's idea of democratic pluralism, the central author of this view was Horace Kallen. It is important to note that even though this theory, unlike the previous two, originated in a more scholarly climate, it did, nevertheless, have an ideological dimension. Kallen was born in Germany of Jewish parents and came to the United States as a child. After graduate school he become a professor of philosophy and psychology. It was Kallen's view that each individual culture, as a unit, contributed something unique, positive, and valuable to American society. It was also his view that although a man may choose his social relationships and identities voluntarily, he can not choose his ancestry, and therefore it will be unlikely that a man will forget if he is German, Italian, Chinese, etc. Kallen believed that:

> Cultural pluralism is possible only in a democratic society whose institutions encourage individuality in groups, in persons, in temperaments, whose program liberates those individuals and guides them into a fellowship of freedom and cooperation . . . What is inalienable in the life of mankind is its intrinsic positive quality – its psycho-physical inheritance. Men may change their clothes, their politics, their wives, their religion, their philosophies, to a greater or lesser extent: they can not change their grandfathers. Jews, or Poles, or Anglo-Saxons, in order to cease

> being Jews, or Poles, or Anglo-Saxons, would have to cease to be. The selfhood which is inalienable in them, and for the realization of which they require "inalienable" liberty, is ancestrally determined, and the happiness which they pursue has its form implied in ancestral endowment.[17]

The idea of cultural pluralism was later adopted by another immigrant writer, Louis Adamic. He employed the poet Walt Whitman's phrase "a nation of nations," to underline the significance of America's multi-cultural composition. One of his goals was to make Americans conscious of what they owed to *all* its ethnic groups, not just Anglo-Saxons. He believed that the children of immigrants must be taught to be proud of their cultural heritage otherwise they would grow in a sense of ethnic inferiority and rootlessness. Other proponents of cultural pluralism included Isaac Berkson (1920) and Julius Drachsler (1920).[18]

The cultural pluralism doctrine has been of great ideological aid to many minority groups in asserting their identities. However, as a scientific theory, cultural pluralism can not confine its reliance to the origins of a phenomenon (in this case, cultural groups), (although it is scientifically useful to know this). A sociological theory of cultural pluralism must direct its attention to the question of why and under what social conditions and political and economic pressures do particular cultural groups retain their distincitive character while existing in the context of a larger society.

Emerging Culture

The fourth theory of American ethnicity, "emerging culture," may be represented by the following equation, $A <-> B = AB$. In this case, the product of the interaction of the two status cultures, is represented by AB. AB stands for a cultural form that is neither A nor B, but is a new form combining A and B in a dynamic relationship. In this process, an Italian becomes an Italian-American, an Arab becomes an Arab-American, a Vietnamese becomes a Vietnamese-American, and so forth. Although each group remains different from one another, they are also different from the original group in the sense that an Irish-American is different from an Irishman, a Black-American in different from a Black-African, a Japanese-American is different from a Japanese, etc. In the context of the emerging culture theory, the culture of the United States emerges a little different; its values are altered; its norms are transformed (however slight); the American way of life is in some way modified with the arrival and incorporation of each new immigrant group. This process happens over and over again. Each group moves toward the other in some respects. For example, the immigrant newcomer acquires the language of the dominant status culture of the host society, and the latter, in dealing with the former in political and economic contexts, adapts itself accordingly. The image presented is a dynamic one, continually changing and evolving as new groups enter the "emerging American culture." A new culture arises from this process for each group including the Anglo-American who is no longer viewed as just an American, but rather as an ethnic American.

Like cultural pluralism, and unlike Anglo-conformity and melting pot, the theory of emerging culture began with scholars of American society. Nathan Glazer and Daniel Moynihan (1970), Francis X. Femminella (1976), Andrew Greeley (1975), and Michael Novak (1972) have contributed to this view in one way or another.[20] All have realized the continuing significance of the role of ethnicity in modern American culture, and that American culture could not be fully understood in terms of "straight-line" assimilation.

It is the contention of Glazer and Moynihan that existing groups, through their experience in the nation, acquire different meanings. This happens first, when each ethnic group becomes a community of membership. This provides each individual with a way of knowing who he or she is. Although still located within the larger society, they derive a large part of their identity from the ethnic group. Secondly, each ethnic group becomes politically organized. As hypenated-Americans they can politically acquire their share of society's reward. Regarding ethnicity, Glazer and Moynihan state:

> Ethnicity is more than an influence on events; it is commonly the source of events. Social and political institutions do not merely respond to ethnic interests; a great number of institutions exist for the specific purpose of serving ethnic interests. This in turn, perpetuates them.[21]

Michael Novak, in his book, *The Rise of the Unmeltable Ethnics* (1972), combines a political radicalism with a cultural conservatism in defining an ethnic group:

> What is an ethnic group? It is a group with historical memory, real or imaginary. One belongs to an ethnic group in part involuntarily, in part by choice. Given a grandparent or two, one chooses to shape one's consciousness by one history rather than another. Ethnic memory is not a set of events remembered, but rather a set of instincts, feelings, intimacies, expectations, patterns, of emotion and behavior; a sense of reality; a set of stories for individuals – and for the people as a whole – to live out.[22]

Because the theme of emerging culture combines both notions of Anglo-conformity and cultural pluralism, a sociological theory in this area must focus on the processes by which groups adapt to the diversity of new environments. Concerning a scientific theory in this mode, Greeley (1975) suggests:

> . . . one can only begin to explain the considerable cultural diversity that exists among American ethnic groups if one begins to investigate the natural history of such groups. There seems to be no way in which sociologists and historians can avoid cooperating with each other on this project . . . Perhaps the single most important issue to be faced by the historian and sociologist is the question of family structure and childhood socialization practices, for these two phenomena represent the basic mechanisms by which ethnic culture and implicit ethnic heritage are transmitted.[23]

Impact-Integration

The fifth theory of American ethnicity, "impact-integration," may be represented by the formula $A < - > B = ab$. In this process, occurring between two ethnic status cultures, a synthesis occurs which unites but does not homogenize the two groups. This "collision" of the two groups impacts one into the other so totally that they become integrated.[24] Each cultural group is in some ways like the original cultural group but has changed as a result of its intersecting experiences with other groups. The final process is an integrated, yet dynamic, synthesis of groups. Impact-integration is represented similarly to the formula given for the emerging culture theory. This can partly be explained by the fact that the former in some respects grew out of the latter. Although they are by no means alike, the theory of impact-integration adds explanatory power to the theory of emerging culture by more closely specifying the dynamics involved in "inter- and intra-ethnic group dynamics." It is from this focus that a new theoretical explanation is generated. It acts to enhance the emerging culture theory and adds precision to it by complementing it with a micro-level analytical component. The difference is largely one of emphasis on the "process character" of the interaction. Nathan Glazer first systematically applied the term *integration* to the study of ethnic groups. For him, immigrants are integrated with Americans when: (1) they no longer present any special problem; (2) their old-nation political interests are subordinate to United States interests; and (3) when, in the United-Statesian culture which they have changed, they as well as old United Statesians are at home.[25]

Although Nathan Glazer adapted many of the parameters of the terms "integration" to the study of American culture, the most precisely articulated version of this theory was presented by F.X. Femminella. The term "impact" was used by Femminella in denoting the process by which certain cultural factors of ethnic groups come together. In this context, the term suggests *"a booming collision* resulting in a forced entanglement."[26] The complex forces of this "cultural collision," however, yield to the dynamics of a creative aftermath. The reaction of the dominant ethnic group in the society may be one of territoriality because it views the immigrants as invading strangers. Femminella describes this process.

> The core of the dominant ethnic group of a society reacts territorially to the immigration of a large number of newcomers. It observes the different, sometimes mutually exclusive, cultural systems of the migrants, and perceives them, ideologically, as adversaries. This "boundary crisis" may be heightened if there is competition for limited rewards, otherwise absorption may be facilitated. Territorial defensiveness takes various forms and goes on in many ways.[27]

The dominant group counters with psychic distantiation and territorial defensiveness. This may lead to overt patterns of emphasizing its own priority, superiority,

> and appropriateness to the country. Thus, the dominant group may deprecate the newcomers and attempt to frustrate their attempts, seeking to cast the immigrants into role of "estranged intruder." The immigrants meanwhile are expected to pay a price for admission; they can legitimize their presence by social and psychological subordination or submission. However, they often refuse to do this. They have been toughened and deepened by their suffereings, their courage, their decisions associated with the very act of immigration . . . No ethnic group has ever completely submitted; this is confirmed by empirical evidence.
>
> But, the result of this process is not a dark and grim affair; the struggle is heated but not hopeless and meaningless. One may take an optimistic view, for out of this impacting comes a new synthesis for an emerging culture.[29]

In this sense, conflicts of an ethnic or racial nature are viewed rather differently than they were in the earlier theories of American culture. Here, they are viewed as a very important part of American history. For out of the process of impacting and integration evolves a new synthesis which gives meaning and importance to the developing nation.

Sociological study in the theory of impact-integration would examine the changes brought about to the people in the society as they experience various forms of social conflict. Sociologists have already provided us with general descriptions about these changes in the newcomers. Social scientists have described the confusion, the alienation and the fears that the immigrants experience when first settling, and the comfort and security they derived from moving into close physical proximity to friends and relatives. These are immigrant communities.

The Sociological Perspective

The sociology of ethnicity, like the other subfields of sociology, draws much of its background theory from the major theoretical perspectives of the discipline. Although there are presently five theoretical perspectives in sociology, throughout its history, two have been ubiquitous: functionalism and conflict.[29] Each of these perspectives attempts to meet the main goal of the sociological endeavor, that of studying and making sense out of the social dimensions of life.

Functionalism

The functionalist, or social order perspective, has a classical tradition of interpretive and explanatory theory running from Comte to Durkheim and Parsons.[30] We may refer to its basic stance toward society as organicism.[32] Society is viewed as a system of interdependent parts; each part of the system serves a function; there is a division of labor among the parts of the system such that differentiation and specialization of parts develop; and finally, social systems tend toward a state of order and equilibrium.[33] Functionalists view society as a social system with various needs of its own which must be met if the needs and desires of its individual members are to be met.[33] Human behavior, therefore, is to be viewed as a series of actions contributing in one way or another to the maintenance of the system.[34] A distinctive feature of this form of theory is that it explains phenomena on the basis of its consequences, i.e., structures arise and are maintained because of the consequences they have.[35]

Ralf Dahrendorf has suggested that the essential assumptions of the structural-functional model can be summarized as follows:

1. Every society is a relatively persisting configuration of elements;
2. Every society is a well-integrated configuration of elements;
3. Every element in society contributes to its functioning;
4. Every society rests on the consensus of its members.[36]

Conflict Theory

The conflict perspective has a classical tradition of interpretive and explanatory theory running from Machiavelli and Hobbes to Marx and Weber.[37] After extracting out its main causal propositions from extraneous political and philosophical doctrines, the essential elements of this tradition become evident. The sociologist Randall Collins has described these elements.

> Machiavelli and Hobbes initiated the basic stance of cynical realism about human society. Individual behavior is explained in terms of their self interest in a material world of threat and violence. Social order is seen as founded on organized coercion. There is an ideological realm of belief (religion and law), and an underlying world of struggles over power; ideas and morals are not prior to interaction but are socially created, and serve the interests of the parties of the conflict.[38]

Marx added more specific determinants to the lines of division among conflicting interests and indicated the material conditions that mobilize particular interests into action and that make it possible for them to articulate their ideas.[39] The Weberian strain of conflict theory differs somewhat from the Marxian. While Marx, for instance, argued that the economic base of society was the most important factor in understanding social relationships between groups, Weber attempted to show that the ethos of social competition and achievement, regardless of its sources, is an important intervening variable affecting social relationships and social structure. In other words, conflict theories tend to view societies as the setting within which various struggles take place.[40]

Ralf Dahrendorf has suggested that the essential assumptions of the conflict model can be summarized as follows:

1. Every society is subjected at every moment to change; Social change is ubiquitous;
2. Every society experiences at every moment social conflicts; social conflict is ubiquitous ;
3. Every element in society contributes to its change;
4. Every society rests on constraints of some of its members by others.[41]

Four Sociologies of Ethnic Intergroup Processes

There are four previous works that have been major attempts to bring the sociological perspective to bear on the study of ethnicity. For this reason, a brief sketch of each will be presented here.

One of the first major attempts to connect the study of ethnic, racial, and religious minorities with the study of society in a systematic way was Milton Gordon's *Assimilation in American Life.* The central theme of this work is that assimilation is not a single process but a number of different subprocesses or dimensions. The most important forms of assimilation are cultural assimilation and structural assimilation. *Cultural assimilation* refers to the fact that all incoming minority groups must to some degree learn the appropriate and required modes of action, dress, language, and other day-to-day norms of culture. It may be useful to think of cultural assimilation as another way of describing the process through which Chinese become Chinese-Americans, Polish become Polish-Americans, and so forth. Gordon contends that while some degree of cultural assimilation always occurs, the process may continue indefinitely and never be complete.[42]

Structural assimilation refers to the degree to which minorities attain entrance into the major institutions of the society, especially on a primary group level. In addition to these two important types of assimilation, which may occur at different rates, Gordon presents five other ways of measuring assimilation. They are:

1. Group intermarriage or amalgamation;
2. Identificational assimilation, or the degree to which minority groups think of themselves as Americans;
3. The absence of prejudice;
4. The absence of discrimination by the majority group;
5. The absence of power and value conflicts between groups.[44]

Gordon's comparison largely involved the first three theories of American Ethnicity, namely, Anglo-conformity, melting pot, and cultural pluralism. His comparison of these three theories is made on the basis of his dual notion of cultural and structural assimilation.[44]

R.A. Schermerhorn's work entitled *Comparative Ethnic Relations* does not concern itself specifically with the theories of American ethnicity, however the theoretical framework developed in this book has significant implications for theories of ethnic group interaction in the United States. Schermerhorn provides us with a complex and comprehensive typology of the structure of intergroup relations in plural societies. By utilizing the concepts, "superordinate," and "subordinate" ethnic groups, he is able to speculate about the possib forms that ethnic group relations take on, given the social structural contingencies existing in particular societies. Schermerhorn integrates a functionalist social order perspective with a power conflict perspective to guide the development of his theoretical framework. The propositions derived from his study have definite applicability to the comparative and cross-cultural analysis of societies, including the United States.[45]

In *American Pluralism,* William Newman's purpose is to analyze majority-minority group relations in the United States. He employs many of the concepts devised by both Gordon and Schermerhorn to interpret intergroup relations in the context of pluralistic societies. First, Newman provides a basic framework for analysis and attempts to locate some key definitions and typologies within that framework. Second, he assesses previous theories about the processes of group relations in plural societies. He focuses on assimilation, amalgamation, and cultural pluralism as alternative interpretations of American society. These three notions are examined both in terms of their social significance as social doctrines and as sociological theories. After making his assessments, he offers an alternative theory. His major argument is that social conflict theory provides a viable theoretical alternative that avoids the shortcomings of previous theories. A model for the analysis of intergroup relations is provided with a related set of theoretical propositions about social conflict. Finally, the book addresses some of the consequences of social pluralism.[46]

E.K. Francis's work, *Interethnic Relations* is the most fully developed contribution to sociological theory construction in the area of ethnicity to date. He has consolidated a conceptual framework, standardized terms, and codified the research carried out in several different sciences. The work acknowledges, is in the tradition of, and goes beyond R.A. Schermerhorn's work in ethnic relations. Francis provides at least one hundred and three empirically testable propositions dervied from the theoretical framework he developed in the early segment of the book. His analysis of ethnic relations contains a massive amount of empirical material depicting types of ethnic interaction in tribal, empire, nation-state, industrial, and modern society. Its relation to the present study can be viewed in the context of current attempts to produce useful scientific theory for the study of ethnic relations in contemporary society.[47]

None of the above studies, however, has actually attempted to identify, analyze, and compare particular theories of American ethnicity through an exploration of the work of its central theoretical figures. Moreover, while the above works all make a consistent effort at theory construction, none of them has attempted to analyze the deeper assumptions that they may have about the nature of man and society and the corresponding influence that these theories *exert upon* of American ethnicity.

Two Anthropologies of Ethnicity.

Up to this point, we have talked much about the aspects surrounding the development of social theory in general and ethnicity theory in particular. But we have as yet said little about the subject matter of the theories of American ethnicity, namely, *ethnicity* itself. What is it? This, of course, is what we will be focusing on as we examine the writings of the theorists cited in this book. However, as noted on page one, the meanings imputed to the term ethnicity have at times been tenuous enough to refer to it as a "term on the move". Therefore, it becomes useful to keep this point in mind during the examination of different theorists. In short, what is ethnic about ethnicity? The following two approaches taken from the work of anthropologists offer ways of thinking about this question.

1. *Ethnicity as a cultural system*

It has not been uncommon to find that ethnic factors become tied in and overlapped with other social variables such as social class, kinship, political interest groups, nationality, and a host of others. The result of this situation is that ethnicity itself becomes difficult to identify and describe as it attaches itself to a host of other social, psychological, and cultural variables. In illustrating this point, the anthropologist Aronson (1976) has conducted a conceptional analysis aimed at extracting the extraneous political and social variables from ethnic phenomena to see what actually remains of ethnicity itself. His conclusion is that ethnicity is best viewed as an "ideology of and for value dissensus and social disengagement from an exclusive socio-political arena, that is, for pursuing major values deemed not shared by others in the arena."[48] In this way, ethnicity can represent a self-enclosed cultural system of values for a particular group or groups in society.

2. *Ethnicity as ethnos*

This anthropological view relies upon the idea of *ethnos* used by eastern European and Soviet social scientists. Soviet social scientists understand this to mean "stable human communities, tied together by unity of territory and history of their formation, and by a common language and culture – all which are manifested in a certain self-consciousness or self-identification based on ethnicity."[49] Noticeably absent from this definition are elements of migration common to most American ethnic groups. Nevertheless, the significant contribution of those who work under the rubric of ethnos theory is the historical approach that is employed with its emphasis on the elements of fundamental significance to the persistence of ethnic groups. One of the main tasks of such studies is "the reconstruction of *ethnogenesis,* i.e., of the components that constitute a certain ethnos, their balance and mode of integration, the subsequent ethnic history of the given unit, inclusion into it of new groups, transformations of its culture, etc., and finally of modern ethnic process – mutual relations of this entity with others, the ways and perspectives of its modern development."[49]

These important components of ethnicity that have been fashioned out of an anthropological perspective are an important key to giving a more total understanding to the study of ethnic intergroup processes in the United States. However, it is critical to remember that while ethnicity is not an easy term to define, one thing is clear. To get a full sense of its meaning for the individual and society, one must go beyond a strictly anthropological, or sociological, or psychological analysis alone. As with the study of other types of complex phenomena, the problem of ethnicity does not respect disciplinary boundaries. The work of the intellectuals explored in the following chapters illustrates this point. Among them are an historian, an anthropologist, a philosopher-psychologist, a political scientist and a sociologist. A solid meaning for ethnicity in American society begins to crystallize through their successive approximations of the processes that occur when people of different ethnic groups come together. The meaning of ethnicity is never spelt out precisely in any one place. It is between the lines of the theories that follow. Therefore, it is up to you, the reader, to engage yourself in an active search for the meaning of ethnicity in American society as you progress through the remaining chapters of this book.

Conclusion: The Interdependency of Theory Elements

In this book the work of five individuals will be viewed as representative of each of the five models presented here in Chapter II. Although together their work spans a broad segment of history, there are common strands of thought running throughout. Following a brief sketch of the biography, major influences, and summary of the major works of each theorist, specific focus will be given to their central works which espouse a theory of American ethnicity. This will lay the groundwork for the identification of each writer's theory of American ethnicity, and a clear explication of the elements therein. Two elements have been abstracted from their writings: (a) propositions and assertions concerning the processes that occur when people of different ethnic groups come together, and (b) domain assumptions concerning the nature of man and society. This is accomplished by a process of critical analysis in which the above mentioned elements will be drawn out and then ordered in accordance with a model.[50] The result of this process yields five sets of elements that constitute the essentials for our comparative analysis. The final elements will be interpreted in terms of the dual orientation of macro-sociological theory.

Beyond Assimilation

Five theorists were chosen. Each has a different background (cultural, personal, social); each wrote in a different time period; each wrote from a different institutional context, with different freedoms, different constraints, different values, different dispositions, and different intentions. They all, however, wrote about one thing in common. All wrote of ethnic intergroup processes within the American socio-cultural context.

More importantly, these theories mark the different stages in the development of theories of American ethnicity. There is a line of progression (that this study will attempt to bring out) which leads away from assimilation as the major process guiding American culture, and moves toward "ethnic integration" as a central axis. One way of illustrating this evolutionary shift is by focusing on a symbol which has become a permanent part of the history of American culture, namely, "the melting pot." Just as Frederick Jackson Turner's concept of the "frontier" was the symbol of an early period of American history, the "melting pot" represents the second phase, and "ethnic integration" is beginning to emerge as the third.

This symbol, the melting pot, is a useful pivotal conceptualization with which to view the selection of the data for this study. Each writer, in developing his theory, has touched base with the melting pot in a uniquely different way. Frederick Jackson Turner used the words melting pot but once, yet, he, of all the theorists, is considered by many to be its strongest proponent.[51] Henry Pratt Fairchild's central piece is entitled *The Melting Pot Mistake,*[52] while Horace Kallen's is called *Democracy Versus The Melting Pot*[53]. Each represents a reaction against the melting pot but from dramatically different perspectives. Nathan Glazer and Daniel P. Moynihan's *Beyond the Melting Pot*[54] *and* Francis X. Femminella's *The Immigrant and the Melting Pot*[55] are what may be referred to as contemporary reactions to the melting pot. It is to these five major works that we now turn.

Notes

1. Alvin Gouldner, *The Coming Crisis of Western Sociology,* New York: Avon, 1970, p. 29
2. Ibid., p. 32.
3. Ibid., p. 34.
4. See Francis X. Femminella, "The Immigrant and the Melting Pot," in M. Urosfsky (ed.), *Perspectives in Urban America,* New York: Doubleday, 1973, p. 45.
5. See Karl Mannheim, *Ideology and Utopia,* London: Routledge and Kegan Paul, 1929.
6. See Max Weber, " 'Objectivity' in Social Science and Social Policy" in *The Methodology of the Social Sciences,* translated by Edward Shils and Henry Finch, New York: Free Press, 1949.
7. Thomas F. Pettigrew, "Ethnicity in American Life," in *Ethnic Groups in the City,* edited by Otto Feinstein, New York: D.C. Heath and Co., 1971, pp. 29–33.
8. This definition is adopted from "Definitions of Ethnicity," by Wsevolod Isajiw, *Ethnicity* 1, 111–124 (1974), and *Comparative, Ethnic Relations: A Framework for Theory and Research,* by R.A. Schermerhorn, New York: Random House, 1970: 123.
9. This mode of analysis is adapted from William M. Newman, *American Ethnicity: A Study of Minority Groups and Social Theory,* New York: Harper and Row, 1973.

10. Madison Grant, *The Passing of the Great Race,* New York: Scribner, 1971, p. 79.
11. See Henry Pratt Fairchild, *The Melting Pot Mistake,* New York: Little, Brown & Co., 1926; Howard C. Hill,"The Americanization Movement," in *American Journal of Sociology,* 24, May, 1919; and Ellwood P. Cubberly, *Changing Conceptions of Education,* Boston: Houghton and Mifflin, 1929.
12. Cubberly Ibid., pp. 15–16.
13. Hector St. John de Crevecour, *Letters From An American Farmer,* (New York, 1912) p.43. originally published 1782.
14. Frederick Jackson Turner, *The Frontier in American History,* New York: Holt and Co., 1920, pp. 22–23.
15. Israel Zangwill, *The Melting Pot,* New York: Macmillan, 1929.
16. See Ruby Joe Reeves Kennedy, "Single or Triple Melting Pot, Intermarriage Trends in New Haven", in the *American Journal of Sociology* 49 (January 1944): 332; also Herberg, op. cit.
17. Horace Kallen, *Culture and Democracy in the United States,* New York: Arrow Press, 1924, 1970, pp. 122–23.
18. See Louis Adamic, *My America,* New York: Harper and Row, 1938; Isaac Berkson, *Theories of Assimilation,* New York: Columbia University, 1920; Julius Drachsler, *Democracy and Assimilation: The Blending of Immigrant Heritages in America,* New York: Macmillan, 1920.
19. Francis X. Femminella, "Societal Ramifications of Ethnicity in the Suburbs", in La Gumina, *(ed.), Ethnicity and Suburbia: The Long Island Experience,* Garden City: Nassau Community College 1980.
20. Nathan Glazer and Daniel P. Moynihan, *Beyond the Melting Pot,* Cambridge: MIT Press, 1970; Francis X. Femminella, "The Immigrant and the Melting Pot," op. cit., Andrew Greeley, *Ethnicity in the United States,* New York: John Wiley, 1974; and Michael Novak, *The Rise of the Unmeltable Ethnics,* New York: Macmillan, 1972.
21. Glazer and Moynihan, 1970, p. 310.
22. Novak, op. cit., p. 48.
23. Greeley, op. cit., pp. 311–312.
24. Femminella, "Ethnicity in the Suburbs," op. cit.
25. Femminella, op. cit., p. 62.
26. Femminella, "The Impact of Italian Migration and American

Catholicism," *American Catholic Sociological Review,* Vol. 22, No. 3, p. 233.

27. Femminella, "The Immigrant and the Melting Pot," op. cit., pp. 62–63.
28. Femminella, "Ethnic Dimensions of Citizenship," a paper read at the White House, Washington D.C., 1976, p. 21.
29. See, for instance, Herman Strasser, *The Normative Structure of Sociology,* London: Routledge and Kegan Paul, 1976; Jonathan Turner, *The Structure of Sociological Theory,* Homewood, Ill.: The Dorsey Press, 1974; Raymond Aron, *Main Currents in Sociological Thought,* 2 Vols., New York: Basic Books, 1965.
30. See, for instance, Auguste Comte, *A General View of Positivism,* Translated by John H. Bridges, New York: Spielder, 1957; Emile Durkheim, *The Rules of Sociological Method,* New York: Free Press, 1964; Talcott Parsons, *The Structure of Social Action,* 2 Vols., New York: Free Press, 1968.
31. Herbert Spencer, *Social Statics,* London: John Chapman, 1851.
32. See Randall Collins, "Two Approaches to Comparative Politics", in *State and Society: A Reader in Comparative Political Sociology,* R. Bendix, et al., eds., Boston: Little, Brown, 1968.
33. William Chambliss, *Sociological Readings in the Conflict Perspective,* Reading, Mass.: Addison-Wesley, 1973, p. 4.
34. Parsons, *The Structure of Social Action. op. cit.*
35. Jonathan Turner, *The Structure of Sociological Theory.* Homewood, Ill.: The Dorsey Press, 1974.
36. Ralf Dahrendorf, "Toward a Theory of Social Conflict", *Journal of Peace and Conflict Resolutions,* XI, 1958, pp. 170–183.
37. Strasser, *The Normative Structure of Sociology;* Turner; *The Structure of Sociological Theory;* Aron, *Main Currents in Sociological Thought.* op. cit.
38. Randall Collins, *Conflict Sociology: Toward an Explanatory Science,* New York: Academic Press, 1975, p. 57.
39. See, for instance, Karl Marx and Frederich Engels, *The German Ideology,* translated by C.J. Arthur, New York: International Publications, 1970.
40. See, for example, Max Weber, *The Theory of Social and Economic Organization,* New York: Oxford University Press, 1947.
41. Dahrendorf, pp. 170–173.

42. Gordon, *Assimilation in American Life,* op. cit.
43. Ibid.
44. Ibid.
45. Schermerhorn, *Comparative Ethnic Relations,* op. cit., *pasim.*
46. William Newman, *American Pluralism,* op. cit., passim.
47. E.K. Francis, *Interethnic Relations.*
48. Aronson, Dan R. "Ethnicity as a Cultural System: An Introductory Essay", in *Ethnicity in the Americas,* Frances Henry ed., Mouton Publishers: The Hague: Paris. 1976, p. 14–15.
49. S.A. Arutiunov and Y. V. Bromley, "Problems of Ethnicity in Soviet Ethnographic Studies," in R.E. Holloman and S.A. Arutiunov eds., *Perspectives on Ethnicity,* The Hague: Mouton Publishers, 1978, p. 11, 12.
50. The following loosely constructed model may be used as a guide in attempting to systematically tease out (a) "domain assumptions" from the infrastructure, and (b) "process assertions" from the surface structure of the selected theories of American ethnicity. This entails a formalizing of the theories that are the subject of study; that is, it involves identifying the surface structural "process assertions" including concepts, propositions, and postulates, and infrastructural "domain assumption," which together comprise the structural elements of any theory of American ethnicity. Applying this model will yield five distinct sets of elements (concepts, propositions, postulates, etc.). Each set individually constitutes a group of entities suitable for comparative analysis. The following model has been used as a guide.

    A. Surface Structure
        1. Concepts
            a) Central concepts in each of the selected theories of American ethnicity
                (1) Ethnic group
                (2) Immigrant
                (3) Alien
                (4) Foreign
                (5) Race
                (6) Nationality
                (7) Culture

b) Definitions and meanings: dimensional consideration
   (1) Historical status of the term
   (2) Type of sentiment the term illicits
   (3) Particular groups denoted by the term
   (4) Similarities and differences of meaning between terms
   (5) Categorical relations
      (a) Dominant-subordinate
      (b) Newcomer-host
      (c) Majority-minority
      (d) Indigenous-colonial
      (e) Culture-subculture
      (f) Core-peripheral
      (g) Metaphors employed in the interpretation
      (h) Relation of terms of culture, personality, and social structure
      (i) Stage dimensions of the process *i.e.* Robert E. Park's stages of assimilation[49]
      (j) Directional dimensions, *i.e.,* one-way assimilation
      (k) Relation to core values-democracy, liberty, union, etc.
   (6) Characteristics attributed to the concept
      (a) Biological
      (b) Psychological
      (c) Cultural
      (d) Social

c) Process concepts in each selected theory of American ethnicity
   (1) Assimilation
   (2) Americanization
   (3) Integration
   (4) Incorporation

2. Propositions: Process Assertions
   a) Processes that occur when people of different ethnic groups come together in the United States
   b) Structure of the total process: Stages
   c) Explication of each stage
   d) Relation to other societal processes

e) Context in which the process occurs
f) Nature of the process
g) Power relations between groups
3. Postulates
a) Disciplinary orientation of key postulates
(1) Biological
(2) Psychological
(3) Political
(4) . . . .
b) Postulates guiding model of society
(1) Organicism
(2) Evolutionism
(3) . . . .
c) Other more specific postulates concerning Man and Society

B. Infrastructure

The infrastructure of the theory is, for the most part, implicit. The elements comprising this level of theory (domain assumptions, sentiments, and world hypotheses) are lodged in a position bordering both the conscious and unconscious levels of the theorist's mental frame. In order to *know* them, one must literally live with and inside of the theorist. One must know his deepest sentiments on life; those that shape this habits and writing style, those that shape his view of the social world and the assumptions about the domain within which he is working, and those which inevitably shape his theory. Obviously, this is a somewhat impossible task. There are no clear lines; all are either very fine as to be almost invisible, or, very fuzzy and perceptively unavailing. They are, however, extremely important. It is these sentiments, domain assumptions, and world hypotheses that resonate congenially or produce a painful dissonance in the individual who experiences the theory. This, oftentimes, has more of an influence on the career of a theory and its acceptability, than its levels of scientific validity and strict adherence to the canons of science. (Gouldner, 1970).

It is at this level of theory that biography and social structure intersect. On the one hand, there is the theorist, the individual. He is a human being with a set of sentiments that "entail a hormone eliciting, muscle-tensing, tissue embedded, fight or flight disposition of the total organism". (Gouldner, 1970, p. 37.) On the other hand, there is the social structure; as the theorist works within it, it also works within the theorist. It deposits within the theorist an essential core of cultural artifacts and symbols, values and beliefs, statuses and roles, as well as other conditioning elements of his social action. In short, it provides him with the necessary baggage to embark on his journey and labors as a writer of social theory.

C. Domain Assumptions
   1. Foundational elements in any universal assumptive framework concerning "nature" (of the universe, man and society.)
      a) Time
      b) Space
      c) Process
      d) Change
      e) Order
      f) Patterns
      g) Structure
   2. Location of the major metaphors used by the theorist.
   3. Assumptions resonant and assumptions dissonant with contemporary sociological theory
      a) Continuity-discontinuity
      b) Convergence-divergence
      c) Focus on the "whole" – foucs on the "part"
      d) Stability-disorganization
      e) Order
      f) Change
      g) Power
      h) Integration
      i) Interdependence
      j) Equilibrium
      k) System
      l) Pattern Maintenance
      m) Consensus
      n) Dissensus

o) Differentiation
p) Specialization
q) Constraints
r) Struggle
s) Confrontation
t) Cleavages
u) Antagonisms
v) Status quo
w) Homeostasis
x) Dialectical
y) Emancipatory
z) Contradictory

51. It was not until after Israel Zangwill produced his play entitled *The Melting Pot,* in 1909, that Frederick Jackson Turner used those words in his essay entitled "Middle West Pioneer Democracy", in 1918. In fact, Turner, in this essay, rejects the melting pot as a way of typifying ethnic intergroup processes in the United States.
52. Henry Pratt Fairchild, *The Melting Pot Mistake,* Boston: Little, Brown, and Co., 1926.
53. Horace Kallen, "Democracy Versus The Melting Pot", in *Culture and Democracy in the United States,* New York: Arno Press, 1970 (1925).
54. Nathan Glazer and Daniel P. Moynihan, *Beyond the Melting Pot,* Cambridge: MIT Press, 1970.
55. Francis X. Femminella, "The Immigrant and the Melting Pot", in M. Urofsky (ed.), *Perspectives in Urban America,* New York: Doubleday, 1973.

PART TWO

THE PROGRESSION OF KEY IDEAS

III Frederick Jackson Turner

Biography

Frederick Jackson Turner was one of the most prominent historians of the United States. He was born in Portage, Wisconsin in 1861.[1] His father, Andrew Jackson Turner, and his mother, Mary Hanford Turner, were pioneers who had come to Wisconsin from upstate New York. Turner's father was a newspaper editor who was active in area politics. He was also a keen local historian.[2]

Portage, located between the Wisconsin and Fox Rivers, was a frontier village the nucleus of which was formed by people of diverse origins.[3] Some were native to the area while others, originally journeying westward, had decided to settle there. Turner recalled that the social composition of Portage included Indians, Irish, Pomeranians, Scots, Welsh, Germans, New England Yankees, a few Southerners, a few Negroes, some Englishmen, one or two Italians, and many Norwegians and Swiss.[4] Such a simple, democratic environment, on the edge of the wilderness, served to develop in the young Turner a sensitivity to and interest in the processes by which civilization replaced the forest life of Indians, trappers, and fur traders.[5] James D. Bennett's remarks sum up the early vision of American development that the young Turner acquired from his early years in Portage, Wisconsin.

> In the small town of Portage, then, Fred Turner could see the world in microcosm; a veritable parade of nationalities filled the streets, proclaiming the traits and characteristics of a dozen nations. But, by the passing of time, the careful observer could note that nationalistic distinctions became less noticeable and could actually see the development of a new national character that recalled European origins, of course, but that exhibited many differences unique to the time and place. Turner was witnessing the very process of American development in his hometown.[6]

In 1878, Turner graduated from Portage High School. He was awarded a prize for his graduation oration entitled, "Power of the Press".[7] Between the time Turner graduated and the time he left for college, he worked as a typesetter in his father's newspaper office.[8] In 1880, he entered the University of Wisconsin. As an undergraduate, he began to study the history of Wisconsin from the Draper Collection at the State Historical Society of Wisconsin. He received his Bachelor of Arts degree in 1884, and immediately began work as a newspaper correspondent for Chicago and Milwaukee newspapers. He was awarded his Master of Arts degree by the University of Wisconsin in 1888. In that year, he enrolled as a graduate student at Johns Hopkins University. The next year, he became an assistant professor of history at the University of Wisconsin and was married to Caroline Mae Sherwood in Chicago. They were to have three children. Turner was awarded his Doctor of Philosophy degree from Johns Hopkins University in 1890. He remained a professor of history at the University of Wisconsin until 1910 when he began his tenure at Harvard University, the same year in which he became president of the American Historical Association. He retired from Harvard in 1924. Turner died on March 14, 1932 in Pasadena, California at age 71.[9]

Major Influences

Turner decided to attend the University of Wisconsin at Madison. It was there he received a classical training and further cultivated the foundations of his literary style. He occupied himself with the works of Milton, Shakespeare, Dickins, Swift, Horace in the "original Latin," Lucretius, Tacitus, Comte, Spencer, Darwin, Macaulay, John Richard Green, Benjamin Franklin, Emerson, George Bancroft, Cooper, and Parkman.[10] The political climate of the University of Madison confirmed the democratic faith that Turner knew so well in Portage. While there, he declared that true progress would require the enlightenment of all and he called for and predicted the appearance of a great epic poet of American democracy. He emphasized a functional, democratic interpretation of art and culture and, as a scholar of Turner observed, he was "breaking with the traditional view that associated great achievements in the arts with a privileged order".[11]

While at the University of Wisconsin, Turner also learned of and applied the scientific method of inductive study to historical data.

This principle had been, until that time, largely applied to natural science phenomena. As a student, he learned of the doctrine of evolution. This allowed him to conceive of society as a growing organism and history as the self-consciousness of that organism. He became exposed to the notion of "multiple hypothesis" by the geologist and president of the University, Thomas C. Chamberlin, who believed that the development of the earth was too complicated to be approached by a single hypothesis.[12]

The most profound scholarly influence on Turner came from his professor of history, William F. Allen. Allen taught his students in the manner of a scientist to do a critical evaluation of the evidence found in primary sources. He emphasized the interrelations of America and Europe. In this respect, Turner would later emphasize the impact of each on the other. Allen's special interest was Roman history. His attention to the expansion of Roman civilization and the movements of people clearly influenced Turner's writings. In 1888, with Allen's guidance, Turner prepared his Master's essay on "The Character and Influence of Fur Trade on Wisconsin".[13]

In 1888, Turner went to Johns Hopkins University. Here he studied and became friends with Woodrow Wilson. He also attended lectures by the sociologist Albion Small, the economic historian Richard T. Ely, and the historian Herbert Baxter Adams. Adams introduced Turner to the "germ theory" of American institutions, that they could only be understood in terms of their European antecedents. However, Turner could not agree with Adams that the similarities America shared with Europe were largely a function of heredity, not environment. Turner, placing more importance on the differences than on the similarities between Europe and America, believed that the wilderness forced the adaptation of the former's institutions to the environmental conditons of the latter. Nevertheless in 1890, under the guidance of Adams, Turner completed his doctoral dissertation entitled, *The Character and Influence of Indian Trade in Wisconsin: The Study of the Trading Post as an Institution.*[14]

Turner's work from this point on was written at a time when the United States was in an almost full swing towards industrialism and mass immigration. Having fully overcome the period of the Civil War and Reconstruction, the nation was gaining great power and its potential role on the world stage was very clear to Turner and his generation. By then, Turner had fully developed his thesis concerning the character of American society.[15]

The Turner thesis, which appeared in its most complete form in 1893, argued basically that one of the most necessary factors, without which American society could not be understood, is the "frontier." In Turner's words, "American history up to our day has been colonial history, the colonization of the great West. This ever retreating frontier of free land is the key to American development."[16] Again, in similar form, Turner remarked: "The existence of an area of free land, its continuous recession, and the advance of the American settlement westward, explains American development."[17] Thus the development of American society constituted an evolutionary process by which unoccupied areas became seeds of civilization, moving from the simple to the complex. As each new area became settled, it would experience the progression of forms engaged in by each previously settled area as it moved from savagery to civilization.[18] Each region followed a transformation process from exploration, to hunting and trapping, to trading, to ranching, and to farming. Later transformations include specialized farming, manufacturing, and regional development of cities and towns.[19] The frontier was also a crucible for Turner; it was one in which diverse nationalities became joined together to form a composite nationality. This process of Americanization is one which is effectuated by the mechanism of democracy. Herein lies the foundation of Turner's theory of American ethnicity.[20]

Turner's theory of American ethnicity is often placed within the melting pot model of American society.[21] This cannot be explained by Turner's frequent reference to the term melting pot, but rather to his usage of the term "crucible" and "composite nationality," both of which were likened to the melting-pot notion by later scholars of ethnicity. Of course, no theory fits perfectly into any model and Turner's theory is no exception. Through the course of this exposition and analysis, an attempt is made to provide an accurate identification of Turner's theory of American ethnicity.

Major Works

It is often difficult to reconcile the fact that a historian as prominent as Frederick Jackson Turner did not write many books. He wrote only four major books. Ray Allen Billington, a major scholar of Turner, remarked about this phenomenon and the effect it had on Turner.

> Such popularity placed increasing pressure on Turner to embody his theories in book form. "Will you not," wrote one of his former students in 1915, "confer a benefit on the American people by gathering your fugitive children together between two covers one of these days: I have spent a small fortune (for a professor) and eighteen months trying to get two copies of each article for my alcove and the end is as far off as peace." Such queries greatly troubled Turner. He was, although he never admitted this to himself, virtually incapable of the sustained effort needed to produce a book. He was the intellectual pioneer, constantly seeking new explanations, new means of understanding and illuminating the past, new avenues for exploration that might unearth fresh treasures. To retell twice-told tales, to chronicle well-known narratives, to bother with the endless detail necessary in a long manuscript – these were tasks that he found not only unpalatable but impossible.[22]

Without a doubt, Turner's most important book was *The Frontier in American History.* In it can be found not only his well renowned "frontier thesis," but also his theory of American ethnicity. It is upon this work that our analytical and interpretive energies will be focused. This book is a collection of some of Turner's most important essays, the foremost being his 1893 essay entitled "The Significance of the Frontier in American History".[23] The essays in the book can be viewed as falling into two groups. In "The Problems of the West", "Dominant Forces in Western Life", "Contributions of the West to American Democracy", "Pioneer Ideals and the State University", "The West and American Ideals", and "Middle Western Pioneer Democracy", he expands aspects of his original thesis, emphasizing especially the democracy and nationalism that he held to be the frontier's most enduring contributions to post-pioneer America.[24] In "The First Official Frontier of the Massachusetts Bay", "The Old West", "The Middle West", "The Ohio Valley in American History", and "The Significance of the Mississippi Valley in American History", Turner applied his frontier concept to specific geographical areas.[25]

'The remaining essay contained in this book, entitled, "Social' Forces in American History", is an essay which reiterates Turner's belief in the complexity of human behavior as well as emphasizing the usability of history in the shaping of modern life.[26] For a clearer understanding of the frontier thesis, it is helpful to consider two of Turner's earlier essays. "The Significance of History", which appeared in 1891, and "Problems in American History", which appeared in 1892, have been called logical antecedents to the 1893 essay.[27] In the 1891 essay, he expressed his own beliefs as to the uses of history. Filmur Mood called this essay the statement of Turner's professional credo.[28] Turner made a statement about the utility of history and the necessity of each generation to rewrite history.[29] In the 1892 essay Turner identified the areas which he felt offer the greatest opportunity for study in United States History.[30] "American history", he contended, "needs a corrected and unified account of the progress of civilization across the continent with the antecedent results".[31] He directed future historians to study the vital forces which created and shaped the laws and institutions of the United States.[32] In this essay, he first referred to the retreating frontier and to free land. The next year, he completed his famous essay, "The Significance of the Frontier in American History".

While Turner did write many other essays, his major ideas in these essays can be found in all of the books that he wrote. Aside from *The Frontier in American History,* Turner's major books were: *Rise of the New West,*[33] *The Significance of Sections in American History,*[34] *The United States 1830–1850: The Nation and its Sections,*[35] and Turner's doctoral dissertation entitled *The Character and Influence of Indian Trade in Wisconsin: A Study of the Trading Post as an Institution.*[36]

Turner's *Rise of the New West: 1919–1929* was a transitional book that linked the frontier hypothesis of Turner's early fame with his later theory of the role of sections in the history of the United States. At the time of his death, he was working on the volume, *The United States, 1830–1850: The Nation and its Sections,* which brought him his second Pulitzer prize in History. His first was awarded in 1932 for *The Significance of Sections in American History.*[37]

The Frontier in American History

Turner's most recognized, quoted, and central work is entitled, "The Significance of the Frontier in American History." In this piece,

Turner espouses his frontier thesis in complete form for the first time. Within this essay, published in 1893, Turner identifies not only the elements of a theory of the character of American society, but he also reveals elements of a theory of American ethnicity.

Integral to Frederick Jackson Turner's social theory is his conception of the role that Europeans play in the formation of the character of American society. Since it was largely the Europeans who immigrated to the United States during the period in which Turner was writing, and, since American institutions did have many of their roots in those of European structure, Turner naturally stresses the importance of the reciprocal relationship between European life and American settlements. He makes use of the term "Americanization" in referring to the effect of the frontier on the European immigrant. In this now famous essay Turner asserts three things. First, the American environment modified and developed European life. Second, Americanization occurs via the frontier. Third, the wilderness. Thus, he colonist, who then sets out in mastering the wilderness. Thus, he clearly suggests that the result of this process is an outcome very different from that noted on the European continent.

It is important to take note of the usage of the term "Americanization" because, as will be seen later, all theorists of American ethnicity have made reference to it, often in very different ways. The meaning of the term is very much a function of the historical context in which it occurs. For Turner, Americanization is a process whereby the European is transformed through interaction with the conditions of the American frontier. The frontier is the force of Americanization in this first period of American history, just as the melting pot idea will be later recognized as a force of Americanization during the next period of American history.

The assertions to be abstracted from Turner's early essays concerning the processes that occur when different ethnic groups come together in the United States are: (1) The immigrants become Americanized (2) The immigrants are reacted upon by American life – namely the frontier (3) The immigrants are transformed by the wilderness and they in turn overcome and transform the wilderness.

In the same essay, Turner describes the effect of the trader on the Indian. His reference to these groups occurs in the context of an analysis of the power relationships between them. The focus is upon the undermining of the position of the Indian by the trader. He points out the subsequent sale of guns to the Indians. The guns were later used by the Indian to resist the farming frontier. The farming frontier was to follow the trader as part of the natural succession of events in the expanding frontier. The important thing to take note of here is Turner's characterization of the Indians as a social group. Are they foreigners, aliens, migrants, or ethnics? Contemporary definitions of ethnic group, such as the one used in this study would surely include the Indians as an ethnic group. However, Turner used the word *ethnic* rather sparingly. When he did use it, he used it to denote groups in the United States that are descendants of a foreign nationality. Hence, his infrequent use of the term ethnic refers mainly to people of European nations who come to America. During the late nineteenth century, the term ethnic was a term very often used to denote groups possessing certain tribal characteristics that emphasized close physical proximity, and a series of distinct physical and cultural traits. Turner's distinction between ethnic and immigrant is also apparent from his usage of the terms. For Turner it appears that ethnics were immigrants who: (1) were noticeably culturally distinct from the majority of the population in a region, and (2) lived in the United States long enough to have developed distinct patterns of living among those of their "own kind."[38]

Although Turner doesn't refer to the Indians as an ethnic group, they may be treated as such for purposes of identifying and abstracting assertions concerning the processes that occur when people of different ethnic groups come together. Indians also qualify as an ethnic group by virtue of the definition given at the outset of this book. In respect to the relationship between the Indian and the trader, Turner states:

> The trading post left the unarmed tribes at the mercy of those that had purchased firearms – a truth which the Iroquois Indian wrote in blood, and so the remote and unvisited tribes gave eager welcome to the trader. "The Savages," wrote LaSalle, "take better care of us French than of their own children; from us only can they get guns and goods." This accounts for the trader's power and the rapidity of his advance. Thus, the disintegrating forces of civilization entered the wilderness. Every river, valley and Indian trail become a fissure in Indian society, and so that *society became honeycombed* [Author's italics]. Long before the pioneer farmer appeared on the scene,

> primative Indian life had passed away. The farmer met Indians armed with guns. The trading frontier, while steadily undermining Indian power by making the tribes ultimately dependent on the whites, through its sale of guns, gave to the Indian increased power of resistance to the farming frontier.[39]

The central assertions concerning the processes that occur when different ethnic groups come together with respect to this situation can be summarized as follows:

1. An incoming ethnic group may make an indigenous ethnic group vulnerable to exploitation by creating a need within the environment, e.g. need for guns.
2. An incoming ethnic group may place an indigenous ethnic group at its mercy because it possesses essential resources (guns) necessary for survival.
3. An indigenous group may welcome an incoming group because it needs the material resources they possess (guns).

These three assertions may be synthesized to yield the more general assertion that – an incoming ethnic group makes an indigenous ethnic group dependent upon it by intervening in its territory and introducing objects which upset a formerly balanced state of affairs of a group (i.e., territorial respect between tribes). In short, one ethnic group (French traders) is establishing a power relationship over another (Indians).

In 1910, Frederick Jackson Turner delivered a commencement address at the University of Indiana. His subject of discourse was the "Ideals of the Pioneer." The sketch of the pioneer is one of extreme individualism, strength, and conquest. His adept resourcefulness and inventiveness of new ways earned him the title of "the trailmaker of civilization".[70] The pioneer was dedicated to the ideals of non-conformity and change as testified by his rebellion against the conventional. He built a new society and broke new soil. Moreover, he valued social restraint, freedom from governmental interference, and personal development based on competition. In conjunction with these things, he also valued democracy. Beginning as a belief in simplicity, economy, rule by the people, a hatred of aristocracy and special privilege, the pioneer's thoughts on democracy came to proclaim the usefulness of legislation as support for the general conditions of his success.

There were however, certain things that began to alarm the pioneer. One was the radical movement toward reconstruction of society by the revolution of socialism. Another was the insurgence of hordes of immigrants. Turner describes this:

> These recent foreigners have lodged almost exclusively into the dozen great centers of industrial life, and there they have accentuated the antagonisms between capital and labor by the fact that the labor supply has become increasingly foreign born, and recruited from nationalities who arouse no sympathy on the part of capital and little on the part of the general public. Class distinctions are accentuated by national prejudices, and democracy is thereby invaded. But even in the dull brains of great masses of these unfortunates from southern and eastern Europe the idea of America as the land of freedom and of opportunity to rise, the land of pioneer democratic ideals, has found lodgement, and if it is given time and is not turned into revolutionary lines it will fructify.[41]

Turner is making several points here. First, host ethnics become replaced by incoming ethnics in the labor market. Second, this action (the entrance of new ethnics) causes a lowering of the general standard of living. Third, the recently arriving ethnics have lodged themselves almost exclusively in industrial urban areas. Fourth, new ethnics (recent arrivals) have accentuated the antagonisms between labor and capital. Fifth, these new arrivals have little inclination to sympathize with capital or the general public. Sixth, these groups (from southern and eastern Europe) are unintelligent (have dull brains). And finally, if revolutionary action is kept from occurring, over time the idea of America as a land of freedom and opportunity will come to fruition. All of the above processes, according to Turner, occur when different ethnic groups come together in the United States. They are not generalized propositions. It is not stated that these processes will occur whenever any ethnic groups come together in this type of situation. They are, rather, a set of descriptive statements that account for what Turner has observed. They are, of course, shaped by his perspective – his way of perceiving social phenomena, his perspective organization of facts, and his assumptions concerning the nature of the society with which he is dealing. Some statements are more interpretive and thus reveal domain assumptions. "That foreigners have settled in urban centers" is less interpretive in character than asserting that "they have dull brains." Turner's lack of general explanatory statements or principles is not surprising. He is a late nineteenth century historian who could not be expected to attempt such a formalized theoretical venture. He does, of course, attempt to answer the "why" of social events, yet when he does, it is clearly an interpretive gesture.

In 1911, Turner delivered an address to the American Historical Association entitled, "Social Forces in American History." His opening statement was a powerful comment on the state of the nation. "The transformations through which the United States is passing in our day are so profound, so far reaching, that is it hardly an exaggeration to say that we are witnessing the birth of a new nation in America".[42] The social forces which contributed to this great transformation are those mentioned earlier, such as industrialization, urbanization, world structuralization, and immigration with its attendant movement of Americanization.

These are inextricably intertwined themes in the development of the society; however, it is the last of these, the influx of immigrants on which Turner focuses. Moreover, here for the first time, he employs the term "ethnic." A possible explanation for its usage may be due to its introduction and more frequent usage by some leading American social scientists. Turner's first use of the term ethnic comes in a discussion of the immigration of 1907, when he says:

> Thus it is evident that the *ethnic* [Author's italics] elements of the United States have undergone startling changes; and instead of spreading over the nation, these immigrants have concentrated especially in the cities and great industrial centers in the past decade. The composition of the labor class and its relation to wages and to the native American employer has been deeply influenced thereby; the sympathy of the employers with labor has been unfavorably affected by the pressure of great numbers of immigrants of alien nationality and of lower standards of life.[43]

With respect to the immigrants, this quote represents a significant historical transiton. The frontier is no longer the symbol of national development, or, the explanation for the character of American society and community. The first period of American history has drawn to a close. The new period of the urban frontier is being ushered in for which the symbol "melting pot" has begun to assume a larger interpretive role in explaining American historical development and the character of the American community. Turner's perspective on the immigrants testifies to this change. He submits first, that the ethnic elements of the United States have undergone startling changes. Presumably, this is a comment on the national origins of the newer waves of immigrants. Second, he observes that they are concentrating in the cities rather than spreading across the nation. In short, this is a transition to urbanization. Third, he states that this has influenced the relation between the native American and the labor class which is made up largely of the "new ethnic elements." Fourth, he interprets the reaction of native American employers to the new ethnic elements in labor as growing increasingly unsympathetic.

By 1910, Turner was probably aware of much of the work beginning to be done on ethnic populations in urban areas. He delivered an address in that year when many of the nativist movements were underway. Turner's writing over those last twenty years revealed a noticeable change in attitude concerning immigrants and ethnics. It moved from a posture of patience, understanding, and hope to an attitude of sympathy and condescension. I believe we can express with some certainty that his attitude toward the immigrants differed before and after the closing of the frontier, a transition that was mirrored by a change in the national origin of the immigrant population.

The final paragraph of Frederick Jackson Turner's major work, *The Frontier in American History*, helps us to understand the significance of the pioneer experience on the development of democracy in the United States.

> This then is the heritage of the pioneer experience, – a passionate belief that a democracy was possible which should leave the individual a part to play in free society and not make him a cog in a machine operated from above; which trusted in the common man, in his tolerance, his ability to adjust to differences with good humor, and to work

> out an American type from the *contribution of all nations* [Author's italics] – a type for which he would fight against those who challenged it in arms, and for which in time of war he would make sacrifices, even the temporary sacrifice of individual freedom and his life, lest that freedom be lost forever.[44]

Turner, like Walt Whitman, Oscar Handlin, and John F. Kennedy, recognized the fact that America (the American type) was formed from the contribution of all nations.

Turner's Theory of American Ethnicity

Frederick Jackson Turner's theory of American ethnicity espouses a specific set of propositions concerning the processes that occur when different ethnic groups come together in the United States. These propositions and the concepts which help comprise them resonate with a set of domain assumptions.

The procedure at this point will be to strip down Turner's theory to its basic process assertions. These process assertions will be stateable in serial order. They can be viewed as a sequence of stages. Turner's conceptual schemes are very consonant with this view; for example, his description of frontier building takes the form of stage sequencing from savagery to civilization as he traces the trail of the buffalo, Indian, trapper, trader, farmer, and so forth.[45] The stages that are listed represent a pared down formalized version of Turner's theory of American ethnicity. As each stage is presented, an attempt is made to elaborate on the concepts used, the way they are organized, the relationship between the process assertions (propositions), and the grounding of these statements in a set of postulates and domain assumptions.

Turner's stages of the process that occurs when people of different ethnic groups come together in the United States may be systematically represented by these five terms:

1. Diversity
2. Conflictual encounter
3. Competition
4. Compromise
5. Unity

These processes can be further elaborated.

1. Turner recognized the 'heterogeneity' of the population of the U.S.. His sentiment toward this heterogeneity was positive. Turner grew up in an environment with a diverse social composition. He often recalled that the ethnic diversity in his hometown of Portage included Indians, Irish, Pomeranians, Scots, Welsh, Germans, New England Yankees, a few Southerners, a few Negroes, some Englishmen, one or two Italians, and many Norwegians and Swiss.[46] He never had much of a problem accepting phenomena that were neither monadic nor homogeneous. Even in science, when he became exposed to the notion of "multiple hypotheses" at the University of Wisconsin, it became incorporated into his formerly linear way of conceptualizing such phenomena.[47] Turner was also comfortable in viewing the fringe of the frontier as an area of savagery and disorder. Accustomed to the acceptance frame of diversity, Turner was able to view American society as follows:

> This, then, is the real situation: a people composed of heterogeneous materials, with diverse and conflicting social ideals and interests. . . .[48]

Although Turner could recognize diversity, he couldn't view it as constant, or as an eventual outcome. Instead, he viewed it as part of a process in which the end result was not plagued by heterogeneity, diversity, or disorder. He didn't necessarily correlate diversity and heterogeneity with disorder; however, he did seem to view it as being less unified and harmonious. Even with regard to the frontier, this process view was evident. The frontier became "the meeting point between savagery and civilization.[49] Civilization meant order, and Turner made it clear that order was associated with progress. The frontiersman was symbolic of this. He could impose order upon chaos. He mastered the wilderness and transformed it. Regarding the frontiersman, he said: "He knew how to preserve order, even in the absence of legal authority".[50]

As frequently happened in Turner's work, whether it concerned "sectionalism," "the froniter," or "ethnicity," diversity, heterogeneity, and disorder always gave way to civilization, unity, and order. Although this is the case, it is interesting to note Turner's slight preservation of a small aspect of diversity, an aspect which becomes modified yet maintained in a different state. It becomes evident as he describes the West.

> The wilderness disappears, the "West" passes on to a new frontier area, a new society has emerged with its contact with the backwoods. Gradually, this society loses its primitive conditions, and assimilates itself to the type of older social conditions of the East; but, it bears within it, *enduring and distinguishing survivals of its frontier experience* [Author's italics].[51]

Some primitive diversity is conserved even after the transformation to unity occurs.

Turner's way of conserving diversity and heterogeneity is sometimes done by relying on the notion of differentiation. Firmly grounded in the concepts of organicism and evolutionism this notion appears in Turner's work. Here it appears with respect to institutions.

> . . . we have the familiar phenomena of the *evolution* of institutions in a limited area such as the rise of representative government; the *differentiation* of simple colonial governments into *complex organs;* the progress from primitive industrial society without division of labor, up to manufacturing civilization.[52]

For Turner, the doctrines of organicism and evolutionism were the reconciling forces for forms of heterogeneity and diversity. His training in these areas was well documented along with the great value he placed on them.

> What Newton did for the mind of man in his age – what Copernicus in his – only in greater degree have Darwin and Spencer done for our own – they have given us a new world – and from this enlarged conception of things must come a new era, broader ideas of religion, government etc.[53]

As a student, he conceived of society as a growing organism and history as the self-consciousness of that organism.[54] With these two doctrines in hand, Turner was able to view all forms of diversity, heterogeneity, and disorder as temporary states. 'Progress' and 'advance' were always taking place.

Accepting the fact that Turner could conserve a small amount of diversity through a transformation in which the process of differentiation played an important role, then, we can begin to understand his notion of a "composite nationality." In this case, diversity becomes subsumed under a larger form of order.

1. In this first stage of the ethnic intergroup process, Turner is describing the elements of the process just before it begins. That is, his assertion that *the population is heterogeneous and that different groups of people have diverse interests and ideals,* is a description of the conditions that exist as people *begin to come together.* It is a view of the landscape of the American community as being comprised of immigrants from many lands. All had different ideals and interests. To this extent they were alike. Turner does, however, make a distinction between immigrants. This distinction, however, is not merely on the basis that they are of different nationalities. The distinction is wider than that. There are immigrants, and there are "alien" immigrants. Toward the first type the sentiment is positive, while toward the second type the sentiment is mixed. Remarking about the "immigrants" of German and Scandinavian nationality, he says:

> To the old native democratic stock has been added a vast army of recruits from the Old World. There are in the middle west alone four million persons of German parentage out of a total of seven million in the country. Over a million persons of Scandinavian parentage live in the same region. The democracy of the newer west is deeply affected by the ideals brought by those immigrants from the Old World.[55]

The difference of sentiment expressed between these "immigrants", on the one hand, and the "alien immigrants", on the other, becomes clear.

> Tides of *alien* [Author's italics] immigrants were surging into the country to replace the Old American stock in the labor market, to lower the standards of living and to increase the pressure of population upon the land.[56]

And here he continues: ". . . . labor has been unfavorably affected by the pressure of great numbers of immigrants of *alien nationality* [Author's italics] and of lower standards of life".[57]

The important difference here is that the latter type does not seem to be conforming to a model in which order will surely prevail. These latter alien immigrants were those largely from southern and eastern Europe who came to the United States around the turn of the century. Turner's sentiment toward them is reflective of many other writers of that time who also feared the seemingly impending social disorganization which these immigrants would bring.[58]

It appears from the analysis of Turner's first stage of the ethnic intergroup processes that he is capable of reorganizing the wide diversity of the American landscape, the heterogeneity of its populations, the savagery of the wilderness, and the disorder of much of the initial stage of social life of the West. However, Turner's ability to view these conditions as permanent characteristics of American life rather than as a temporary state of affairs, is very limited. He can only cope with these conditions by alluding to concepts such as 'advance' and 'progress,' for in this way, the temporality of these conditions is made clear. The grounding for his conceptual scheme is found in the doctrine of organicism and evolutionism.

These two views profoundly shape the development of his theory. While evolution legitimates the notion of forward progress and advance, organicism copes with diversity by refining it and imposing a process of differentiation upon it. The remaining four stages of his theory are also heavily guided by these two doctrines.

2. Frederick Jackson Turner's second stage is illustrative of the *confrontation* which occurs between the different ethnic groups. These groups have "diverse and conflicting social ideals and interests."[59] There is no question that ideals and interests of ethnic groups are different. However, one should note Turner's tendency to always focus on those that differ, and not on social ideals and interests which are the same (and there are many). All immigrants, for example, just by the nature of being immigrants, share a common value tied to the act of migration. This orientation of Turner's, to focus on differences rather than similiarities, was evident in his early scholarly work with Herbert Baxter Adams in which Turner was noted as having placed an emphasis on the differences more than the similarities between Europe and America.[60]

Turner often takes note of the conflictual encounters between immigrant groups, although again, he views this as a temporary state. He often points out the "grave anxiety" caused by the coming of the Germans and Scots-Irish to Pennsylvania,[61] and of the Puritans in New England as they pushed away the Scots-Irish Presbyterians,[62] or the "stubborn" Pennsylvania Dutch as they refused to assimilate, problematically affecting state politics.[63] Even in the Middle West, he points out the conflict over social ideals between the Germans and Puritans.

> In some of their social ideals, they came into *collision* with the Puritan element from New England.[64]

And again, in Milwaukee, he points out the "resistance" of Germans to native American efforts to enact rigid temperance legislation.

It is important to take note of Turner's implication that conflict exists because people are heterogeneous and have diverse ideals, and not because conflict is a normal state of affairs. In other words, it is not the conflicts that are the essence of the American social world, these are only temporary; but rather it is the forward progress and composite unity that is the essence of the American social world.

It would be difficult to label Turner's theory of American ethnicity as a theory of assimilation in the same sense in which later authors refer to the meaning of assimilation. Turner's meaning of assimilation is limited to what happens on the frontier. In the end, a total assimilation in the sense in which later authors refer to it, does not occur from Turner's perspective. Not only does he affirm the persistence of an inherited morale, but he also dismisses the melting pot as an adequate notion to explain what was happening in American society.[65]

3. Turner's third stage of interethnic group processes in the United States involves the activity of *competition.* The appearance of this is not surprising for it is a core value of American life which has permeated nearly all works on American social character. Following Turner:

> Both the native settler and European immigrant saw in this free and *competitive* movement of the frontier, the chance to break the bondage of social rank and to rsie to a higher plane of existence.[66]

Concerning the Germans and Puritans, he asserts that there was a "steady contest" between them before a compromise was reached.[67]

This third stage of competitive relations between ethnic groups is grounded within the deeper assumptions about the nature of man and society. Turner developed a set of positive sentiments toward another core American value, that of individualism. This becomes expressed in his assumption that "society becomes atomic."[68] Atomistic theory emphasizes the autonomy of the individual and his inherent reason as the determinant of behavior. In this way, the individual can be defined in relation to the community, yet his actions need not be totally determined by the community. Atomistic theory not only grounded Turner's concept of the relationship between man and society, but it also conserved the American value of individualism – one that is essential for the process of competition in American life.

4. Turner's next stage in the process of ethnic intergroup relations in the United States is exemplified by the word *compromise.* This marks the phase in which group relations become reordered. Among the many processes that occur within this stage are Americanization, mixing, fusion, reorganization, and equilibrium. This is by far the most comprehensive of the five Turner stages. This is a stage in which *turbulent forces* give way to *equilibrating forces.* The words "crucible" and "witch's kettle" are used in different cases to symbolize the place where turbulent forces come together.[69] For example, Turner says: "In the crucible of the frontier the immigrants were Americanized, liberated, and fused into a mixed race."[70] And here again, he expresses metaphorically these forces: "The forces of reorganization are turbulent and the nation seems like a witch's kettle."[71]

The forces of reorganization that he refers to here but does not specify, include the equilibrating forces. Among these are mutual education, cooperation, and democracy. Concerning mutual education he states:

> In the midst of the more or less antagonism between "bowie knife Southerners", "cow-milking Yankee Puritans", "beer drinking Germans", and "wild Irish-men", a process of mutual education, a giving and taking, was at work.[72]

Concerning democracy as a mechanism for compromise and placing it within the context of sentiments that stress individualism and non-determinism, Turner states:

> This then is the heritage of the pioneer experience, – a passionate belief that a democracy was possible which

> should leave the individual a part to play in free society and not make him a cog in a machine operated from above; which trusted in the common man, in his tolerance, his ability to adjust to differences with good humor, and to work out an American type from the contribution of all nations.[73]

Turner has a way of reconciling the sharp movement from turbulent to equilibrating forces. This is done by a grounding in the assumption that:

a) Society is plastic;[74]
b) "All were accepted and intermingling components of a forming society, plastic and absorptive."[75]

5. The final phase of Turner's process of ethnic intergroup relations, a process which yields a "composite nationality," is denoted by the term *unity*. As mentioned earlier, Turner was largely influenced by the doctrines of organicism and evolutionism. These are also grounding assumptions for the final stage, that of unity. Following Turner: "The diverse elements are being fused into a national unity".[76] And within the same paragraph, the organic notion of equilibrium is employed. Remarking about the diversity and heterogeneity of the population, Turner describes the process in which, over time, the vacant spaces of the continent become filled, the people are thrown back upon themselves, after which they begin "seeking an equilibrium".[77]

Turner's final product, although having a seemingly unified and harmonious character, and symbolized by the term composite nationality, does not totally wipe out diversity. Just as there are limitations placed on the meaning of Turner's concept of assimilation, there are also limitations placed on his ability to visualize, project, and accept total homogeneity. There are two assertions in particular that make this evident. In the first, he dismisses the melting pot as representative of the process of nationality formation in the United States. And in the second, he asserts the persistence of an inherited morale among ethnic groups.

> In the outcome, in spite of the slowness of assimilation where different groups were compact and isolated from the others, and a certain *persistence of inherited morale,* there was the creation of a new type which was neither the sum of all its elements, *nor a complete fusion in a melting pot* [Author's italics].[78]

Turner could not bring himself to totally assimilate the immigrants because he knew very well that there was a lasting immigrant character to American society. His theory of the frontier often described the great contributions made by immigrants to frontier building and westward expansion and development. He knew the legacy of the immigrants would not disappear and although groups worked together to build the frontier and assimilated with each other, he stopped short of describing or projecting a total assimilation.

Turner Typology

Concepts: Immigrant, Alien Immigrant, Alien Nationality, Ethnic Elements, Native Stock, Assimilation, Americanization

Process Assertions:

(1) Diversity, Heterogeneity
- (a) Social Interests
- (b) Social Ideals

(2) Conflictual Encounter
- (a) Territoriality
- (b) Resistance

(3) Competition
- (a) Individualism
- (b) Mutual Education

(4) Compromise
- (a) Turbulent Forces
  1. Crucible, Witch's Kettle
  2. Mixing, Fusion
- (b) Equilibrating Forces
  1. Reorganization
  2. Democracy, Cooperation

(5) Unity
- (a) Composite Nationality
- (b) National Unification

Postulates

(1) Organicism
  (a) Spencer
  (b) Society as a Growing Organism
  (c) Complex Organs, Differentiation

(2) Evolutionism
  (a) Darwin
  (b) Progress, Advance
  (c) Differentiation

Domain Assumptions:

(1) Society is Atomic

(2) Society is Plastic

(3) Society is Absorptive

(4) Individualism, Anti-Determinism

(5) Alien Immigrants – "Dull brained," (Differing immigrant sentiments)

(6) Persistence of Inherited Morale and Non-Melting Pot.

Notes

1. Some excellent biographical sources on Frederick Jackson Turner include Wilbur R. Jacobs, *The Historical World of Frederick Jackson Turner,* London: Yale, 1968; James D. Bennett, *Frederick Jackson Turner,* Boston: Tyayne, 1975; and Filmur Mood's introduction to *The Early Writings of Frederick Jackson Turner,* Freeport, NY: Books for Libraries Press, 1938, reprinted 1969; also Wilbur R. Jacobs, ed., *Frederick Jackson Turner's Legacy,* San Marino, 1965.
2. Jacobs, Ibid., pp. 6–7.
3. Bennett, Ibid., p. 17.
4. Jacobs, Ibid., p. 61.
5. *Wisconsin Magazine of History,* 1935, p. 96.
6. Bennett, Ibid., p. 18.
7. Jacobs, Ibid., p. xix.
8. Bennett, Ibid., p. 13.
9. Bennett, Ibid.

10. Jacobs, Ibid., p. 8.
11. Merle Curti, "Frederick Jackson Turner," in *Wisconsin Witness to Frederick Jackson Turner: A Collection of Essays on the Historian and his Thesis,* compiled by O. Lawrence Burnette, Jr., Madison, 1961, pp. 178–179.
12. Ibid., pp. 179–180.
13. Ibid., p. 181.
14. Ibid., pp. 182–183.
15. Ibid., p. 185.
16. Frederick Jackson Turner, *The Aegis* (Madison), 7, pp. 48–49, November 4, 1892.
17. Turner, *The Frontier in American History,* Huntington, New York: Krieger, 1976, p. 1.
18. Ibid.
19. Curtie, op. cit., p. 190.
20. Turner, op. cit., p. 4.
21. See Milton Gordon, *Assimilation in American Life,* New York: Oxford University Press, 1964.
22. Turner, *The Frontier in American History,* p. xiii.
23. Turner, "The Significance of the Frontier in American History," read at the meeting of the American Historical Association, Chicago, July 12, 1893.
24. Billington, Preface from *The Frontier in American History,* p. xi.
25. Ibid.
26. Ibid., p. xii.
27. Bennett, op. cit., p. 37.
28. Mood, op. cit., p. 36.
29. Ibid., p. 39.
30. Ibid., p. 40.
31. Turner, "Problems in American History," *The Aegis* 7 (November 4, 1892): 48–52.
32. Bennett, op. cit., p. 40.
33. Turner, *Rise of the New West,* New York: Harper, 1906.
34. Turner, *The Significance of Sections in American History,* New York: Henry Holt, 1932.
35. Turner, *The United States 1830–1850: The Nation and its Section,* New York: Henry Holt, 1935.
36. Turner, *The Character and Influence of Indian Trade in Wisconsin: A Study of The Trading Post as an Institution,* Baltimore: Johns Hopkins University, 1891.

37. Bennett, *Frederick Jackson Turner,* p. 80.
38. Turner's only use of the word ethnic appears on p. 51 of this chapter.
39. Turner, "The Significance of the Frontier in American History," p. 13.
40. Turner, "Pioneer Ideas and the State University," in *The Frontier in American History,* p. 270.
41. Ibid., pp. 277–278.
42. Turner, "Social Forces in American History," p. 311.
43. Turner, "Social Forces in American History," p. 316.
44. Turner, "Middle Western Pioneer Democracy," p. 359.
45. Frederick Jackson Turner, *The Frontier in American Life.*
46. James O. Bennett, *Frederick Jackson Turner,* Boston: Tyayne, 1975, p. 17.
47. Merle Curti, "Frederick Jackson Turner," in *Wisconsin Witness to Frederick Jackson Turner,* pp. 179–80.
48. Turner, "The Problem of the West," p. 321.
49. Turner, "The Significance of the Frontier in American History", p. 2.
50. Turner "The Problem of the West," p. 212.
51. Turner, ibid., p. 205.
52. Turner, "The Significance of the Frontier in American History."
53. Jacobs, *The Historical World of Frederick Jackson Turner,* p. 9.
54. See, for example, Turner's "The Significance of the Frontier in American History" and "The Problems in American History."
55. Turner, "Contributions of the West to American Democracy," p. 265.
56. Turner, "Pioneer Ideals and the State University," p. 271.
57. Turner, "Social Forces in American History," p. 316.
58. See, for example, Henry Pratt Fairchild, *The Melting Pot Mistake.*
59. Turner, "The Problem of the West," p. 221.
60. Merle Curti, "Frederick Jackson Turner," pp. 182–83.
61. Turner, "The Old West," p. 109.
62. Ibid.
63. Ibid., p. 110.
64.. Turner, "The Middle West," p. 138.
65. This is demonstrated clearly in a later process assertion.
66. Turner, "The Middle West," p. 154.
67. Turner, Ibid., p. 138.

68. Turner, "The Problem of the West," p. 212.
69. Turner, "The Problem of the West," p. 221.
70. Turner, "The Significance of the Frontier in American History," p. 23.
71. Turner, "The Problem of the West," p. 221.
72. Turner, "Middle Western Pioneer Democracy," p. 349.
73. Ibid., p. 358, 359
74. Ibid., p. 349.
75. Turner, "Middle Western Pioneer Democracy," p. 351.
76. Turner, "The Problem of the West," p. 221.
77. Ibid.
78. Turner, "Middle Western Pioneer Democracy," p. 349.

IV Henry Pratt Fairchild

Biography

Henry Pratt Fairchild was born in Dundee, Illinois, on August 18, 1880.[1] He was the son of Arthur Babbitt Fairchild and Isabel Pratt. His first paternal American ancestor was Thomas Fairchild who came to North America from England in 1638 and settled in Stamford, Connecticut. His father was an educator and a significant influence on Henry Fairchild's early intellectual training. Fairchild attended school close to home in his town of Crete, Nebraska. He received his preliminary education at the public schools there and also received his A.B. degree in 1900 from Doane College in the same community. Following this, between the years 1900–1903, he was an instructor at the International College, Smyrna (later Izmir), Turkey. When he returned to the United States he travelled for three years throughout Nebraska in the capacity of State Secretary of Doane College. He was enrolled at Yale University as a graduate student and between 1906 and 1909 he taught in Greece and completed his Ph.D. dissertation on Greek Immigration to the United States. He was professor of economics and sociology at Bowdoin College from 1909–10, assistant professor of economics at Yale University from 1910–11, and assistant professor of the science of society at the latter school during 1912–18. Additionally, he was secretary of the Bureau of Appointments at Yale University in 1917–18.

During the First World War, 1918–19, Fairchild served as the director of the personnel department at the War Camp Community Service, New Haven, Connecticut, in which he trained men for non-combat service, making use of his abilities as a horseman to teach equestrian drill and horseback riding. In 1919 he joined the faculty of New York University as professor of social economy and director of the Bureau of Community Service and Research, positions he held until 1924. In that year he was named professor of sociology at New York University and in 1938 he was additionally named chairman of the department of sociology at the New York University Graduate School of Arts and Sciences, continuing in both posts until his retirement as professor emeritus in 1945.

Fairchild's religious affiliation was with the Congregational Church. Politically, he was an independent. Playing tennis was one of his recreations; he was also interested in folk music and played guitar. He was married in New Haven, Connecticut, on June 2, 1909, to Mary Elenor, daughter of Charles Townsend, a businessman of that city. Fairchild had one daughter. He died in North Hollywood, California, on October 2, 1956.

Fairchild was very active in many civic organizations and societies within his fields of interest. He was president of the Eastern Sociology Conference in 1931–32, the People's League for Economic Security during 1934–38, and the Film Audiences for Democracy in 1939–40. He served as chairman of the Commonwealth Federation of New York during 1934–38, chairman for the National Council for the Arts, Sciences and Professions in 1942, and vice-president of the Planned Parenthood Federation from 1939–48. He was a member of the executive committee of the American Political Federation, and secretary of the National Council of American-Soviet Friendship. He was a member of the American Sociological Society (pres. 1936), the American Eugenics Society (pres. 1929–31), American Association of University Professors, and the Population Association of America.

Major Influences

Sources for this are virtually non-existent, however it is possible to piece together one set of influences that guided Fairchild's interests and study. Probably the most significant intellectual influence that Fairchild received took place during his graduate training at Yale University. It was here that he came after spending several years abroad in lands very different from his own, with people of a culture very remote from his own. This experience helped to stimulate an interest in Fairchild concerning culture, race, and nationality. The years he spent in southeastern Europe were years marked by large-scale migrations from that area to the United States. He was undoubtedly concerned with the questions that arose pertaining to the mixing of populations. When he returned to the United States, his major areas of study included birth control, immigration, population, and eugenics.[2] It was in these areas that his training at Yale University contributed the most. In attempting to trace the influence at Yale, we find that his doctoral dissertation, entitled *Greek Immigration to the United States*, was completed under the guidance of Professor Albert G. Keller. Keller was a mere six years older than Fairchild. However he possessed a much superior intellectual training, having received his Ph.D. ten years before Fairchild, under the guidance of Professor William Sumner. Aside from Keller, Sumner also had a direct influence on Fairchild. Sumner was a professor at Yale during Fairchild's graduate years. In fact, Fairchild had made informal reference to Sumner. In *Immigration* he says, "The laws of nature seem so much safer a guide than any plan which, as Professor Sumner says, someone has thought out in bed".[3] It is very doubtful that there was a student in sociology at Yale who was immune from the influence of a towering figure such as Sumner. Albert Keller, Fairchild's mentor, was probably the most devout student of Sumner, having co-authored with him and later published a book of personal reminiscences of Sumner's life.[4] Keller also became the William Sumner Professor of Science at Yale University.

The total influence of Sumner and Keller sharpened Fairchild's understanding and skill in the scientific study of society and the application of evolutionary theory to the study of social problems. The specific area of race relations and population was a topic of study for Sumner as well as for Keller.

Major Works

During his career, Fairchild wrote fourteen major books, edited three others, published two editions of a dictionary of sociology, and wrote numerous journal articles. He was the author of *Greek Immigration to the United States* (1911), *Immigration* (1913), *Outline of Applied Sociology* (1916), *Elements of Social Science* (1924), *The Melting Pot Mistake* (1925), *The Foundations of Social Life* (1927), *Profits or Prosperity?* (1932), *General Sociology* (1934), *The Way Out* (1936), *People: The Quantity and Quality of Population* (1939), *Economics for the Millions* (1940), *Main Street: The American Town, Past and Present* (1941), *Race and Nationality as Factors in American*

Life (1947) and *Versus: Reflections of a Sociologist* (1950). He was also the editor of *Immigrant Backgrounds* (1927), *The Obligations of Immigrants to the Social Order* (1933), *Dictionary of Sociology* (1944), and *Anatomy of Freedom* (1957).

Throughout most of his work Fairchild's major concern was with issues of population, immigration, race, and nationality. Even his textbooks on sociology (1916, 1924, 1927, 1934) mirror this fact. For instance, he devotes seven chapters to the topic of population in *An Outline of Applied Sociology;* in *The Foundations of Social Life* he devotes a chapter each to "The Great Dispersion" and "The Ways of Heredity"; and, finally, in *General Sociology* Fairchild devotes a major portion of the book to population and immigration. This concern can be traced to his doctoral dissertation when he said:

> The great question which, in the case of the Greeks, as well as of every other class of our alien population, is, will they make good citizens?[5]

This, in effect, is what Fairchild defined as the problem of immigration. He tried to answer this question and deal with this problem in one way or another in most of his works. For instance, two years later, in 1913, he further speculated about the possibility of injury to the United States.

In *Immigration* he states:

> What then are the arguments for and against immigration from the point of view of the United States? The positive arguments for, and the negative arguments against, immigration center around whether the United States needs immigrants. The positive arguments against, and the negative arguments for, immigration have to do with the claim that immigration injures the United States.[6]

By the time *The Melting Pot Mistake* was written in 1925, Fairchild had clearly spelled out the dangers of immigration to the national unity of the United States. Here he advises what must be done to preserve that unity.

> If immigration is to continue, and if our nation is to be preserved, we must all, native and foreigner alike, resign ourselves to the inevitable truth that unity can be maintained

> only through the complete sacrifice of extraneous national traits on the part of our foreign elements.[7]

After The *Melting Pot Mistake* Fairchild continued to stress the "hard facts" of intergroup relations. Working from a science of society frame of reference that he had acquired under Keller and Sumner at Yale, Fairchild treated the factors of race and nationality as the sole and most significant determinants of intergroup relations.

In his text entitled *General Sociology* he states:

> It follows that the ideal human group, from the point of view of security, stability, and efficient functioning, and the most nearly complete satisfaction of desires and cravings of social man, is realized when society, race, and nation coalesce, when the functioning group, the biological group, and the spiritual group are identical.[8]

Fairchild's concern with the problem of immigration carried through until the time of his death. The work that he produced had a definite effect on the establishment and maintenance of immigration quotas. In one of his last works, *The Prodigal Century,* he began to tie his concern with the immigration problem to the issue of eugenics.

> But, supposing that some country, the United States par excellence, were to experience a great upsurge of international humanitarianism and should throw down all its immigration barriers except, perhaps, the most obvious qualitative ones, what good would it do?[9]

He is making the point that although the possibility exists for the United States to open its doors to the masses of people who are overflowing the borders and boundaries of other nations, this would not help to alleviate the root cause of the problem, namely, overpopulation. It naturally follows, for Fairchild, that control measures on population quantity are necessary.[10] He goes still further and espouses "the humanity of eugenics" as a way of controlling the *quality* of the population.[11]

The Melting Pot Mistake

Fairchild's major work, entitled *The Melting Pot Mistake,* is a treatise aimed at rejecting the notion of the melting pot as a symbol that would explain what was and what would happen to American society. Written at the peak of the great immigration of the early twentieth century, this work refused to acknowledge the then increasingly common view that all the immigrants and "old-stock" Americans would become homogenized into a new American type that represented a combination of all their nationalities.

Fairchild lays the groundwork for his argument by asserting that, due to the "present complicated and headlong organization of society",[12] a democratic society like the United States devises all kinds of symbols to help sort out the web of intricate social issues so that an adequate independent judgment can be made of social, economic, and political situations. Labels and symbols aid the citizen by making him associate these situations with the images in his mind. The major dysfunction of these symbols is that they often call out inaccurate images. The citizen's image of an issue is based on the interpreter's symbol usage and it becomes "fundamentally important, then, that the interpreter be both honest and acute, and that the symbols be authentic as well as realistic".[13] From this point, Fairchild makes it evident that the symbol – melting pot – will be the focus of his attack.

This idea (melting pot), according to Fairchild, is a big mistake. The diverse ethnic and social groups have not melted, cannot melt, and never will melt. The major task of his work is to explain why this is true, why the melting pot idea failed, the results of that failure, the hope for escaping the consequences of that failure, and by what means that hope shall be realized.

Fairchild interprets the central problems surrounding the melting pot and immigration, as boiling down to the social matter of *unification.* He reveals a broad domain assumption that runs through his entire theory of American ethnicity, when he states that " . . . in any community, particularly a democratic one, unity is one of the essentials of stability, order, and progress."[14] He assumes this almost intuitively. From this point of view, this would seem to be a quite accurate orientation from which to depart. It is important to take note of this because the next theorist, Horace Kallen, will take a completely different posture on unity. Fairchild was quite skeptical concerning the real purpose of the melting pot symbol other than to "convince the American people that immigration did not threaten its unity, but tended to produce an even finer type of unity."[15]

Thus it is easy to see where he builds his argument against the melting pot in his theory of American ethnicity. It is in the nature of group unity that he looks for answers and solutions. To this extent, his perspective of the social world yields for him a particular type of conception of the nature of group unity, one which conceives of different groups bound together by powerful ties, and each seeking its own interest, oftentimes in opposition to the interests of others.[16]

Several assumptions become apparent from a close reading of Fairchild's assertions concerning groups unity. First, he sees the human species as being comprised of well-defined units by which he means groups. Furthermore, each group is distinct and the bonds between its members are powerful. Second, group interests place them in opposition with other groups. Noticeably missing are the categories – immigrants and ethnics. Fairchild's conceptual scheme treats immigrants from two parameters, race and nationality. That is to say, an immigrant is a member of a particular nationality and race. In this way, Fairchid can continue to build his analysis on the presupposition that race and nationality are key factors in the major theme of social unification. The word ethnic does not appear for the same reason it was infrequently used by Turner. Before the early twentieth century, it wasn't a word commonly thought of as applying to immigrants and their descendents. Furthermore, it didn't pack the explanatory power that race and nationality had. Nevertheless, as Fairchild suggests, it is not the name that is important but the fact that these groups form the basis for world alignments.

During his career, Fairchild served as a special immigration agent in Europe for the United States Department of Labor. The process of immigration fascinated him and led him to write a book entitled, *Immigration* (1913). In *The Melting Pot Mistake,* he talks about immigration and its relationship to group unity. He believed that in order to fully understand the process of immigration, one must go back over the course of human evolution starting with the beginning of man's existence.

> The consensus of opinion of scientists is that if we could go back to the very beginning of man's existence we should find a single small group, living probably somewhere on the high central plateau of Asia. Among the members of this group there would be virtually complete unity, with only such minute individual variations as distinguish the members of any restricted species of animals.[17]

Immigration is described as having an immediate bearing on group unity. His assumptions about the nature of man and society are anthropological in character. First, it is the nature of human groups to be organized. Second, as evolution occurs, group size and number increase. Third, all humans developed from an "original uniform type". Fourth, the members of the original human group were "virtually completely" unified.

Fairchild attempts to trace the processes by which the present scale of human diversity was produced. There was a struggle for existence as the supplies of nature became limited, and therefore man had to compete with others in his environment. As the eventual increase of human beings reached the point where man's original habitat was filled, he then came face to face with a fundamental law of nature – the law of stationary population. Every species except man succumbs to this law, man alone has the option to escape out of his original habitat and move to practically any land surface on earth.[18]

This process of progressive adaptation to different environments is the first basis of group differentiation. It therefore becomes important to explain just why and how his adaptation took place and the nature of the results. In doing so, more anthropological assumptions become salient. Group differentiation as a basis for the process of progressive adaptation occurs in the following way. Every living species, including man, is adapted to some specific environment. Within this environment, some individuals are more closely adapted and approximate an average of the species. Those who are not among this average group, but within close range of it, do continue to exist, although with a specific handicap.

Those who are far from the average do not survive. At any time, there are individuals on the edge of that habitat in close proximity to another environment. As these individuals produce offspring, there will be "some whose variations constitute a handicap in the regular environment but afford an advantage in the adjacent environment."[19] These individuals will have a tendency to drift over to the new environment in order to survive. As this process becomes perpetuated from one environment to the next, the species of man spreads across the globe.

The above process accounts, in part, for the formation and separation of different groups on the face of the earth known as races. Fairchild refers to this historical process of population movement as the "period of race formation". His conclusion in this respect is that "the primary basis of group unity is therefore racial".[20] As he begins to define race, his domain assumptions and theoretical presuppositions begin to take on a biological orientation.

> A human race is a group of men more closely related to each other by physiological kinship than they are to the members of other races, because they have more nearly a common ancestry. The ancestral lines of the members of a single race draw together into a great common stock. It is obvious, then, that race is a relative term. All men are physiologically related to each other. All men have the same general ancestry, and not two men have an identical ancestry except brothers and sister. The question of race is a question of degrees of relationship.[21]

With this definition of the process of race formation as a basis, Fairchild is able to interpret population movements in general. The primary period of population movement is distinguished from other types of population movements by the term "dispersion." It is slow and instinctual with a lack of conscious direction. It is a movement "away from" rather than "to". It is a movement aimed at escaping the law of stationary population and toward the conditions of least resistance.

The process of dispersion caused the formation of racial groups. These groups are characterized by a community of physical kinship and identified by distinct physical features. Moreover, racial traits are hereditary. They are carried by means of genes in the germ plasm of each race.[22] Concerning these racial traits, Fairchild asserts that the observable type is the type from which people usually form their judgments, and, prejudices are based on observable physical traits such as skin color and facial features. However, he believes these to be less important than the non-observable traits, especially the psychological traits, which he believes are also hereditary as they are a function of distinctive features of the brain. These are *organic* differences on which depend intellectual, emotional and psychological traits. Thus Fairchild has established the bases for a theory of inherited traits. While he identifies all these as racial in character, he believes the psychological traits to be the most important from the point of view of social relationships.[23]

Concerning the significant role each of these racial factors plays in group relations, Fairchild clearly sees one as being more important.

> Just as we, individually, choose our friends more for their spiritual traits than for their physical so the relations between groups of men depend much more on their respective reactions to ideas and other psychical stimuli than upon the physical appearance or the anthropological classification of their members. We can quickly get used to novel or even unattractive outward appearances, but we can never quite adjust ourselves to those whose fundamental spiritual processes have nothing in common with our won.[24]

Fairchild identifies the second era of the movement of peoples as the period of *race contact* and *race conflict.* By the end of the previous period of species dispersion, racial traits had embedded themselves as a result of the eventual exhaustion of uninhabited regions of the world. A development of distinctly human culture and civilization began to occur. Thus, a new epoch was introduced that eliminated the necessity of physical adaptation as a condition of movement into diverse environments. The possibility of artificial adaptation was substituted which provided the means for rapid movement of population from one region to another.

According to Fairchild, for many reasons the pressure of population movement did not cease. A result was the emergence of a period of race contact and conflict. "Race mixture" began to occur and cross-racial interactional situations increased. The phenomenon of race mixture began to increase until racial purity was found only in the more isolated corners of the earth. However, this racial mixing did not dilute racial identity. As Fairchild asserts:

> . . . there can be racial identity and racial distinction without racial purity. If only two races are mixed, the resulting type may be almost as distinct and definite as a pure race. As a matter of fact, in spite of the long centuries of race mixture, it still remains true that in most of the great habitation areas of the globe the natives are characterized at least by a typical racial preponderance if nothing more. There is still ample racial unity in the leading human groups to make racial traits and racial affiliations fundamental factors in intergroup relationships.[25]

Like race, nationality for Fairchild, is of equal significance for understanding the social basis of group unity. While racial formation was going on, nationality development began to occur. As civilization became established, the needs and desires of human beings guided its founding. Each civilization developed different ways to satisfy the same types of needs of its members (i.e., food, mating, respect, etc.). This became the second basis of group unity.

Upon designating nationality to this position, Fairchild does concede that there is some confusion surrounding the term. He states:

> This is the confusion between race, and this other fundamental basis of group unity. An indication of this confusion is furnished by the fact that there does not exist even a word to definitely indicate the latter. Of all the available terms, that which comes nearest to the idea is "nationality," and rather than follow the academician's expedient of coining a new term out of his inner consciousness it will be well to take this word, give it a restricted meaning, and see it in as scientific a sense as possible.[26]

So although not completely satisfied with the term "nationality," he still uses it for reasons of his apparent lack of a better word and also his distaste for coining new words. A curious matter would be to consider whether or not "ethnic group" might have suited the notion Fairchild was trying to communicate. His usage of nationality sometimes comes close to the meaning of culture as in this case in which he makes an indirect inference to its meaning.

> Every individual is born with no nationality at all. He has no language, no dress, no moral code, no single one of the manifold accomplishments that compose human culture.[27]

Fairchild does outline a basic distinction between race and nationality. While race is impressed inextricably upon the individual, nationality is not. While race is inherited and biologically transmitted, nationality is acquired. He further defines nationality as follows:

> Nationality, then, is to be thought of as a great spiritual reality, existing much less in the realm of the intellect than in the sentiments and emotions. A certain amount of knowledge is inherent in nationality, but its real essence consists not in what one knows but in how one feels.

> Nationality is a composite body of ideas and ideals, beliefs, traditions, customs, habits, standards, and morals infused with loyalty, devotion, allegiance, and affection. A group of people who possess and are possessed by such a concrete mass of spiritual values embody that nationality, or, in a slightly different use of the word, constitute a nationality, or *are* a nationality.[28] [Authors Italics]

> . . . Nationality is a product of the human mind reflecting itself in group relations. So as long as the human mind continues to develop, and as long as the principle of change remains inherent in group relationships, nationality must continue to be a dynamic factor.[29]

One can not help but notice the similarity of this definition of nationality to other definitions of ethnic group. One of the differences between these is the factor of living as a group within the context of a larger society. Fairchild's definition is void of any consideration that these people or groups that constitute a nationality will upon migration to another society be different than the individuals who did not migrate. Merely referring to this group as a nationality or even as immigrants and attributing to them the characteristics of a nationality of which they are no longer totally a part, refuses to acknowledge a dynamic aspect of group processes. This is where the term ethnic group can cover for this dynamic aspect that Fairchild attributes to nationality but which the term nationality can not justly embrace once members of that group compact themselves within new communities of a different society.

These two factors, race and nationality, are designated by Fairchild to be the major foundational bases of group unity. They act to bind people inextricably together. Therefore, the character of relations propounded by these two factors cannot, Fairchild contends, be dismissed from the minds of the American people "by a lighthearted appeal to the figure of the melting pot".[30]

Fairchild's first use of the word *ethnic* comes in this discussion concerning in-group feelings, particularly in reference to tribes.

> A traveller asking for the name of the tribe will be told, "We are The Men." All other tribes are something less than men. This feeling is a compound of familiarity, pride,

> self-interest, habit, affection, and loyalty. At is worst, it expresses itself as an overweening ethnic egotism and selfishness. At its best, it appears as exalted patriotic devotion.[31]

Nothing approaching a formal definition of the term is offered here. The closest relational meaning for ethnic egotism might be ethnocentrism. At this point, however, ethnic is still embedded in the phenomenon of the tribe as described earlier.[32]

In summary, Fairchild has identified two factors which characterize primary human groups. These two factors form the basis of group unity. The first is race, largely defined as physical similarity. The second is nationality, largely defined as cultural similarity. In moving one step closer to the problem of group unification in general and group unification in the United States in particular, the next area of analysis becomes "group contact". Here, a general law of nature is initially postulated, "Creatures which are similar to each other are drawn or attracted to each other and find pleasure in companionship and some degree of common action."[33] This pivotal law suggests some things about intergroup relations. They are (a) group sympathy, characterized by such things as familiarity, pride, affection, loyalty, self-interest, we-ness, and consciousness of kind; (b) group antipathy, characterized by feelings toward outgroup members which include dislike, disgust, misunderstanding, hatred, fear, and various degrees of hostility.

Fairchild is led to construct a four-fold categorization scheme for universal intergroup relations based on the primary factors of group unity. These four are racial sympathy, racial antipathy, national sympathy and national antipathy. Concening these, he stresses the importance of the matter because his analysis of the process of assimilation rests heavily on it. "Every case of assimilation," he asserts, "is governed by the peculiar factors which condition it, and before predicting the outcome in even the most guarded terms these factors must be fully taken into the reckoning".[34]

An issue which can not be skipped over when dealing with the subject of group contacts is "race prejudice". Fairchild tries to correct the major misconceptions surrounding this term. He believed that most of what is thought of as racial is really not racial at all but rather national. These designate differences in language, dress, habits, foods, religion and family customs which are all national. This is particularly true in the United States.

What Fairchild is trying to point out is that national antipathy far outweighs racial antipathy as a key factor for understanding intergroup relations in the United States. It is the barriers of language, religion, political system, habits, customs, traditions, and national loyalty which have an enormous influence on intergroup relations, "none of which has any necessary connection with race".[35] This is not to suggest that race should be considered lightly, especially with respect to the building of a strong group unity. Harmony reaches its maximum when racial sympathy supports national sympathy. It is clear to Fairchild that racial dissimilarity can constitute an element of weakness to group unity.[36]

The implication of these possible conditions for the United States has occupied Fairchild's mind to the extent that he thought racial dilution in such a democracy is always a risky affair for the nation. As a mass of foreign population comes in contact with a native population, the results will depend on the particular combination of factors that exist among these two populations.

Having developed a theoretical foundation of the universal factors affecting intergroup relations and group unity, Fairchild set out to bring this to bear upon the circumstances that have occurred in the United States. As he embarked upon an analysis of the racial composition of the United States, his central problem immediately became one of tracing the roots of its people. As an organizing gesture, he splits the immigration history of the United States into two periods, colonial and national. The colonial period of immigration was designated as that time slot between roughly 1607–1790. This was considered a relatively small immigration as compared to the later national immigrations. While the former period of immigration amounted to approximately one-fifth of the existent population of America at the time, the latter amounted to approximately one-third of the existent population.[37] Also, while the former period of immigration came exclusively from northwestern Europe, the latter immigration came largely from the southern and eastern sections of Europe.

In tracing the major period of immigration, a clear distinction is made between the pre-1882 era, in which the migrants came from sources which were nearly identical racially (or as Fairchild put it, "at least the racial composition differed in proportion rather than in nature"[38]), and the post-1882 era, in which the predominance of racial purity in the United States was broken. Beginning in 1882 a marked change in the types of immigrants occurred. To this group Fairchild confers the phrase "The New Menace".[39] Large numbers of people from Austria-Hungary, Italy, the Russian Empire, Finland, the Balkan states, Turkey, and Greece began to swell the immigrant ranks. The racial composition of these groups was more diverse. Included were Mediterranean, Alpine, and Slavic races. Thus a significant problem of group unification began to exist in the United States. The Nordic predominance in the United States was profoundly altered. The problem became one of race mixture.

The concern expressed about the results of race mixture are significant and become carried on into a discussion on the effects of race mixture upon the character of society in the United States. In order to conceptualize this process, various analogies are employed, one of which is the melting pot. Surprisingly, Fairchild asserts that in respect to racial mixture, "the analogy of the melting pot is not far amiss."[40]

Upon stating this, he quickly qualifies the remark by first pointing out, that the major part of the problem of the great immigrations of the United States had nothing to do with racial mixture. It had more to do with nationality mixture. And second, the notion of the melting pot is accurate in respect to racial mixture only insofar as it confines itself exclusively to the process, and deals very little with the result. It is the result that is crucially important. In short, the question is, will it be good for anything?

As to the question of result, Fairchild admits that we are very limited in the power to answer this. The conclusions with respect to the results of race mixture are very uncertain. This is so for many reasons among which is that we cannot conduct experiments of this sort with human beings. However, since the facts of heredity are universal, then certain general principles that underlie all species of plants and animals may be applied to humans. Thus, the crossing of races is not necessarily disastrous, unless it is done indiscriminately in which case only one result can be expected – the mongrel.[41]

The implication here is that, in respect to the crossing of races in America, disastrous results are possible. Among these results, the most severe would be a loss of specialization. The specialized genes will either "neutralize or cancel each other out."[42]

Fairchild avoids explicitly stating that one race such as the Nordic race, for instance, is superior to the Mediterranean race. Yet he believes that their interbreeding will produce problems. Also, he is more concerned with the harm of diluting the Nordic and Aryan stocks than that of any other. The reason presumably being that they represent the "American type". Another assumption, then, is that the American type is Nordic and Aryan in terms of race, and, as later expounded, Anglo-Saxon in terms of nationality. Fairchild goes to all lengths to make it clear that he is no way implying that foreign elements are inferior.

> Mongrelization implies no inferiority on the part of the original constituents. So in a human society, the prediction of a mongrel population as the almost certain product of a free-for-all immigration policy carries no more slur against the foreign elements than against the natives. It simply means a loss of specialization on all sides.[43]

The final fear expressed with respect to racial mixing is the possibility that if the results are undersirable, the mistake will be virtually impossible to correct. For this reason and for others already mentioned, all measures taken to curtail and control immigration to the United States are legitimized. The "principle of national origins" is a case in point.[44]

Fairchild reveals a distinct change in thinking from most other Anglo-conformity theorists of American ethnicity. The races of southern and eastern Europe are not judged as inferior to the races of north-western Europe. They are simply incompatible or incommensurable. And since there can be no certainty concerning the possibility for instances of race-mixing yielding a positive outcome, Fairchild believes that the safe thing to do is to avoid it. Later developments in science may bring answers to this question but for now the best position is to stay on the safe side.

When placed in the context of American society, Fairchild's notion of assimilation can not be separated from the notion of Americanization. During this historical period, Americanization takes on a special meaning. Not only did it refer to a process by which immigrants become assimilated into American life, but it was also a movement launched by individuals who believed that assimilation would not occur on its own and that immigrants constituted a threat to the fiber of society unless they become Americanized. He identified the distinguishing features of Americanization as a recognition that assimilation had not been successfully achieved by the natural and spontaneous forces is the society but instead must be accomplished by deliberate artificial means. In short, Americanization was a manifestation of the delegation of assimilation into a "problem."[45]

During the time Fairchild was writing, many attempts were being made to assimilate the immigrant. The most notable of these was the Americanization movement. Americanization became a symbol for a new set of ideas. It was hailed but dimly comprehended by the citizens of the United States.[46] According to Fairchild, the distinguishing feature of Americanization was the recognition of the fact that assimilation had not been achieved, and therefore presumably could not be achieved by the spontaneous play of natural social forces and the determination to bring it to pass by artificial methods.[47] The Americanization movement was, in short, a deliberate effort at maintaining unification.

The Americanization movement largely took the form of an education campaign. Methods ranging from night schools, to worker training, to elementary school methods, were used to Americanize the immigrant. According to Fairchild, the movement largely failed. It failed because it confused means with ends. It mistakenly assumed that knowledge could provide the necessary forces to unite. But the movement wrongly assumed that the problem could be corrected by education. The way in which Fairchild conceptualized nationality limited his ability to see a change in nationality as primarily determined by education. The true test of nationality "is not what you know but how you feel."[48] Thus by stressing the cognitive aspect of education, and denying totally the affective dimension, such reasoning appeared natural to Fairchild.

While critical of the Americanization movement in many of his comments, he was also grateful and encouraging in others. He believed that the movement was "indispensable." However, the false assumption of the movement had been its downfall. It did not grasp the real nature of assimilation. Nevertheless, it did succeed in providing some knowledge about the American nationality via educational programs without which assimilation would be impossible.

Fairchild believed that another false assumption of the Americanization movement was the critical belief that assimilation is a voluntary process. It was as if one only had to decide to become

Americanized and it would be so. Consequently, when the immigrants failed to assimilate in great numbers, they were directly blamed for their non-assimilation as if it were their own fault. A very enlightening example is given to illustrate this aspect of assimilation. If, for instance, an American had to move and reside in a foreign country in the service of his government, could one realistically expect him to forget his feelings and sentiments about his home nation? In the same way, it would be naive to expect the immigrant to forget his nationality. The conditions of assimilation are not under voluntary control as many supporters of the Americanization movement were led to believe. Thus, asserts Fairchild, it would be foolish to blame the immigrant for non-assimilation and equally foolish to take a "holier than thou" attitude toward them.[49] Instead, he suggests that the people of the United States say:

> We have our own ways and you have your ways. Your ways are not our ways. We prefer our ways just because they are our own, and because our whole national life is built upon an around them. It is naturally very hard for you to give up your own ways, even though you want to. But we cannot tolerate the danger of having too many persons in our midst whose ways are different from ours. So if you wish to remain among us we hope that you will utilize every opportunity to learn and adopt our ways, and on our part we stand ready to help you by every means at our command.[50]

Having belabored the point that the Americanization movement has been working without a knowledge of the nature of assimilation and with false assumptions concerning the way to facilitate the process, Fairchild has now to address his critics. They ask: What hope is left for national unity? How is the dilemma incurred by immigration to be solved? In short, is assimilation a useless venture and a futile attempt to do the impossible? Fairchild's answer to these questions is one of optimism. He begins first by positing questions of his own. What are we trying to assimilate the immigrant into? What is an American? What is the meaning of America?

In contemplating the answers to this important set of questions, Fairchild assumes first that every human being is assimilated into that nationality of his birth. Because this process takes place at a very young age, it leaves a deep nationalistic impression on the individual which cannot be voluntarily discarded. Following on from this, the only way that one can be naturalized is by living in that nation. In the case of naturalization, there is a difference between a native and a foreigner. The native has become assimilated into one nationality whereas the foreigner has begun in one nationality and moved to another. This makes it extremely difficult for the foreigner to assimilate because he has already gone through that early period of internalizing a nationality. Therefore, any attempts at naturalization are hard pressed to work. Fairchild states:

> There can be no substitute for the genuine forces of assimilation. The only way in which any individual can be nationalized is to live in the nationality in question.[51]

To accept the proposition that in order for the immigrant to be Americanized he must live in America, it becomes necessary to build a conception of what America is. Then we can judge whether or not the immigrants are living in it. First, America is not merely a geographical area. Second, America is not merely an aggregation of people. Third, America is more than a governmental organization. If America were only made up of these three factors, then the assimilation of foreigners would not be much of a problem. But according to Fairchild, America is more than that.

> American is a nationality, and fortunately also a nation. America is a spiritual reality. It is a body of ideas and ideals, traditions, beliefs, customs, habits, institutions, standards, loyalties, a whole complex of cultural and moral values.[52]

Having defined what America is, the question that follows is – What does it mean to live in America? To this question Fairchild provides these answers. To live in America is (a) to live in an atmosphere of immaterial standards and values, (b) to possess them in one's own character and to be possessed by them, and (c) to live in close spontaneous contact with genuine Americans.[53]

These are the attributes of America – the reality of America, and what it means to live in America. These constitute very highly selective attributes. They are actually, in terms of ethnicity, the attributes of Anglo-Saxon America – the America of Fairchild. This is the America of the superordinate ethnic group. Other groups must either be totally assimilated or restricted from entrance, or both. It was somewhat surprising that Fairchild did not advocate mass deportation since it was clear that he did not seem overly optimistic about the feasibility of large-scale assimilation.

Fairchild's Theory of American Ethnicity

Henry Pratt Fairchild's theory, like Turner's, can be viewed as a series of process assertions. A very significant difference, however, between Fairchild's theory of ethnicity and the others in this book, is its heavy emphasis on assimilation. This occurs, of course, at the expense of other ethnic intergroup processes. Fairchild's main concern is with how people becomes assimilated into the dominant status culture in the United States. Therefore, we find his interest being circumscribed around the interaction patterns between the superordinate Anglo-Saxon Americans and the various, but all subordinate, immigrant groups. This is accomplished initially at a highly abstract level with a type of "grand theory" of group unity constructed within the universal parameters of race and nationality. Fairchild's effort to write a highly objective scientific treatise on the problems of maintaining national unity in the face of massive immigration is distinctly evident throughout his work on the subject. Ideology becomes masked as science and a structured presentation of ideas attempts to be passed off as objectivity. The historical context out of which his piece emerged was one in which social science increasingly became called upon to cast "expert" judgments upon the social problems that began to plague the rapidly urbanizing American nation.[54] Although many books were being written with the intention of warning the citizens of the United States about the impending danger of the huge waves of southern and eastern European immigrants, Fairchild's work was unique.[55] While many books took an explicitly condescending posture toward the "inferior races" that were arriving on the shores of the nation, Fairchild refrained from casting a debilitating label such as 'inferior' upon the new arrivals. Instead, he chose to build an explanation that pointed at the inferiority that would result from the *mixture* of immigrant and old-stock Americans. This mixture, he concluded, would be tragic because of the hard scientific evidence concerning the dangers of uncontrolled inbreeding of more than moderately variant races. Furthermore, a reference to organicism reveals that the "American organism" could not digest the uncontrolled influx of other national substances without a threat to its survival.

Unlike Frederick Jackson Turner who, as an historian, assumed a descriptive mode of discourse and frequently made reference to particular immigrant groups such as Germans or Italians, Henry Pratt Fairchild, on the other hand, assumed a highly generalized sociological approach to the subject of ethnic intergroup relations in which reference to particular national groups was scarce. The identities he uses correspond to his definition of races and are referred to as Alpine, Nordic, Aryan, and Mediterranean. There are two other striking differences between Turner and Fairchild which need only be mentioned at this point and re-examined later in the larger comparative analysis. The *first* difference concerns their references to the character of American society. While Turner is quoted as affirming "the formation of a composite nationality for the American people,"[56] Fairchild, on the other hand, contends "that the attempt to mix nationalities may result not in a new type of composite nationality but in the destruction of all nationality.[57] The *second* important difference concerns the assimilation process. In referring to the antagonism between ethnic groups in American society, Turner states that "a process of mutual education, a giving and taking, was at work."[56] Fairchild pointed to the extraneous national traits of the foreign element in America and firmly concludes that "There can be no 'give-and-take' in assimilation."[59]

The fact that Fairchild's theory was one that stressed assimilation reveals a number of key domain assumptions. His interest was in maintaining the group unity of his own group with complete disregard for the unity of other groups. This he legitimized in the interest of national security and unification. One wonders why Fairchild, who was so compelled to stress the importance of the universal dynamics of group unity, could believe that some groups of human beings should, or would, or even could completely divorce themselves from such a pervasive element as national heritage. Although he did acknowledge that it would be a difficult thing for immigrants to do, he insisted that they must because "We can not tolerate the danger of having too many persons in our midst whose ways are different from ours."[60] The implicit assumption of territorial sovereignty begins to emerge here.

Henry Pratt Fairchild's series of process assertions concerning ethnic intergroup relations can be represented as follows:

1. Sorting of assimilable substances.
2. Contact with assimilatory organs.
3. Transformation of substances, loss of original qualities.
4. No change in structure and character of the American organism.
5. Organization and maintenance of the American organism.[61]

The above process assertions were built upon a metabolic metaphor. Although Fairchild denounced many aspects of the organic analogy, in particular Herbert Spencer's application of it to many social phenomena he modified it into a metabolic analogy which he found useful.

With respect to the term "ethnic", Fairchild, like Turner, only used it once throughout his work. While Turner used the words "ethnic elements" to refer to groups of immigrants in the United States, Fairchild used the term "ethnic egotism" to refer to that characterisitc of a tribe in which it expresses an overwhelming self-interest.[62] Fairchild's meaning for ethnic egoism was remarkably close to that attributed to ethnocentrism.

On examining each of the above five process assertions, it becomes apparent that there were two types of ethnic groups involved in the process. The first, denoted in the metabolic analogy as the assimilating organism, was the dominant ethnic status culture in the society; in this case it was "Anglo-American". The second, denoted in the metabolic analogy as "certain types of substance" or "assimilated material", was the subordinate ethnic status culture in the society, the newcomer, in this case, the new immigrant. This group of new immigrants who entered the country after 1882, was labelled "the new menace" by Fairchild.[63] He viewed them as separate and distinct from the pre-1882 immigrants because the latter resembled the 'American stock' more closely in race and nationality.

1. Fairchild's first process assertion focused on the selection of assimilable substances (immigrants).

> Only certain types of substances will respond to the assimilative agencies in the body of any given organism, and the wise organism will see to it that other substances are not admitted except in strictly limited quantities.[64]

By way of analogy, Fairchild made it clear that only "certain types" of immigrants would be able to assimilate. By this he meant that only those close to the Anglo-American type in the characteristics of race and nationality would be likely to respond to the assimilative process. Moreover, on this basis, he attempted to legitimize immigration restrictions that would "strictly limit" the number of people of certain races and nationalities coming to the United States. The organism was "wise" to do this in the interest of national unity.

The manner in which Fairchild defined race and nationality and grounded them in universal assumptions concerning group unity and group contact allowed him to build the argument that supported limitations on immigrants from southern and eastern Europe. Initially, postulating that "in any community, particularly a democratic one, unity is one of the essentials of stability, order, and progress,"[65] he then examined the bases of a group unit – race and nationality. From here, he moved on to examining the dynamics of these two factors individually and in combination within the context of group contact. The concepts of race sympathy, race antipathy, national sympathy, and national antipathy were generated to interpret the dynamics of group contact. Since his overriding concern was with group unity in general, and national unity in particular, he set his analysis to bear upon the character of the situation in the United States, especially the problem of immigration. He was led to conclude that certain types of race and nationality mixing in the United States could have detrimental and irreversible consequences.

The factor of race was largely defined in terms of physical similarity and was postulated as a biological phonomenon.

> It is strictly and exclusively a biological fact. Whatever influences of race we experience come to us because we are animals.[66]

The problem of mixing races became an area of concern for Fairchild. He believed that racial identity and racial distinction could exist without racial purity.[67] He went as far as accepting the applicability of the melting pot to characterize the process of race mixing.[68] However, his fear resided in the question – Will the result of mixing be good for anything? That is, Fairchild projected that the random mixing of races would result in a series of disastrous consequences such as mongrelization, lack of specialization and other debilitating effects on the species. Fairchild's domain assumption in this regard was that men are exactly like plants and animals in respect to the dynamics of breeding and reproduction. Furthermore, there was no recognition that whereas plants and animals were totally determined by these natural processes, man could rise above them through knowledge and understanding. Following Fairchild:

> The result to be looked for in the offspring is therefore a primitive, generalized type – often spoken of as a "revision", "atavism", or "throwback".[69]

When Fairchild brought these scientific facts to bear on the immigration situation in the United States, he justified his scientific analysis by contrasting pre-1882 and post-1882 immigration combinations. The pre-1882 combinations.

> produced a type with outstanding characteristics; . . . it is a type of peculiar excellence. This is in the English type and it is the American type . . . It is certainly a noble type with a remarkable reward of achievement. . .[70]

The post-1882 immigrant combinations on the other hand, "signalized the beginning of the process of mongrelization of this [English type; American type] type".[71]

In contrast to race, nationality was defined in cultural terms as dynamic.[72] It included such things as spiritual reality, sentiments, emotions, ideas, ideals, beliefs, traditions, customs, habits, morals, loyalty, allegiance, and affection, It was dynamic because "it is a product of the human mind reflecting itself in group relations."[73] On this basis, Fairchild approached the question – Can diverse nationalities be harmonized by mixing them together? His answer was that "the attempt to mix nationalities must result . . . in the destruction of all nationality."[74]

Fairchild's analysis of the dynamics of the factors of race and nationality within the context of group contact led him to conclude that America had no choice but to place heavy restrictions on immigration in the interest of saving the American nationality from destruction.

2. The second process assertion is concerned less with the substance and more with the process of assimilation.

> Second . . . even appropriate substances cannot undergo the process of assimilation except as they come in contact with those organs of the body which are endowed with assimilating power.[75]

This process assertion focused on the fact that assimilation does not occur automatically or spontaneously. This certainly did not agree with Turner's conception of the frontier being the crucible of assimilation in which people of different ethnic groups came together in the act of frontier building and that assimilation followed indirectly. Rather, Fairchild believed that the notion of assimilation could not be separated from the notion of Americanization. Another domain assumption is revealed in that *assimilation will not occur on its own.* It requires a purposeful, intentional effort on the part of the host nationality. Fairchild, therefore placed a great emphasis on the Americanization movement. "It was the organization of deliberate purposeful effort to promote national unification."[74] His assumptions about the nature of the process of assimilation also led him to conclude that the movement, although indispensable, largely failed. It failed precisely because its assumptions did not resonate with the nature of the process. First, the Americanization movement assumed that assimilation was a voluntary process, when, in reality, the conditions of assimilation are not under voluntary control;[77] and second, it confused means with ends, with the result that it largely took the form of an educational campaign.[78] Thus without recognition of these two aspects, the "assimilating power" of the Americanization movement became greatly reduced. Fairchild defined nationality in such a way that one could not easily separate onself from its dynamic influence.

3. The third process assertion concerns the degree of change that the immigrant must undergo in order to be truly assimilated. To this extent, it is a complete transformation.

> Third . . . the final destiny of all assimilated materials is to be transformed into the particular kinds of cells of which the organism is composed and eventually to be incorporated into the body itself. All traces of diverse origin are lost.[79]

There was no question that Fairchild was demanding the total discardment of all national heritage the immigrant might have carried with him to America. Otherwise assimilation could not occur. Fairchild was sympathetic, yet firm, about the "harsh situation" that the immigrant had to face.

> The traits of foreign nationality which the immigrant brings with him are not to be mixed or interwoven. They are to be abandoned. . . a harsh situation, indeed! but a situation of which is determined not by inclination . . . but by the inherent qualities of human nature and social organization.[80]

Fairchild built much of his argument in the *Melting Pot Mistake* upon a theory of human nature, yet, there are certain questions which are noticeably evident and not dealt with. The pervasive nature attributed to nationality is unquestionable. Fairchild takes great pains to stress this enormous determining factor of group life. Yet he does not stop to consider the destructive capacity that the renunciation of one's national heritage could have upon the individual. The slightest appeal to the disciplinary matrix of psychology for such answers is totally absent from his analysis. It is as if some men had the ability to divorce themselves from the psychology of their being by virtue of the fact that they were immigrants. Moreover, the possible effects of such individuals (who could make a complete shift from one nationality to another) on the national character and national unity is not explored. Seemingly, it is supposed that the protected sovereignty of the Anglo-American would assure the well-being of all American peoples including the assimilated "new menace," if only national amnesia was allowed to set in.

4. The fourth process assertion concerns the changes that the American organism must undergo in assimilating the immigrants. It is imperative for Fairchild that it undergo absolutely none.

> Fourth . . . the organism undergoes no change to correspond to the different sources from which its food substances come.[81]

Again, his argument on this aspect of assimilation is grounded in his theory of the nature of group unity. In order for the United States of America to remain unified, it must not dilute the quality of its national character. Fairchild was proposing what is known as a *straight line one-way theory of assimilation.* There can be no give and take in assimilation. It is the immigrant who must do the assimilating. Toleration is out of the question when national unity is at stake.

5. Fairchild's last process assertion hinges very closely on the previous one.

> Finally, in order that the assimilative process may take place, the organism itself must be sound, healthy, and well-organized.[82]

This implies an adherence to the principles of group unity. Fairchild was operating upon a theory of human nature that tied the factors of race and nationality inextricably to group unity. "The strongest possible group unity exists when national solidarity and racial identity are combined."[83]

Fairchild's entire theory of American ethnicity has rested on a set of domain assumptions that resonate congenially with his process assertions. A one-way, straight-line assimilation was a must in order to maintain group and national unity. Assimilation does not occur on its own. Moreover, there were certain power relationships which could be legitimized on the basis of maintaining this unity. Concerning this last point, it is certainly worth noting the relationship between Fairchild's institutional context and his theory. He spent many years as an immigration official.[84]

Fairchild Typology

Concepts: Group Unity, Group Contact, Race, Nationality, Race Sympathy, Racial Antipathy, National Sympathy, National Antipathy, Immigrant, Foreigner, Native, Ethnic-Egoism, Assimilation, Americanization.

Process Assertions:

(1) Sorting of Assimilable Substances
- (a) Problem of Immigration
- (b) Theory of Human Nature and Group Unity
- (c) Legitimization of Immigration Restrictions

(2) Contact with Assimilatory Organs
  (a) Americanization
  (b) False Assumptions
  (c) Power of Assimilatory Organs

(3) Transformation of Substance, Loss of Original Qualities
  (a) New Menace
  (b) Abandonment of National Heritage

(4) No Change in American Organism
  (a) One-Way Straight Line Assimilation

(5) Organization and Maintenance of Organism
  (a) Health of Native-American Type

Postulates:
(1) Organicism
(2) Evolutionism
(3) Group Unity
(Anthropology, Sociology, Biology)

Domain Assumptions:
(1) Racial and National Mixing are Dangers to National Unity
(2) Men are Exactly like Plants and Animals in Respect to the Dynamics of Breeding and Reproduction
(3) Territorial Sovereignty
(4) "New Menace"
(5) Assimilation is Not Voluntary
(6) Assimilation is a Must for Group Unity.

Notes

1. Biographical material on the life of Henry Pratt Fairchild is relatively scarce. Much of this information was culled from *The National Encyclopedia of American Biography* or from the introductions of his books.

2. He later became an advocate of the limitation of population as a necessary measure to serve international peace.
3. Fairchild, *Immigration,* p. 305.
4. A.G. Keller, *Reminiscences of William Graham Sumner*, New Haven: Yale Press, 1933.
5. Fairchild, *Greek Immigration,* p. 240.
6. Fairchild, *Immigration,* p. 388.
7. Fairchild, *The Melting Pot Mistake,* p. 155.
8. Fairchild, *General Sociology,* pp. 36–37.
9. Fairchild, *The Prodigal Century,* p. 196.
10. Fairchild, *People: The Quantity and Quality of Population.*
11. Ibid.
12. Fairchild, *The Melting Pot Mistake,* p. 3.
13. Ibid., p. 9.
14. Ibid., p. 11.
15. Ibid., p. 12.
16. Ibid., p. 13.
17. Ibid., pp. 14–15.
18. Ibid., p. 16.
19. Ibid., p. 19.
20. Ibid., p. 21.
21. Ibid., p. 22.
22. Ibid., p. 27.
23. Ibid., p. 32.
24. Ibid., pp. 32–33.
25. Ibid., p. 36.
36. Ibid., p. 40.
27. Ibid., p. 43.
28. Ibid., p. 50.
29. Ibid., p. 52.
30. Ibid., p. 56
31. Ibid., p. 59.
32. See the discussion on Turner's usage of the term "ethnic elements" in Chapter III.
33. Ibid., p. 60.
34. Ibid., p. 37.
35. Ibid., p. 75.
36. Ibid., pp. 78–79.
37. Ibid., pp. 83–88.

38. Ibid., p. 105.
39. Ibid., p. 107.
40. Ibid., p. 119.
42. Ibid., p. 123.
43. Ibid., p. 125.
44. Ibid., p. 134.
45. Ibid., p. 154.
46. Ibid., pp. 163–65.
47. Ibid., p. 163.
48. Ibid., p. 176.
49. Ibid., p. 176.
50. Ibid., p. 176.
51. Ibid., p. 199.
52. Ibid., p. 201.
53. Ibid., pp. 203–204.
54. See, for instance, Robert Church, *Education in the United States: An Interpretive History,* section on "Higher Education at the Turn of the Century", New York: Free Press, 1976.
55. See, for instance, Madison Grant, *The Passing of the Great Race,* New York: Scribner, 1916.
56. Turner, "The Significance of the Frontier in American History", p. 22.
57. Fairchild, *The Melting Pot Mistake, p. 150.*
58. Turner, "Middle Western Pioneer Democracy", p. 349.
59. Fairchild, *The Melting Pot Mistake,* p. 155.
60. Ibid., p. 116.
61. Ibid., p. 137.
62. Ibid., p. 59.
63. Ibid., p. 107.
64. Ibid., p. 137.
65. Ibid., p. 13.
66. Ibid., p. 22.
67. Ibid., p. 32.
68. Ibid., p. 119.
69. Ibid., p. 123.
70. Ibid.
71. Ibid., p. 124.
72. Ibid., pp. 50–52.
73. Ibid.

74. Ibid., p. 150.
75. Ibid., p. 137.
76. Ibid., p. 154.
77. Ibid., pp. 163–66.
78. Ibid.
79. Ibid., p. 137.
80. Ibid., p. 154.
81. Ibid., p. 137.
82. Ibid.
83. Ibid., pp. 78–79.
84. See, Henry Pratt Fairchild's Biographical Sketch. Supra, p. 66 ff.

V Horace Kallen

Biography

Horace Kallen was an immigrant. He was born in Berenstadt, Silesia, Germany on August 11, 1882.[1] His parents Jacob David and Rebecca (Glazier) Kallen brought him to America in 1887. His parents were Jewish and as a child, he studied the Hebrew Bible and attended Elliot Grammar School in Boston. While living in the Social Settlement in Boston's old North End he attended Harvard University. He graduated magna cum laude in 1903. He did his post-graduate work at Princeton University, Oxford University, and in Paris. In 1908, he received his Ph.D. from Harvard University. Kallen was named by the noted American philosopher William James to edit his unfinished book in 1910. Between 1908 and 1911 he was a lecturer in philosophy at Harvard and instructor of philosophy and psychology at the University of Wisconsin between 1911 and 1918. He then became professor at the New School of Social Research in New York City, where he remained until 1952. In 1952, he was named research professor of social philosophy. He was a member of many organizations, among them were the International Institute of Arts and Letters, the American Jewish Congress, the World Jewish Congress, the International League for the Rights of Man, the American Philosophical Society, and the Society for the Social Study of Religion.

Major Influences

As a child, Horace Kallen studied the Hebrew Bible with its Judaist commentaries. It was upon this foundation and against the background of his Jewish cultural milieu that his vision of America had grown.[2] While attending grammar and high school, he perceived a simplicity, clarity, and beauty in the history textbooks that were used during the 1890's. In this respect, he recalled his "old, agnostic Yankee teacher" in the Elliot Grammar School who had fought in the Civil War and would read his class poetry and bits of Emerson. Viewing America through textbooks, Kallen saw a "pious and heroic generation of Puritans, making their righteousness and providential way, their way of justice and loving kindness, against devilish and blood-thirsty red-skins, upon 'stern and rockbound coasts."[3] He also saw their descendants, a heroic and embattled handful of lovers of liberty, pouring the tea into Boston Harbor, fighting to victory the battles of Bunker Hill, Lexington and Concord, although the odds against them were ten to one.[4] The young Kallen would often go down to the sea wharf to see where the tea had been poured and up to Bunker Hill to fight the battle for himself. He recalls the trouble he often had trying to get his "devout, very learned, and snobbish father" to understand the "why" of his truancies from school so that he could view Boston Harbor and Bunker Hill. He even had trouble understanding it himself. He recalls these experiences, "I only know that in some obscure, obstinate way, defiant of all conscience, they were the true life of my life, the most personal part of my existence. They had to happen and they were more than worth the punishment I endured for their name's sake, Amen".[5]

Freedom and liberty were among the most common of themes in the books that Kallen wrote during his life. In this passage, he speaks of his early passions for these ideals.

> In our household, the suffering and slavery of Israel were commonplace conversation; from Passover to Passover, freedom was an ideal, ceremonially reverenced, religiously aspired to. The textbook story of the declaration of independence came upon me, nurtured upon the deliverance from Egypt and the bondage in exile, like the clangor of trumpets, like a sudden light. What a resounding battle cry of freedom! And then, what an invicible march of Democracy to triumph over every enemy – over the English king, over the American Indian, over the uncivilized Mexican, over the American champions of slavery betraying American freedom, over everything, to be the very day of the history lesson![6]

Kallen's vision of America took a certain power over his developing life, . . . "it spread a glamour which so colored the labor and the strivings of my long hard days that I could not see truly the sordid realities of the daily struggle for bread which I shared with my God-fearing proud father and his long-suffering household."[7]

As Kallen reached high school, his religious sense opened up a period of critical questioning. He became interested in Spinoza's treatise on politics and theology. He also acknowledged Emerson's call for self-reliance. This was carried on as he entered Harvard College. While there, he took particular delight in the works of Edward Everett Hale, Barrett Wendell, George Santayana, and William James. It was also at Harvard that he had his first direct encounter with the near actualities of American politics. He recalls, I "fought my comic fight against the Martin Tomasney of the old English Ward in Boston, whom Lincoln Steffens sanctifies in his autobiography. Martin invited me to join the Hendricks Club and I righteously refused. That was one of the most foolish gestures of the many foolish gestures my life can record . . ."[8]

Kallen occupied part of his time at the Social Settlement in Boston's North End. It was there he made his acquaintance with the Socialist and Anarchist psyche. He attended the meetings of the Socialist Jews and Italian Anarchists. Among these people, he was introduced to the works of Marx and Kropotkin.

After Harvard, Kallen went to teach English at Princeton to young fellows of his age, " . . . and I grew a mustache to disguise the parity – and learned how the merest commonplaces of Massachusetts' Harvard could be the violent heresies of New Jersey's Princeton".[9] Woodrow Wilson had been named president of Princeton at that time. Kallen looked back on those times as having been part of a "conversion" he went through; one he characterized as negative because as he put it, "The God-fearing authorities refused any longer to harbor me and my Jewish heresies."[10] He was dropped from Princeton and then returned to Harvard with his dream of America completely distorted.

> I had seen how the very Americans themselves, the true Americans for whom the traditions of liberty were an inheritance and not a choicé, were occupied in confuting principles by practices, falsifying ideals by facts, and cheating and defeating the promises of the schools by the

> performance of the market-place, the altar and the forum.[11]

At this point, he began to read more history, moving from Thomas Paine and Thomas Jefferson to Barrett Wendell and Henry Adams and to Brook Adams. When he was offered a position to teach philosophy and psychology at the University of Wisconsin, he took it and remained "not easily, not quietly" for seven years. It was during this time that the thoughts and expression of *Culture and Democracy in the United States* began to take shape.

Major Works

Kallen authored and edited many books including *Culture and Democracy in the United States* (1925), *Individualism: An American Way of Life* (1933), *Freedom in the Modern World,* editor (1928), *Arts and Freedom,* 2 Vols. (1942), *Modernity and Liberty* (1947), *The Liberal State* (1948), *Ideals and Experience* (1948), *The Education of the Free Man* (1949), *Patterns of Progress* (1950), *Democracy's True Religion* (1951), *Secularism is the Will of God* (1954), *Cultural Pluralism and the American Idea* (1956), *Utopians at Bay* (1958), *The Book of Job as Greek Tragedy* (1959), and *A Study of Liberty* (1959).

It is very clear, from a gaze at Kallen's list of major works, that the central theme running thoughout his work was that of liberty and freedom. From the time he was a child, Kallen was fascinated by the ideas of liberty, freedom, democracy, and equality. And this became reflected in many of his works including *Culture and Democracy in the United States,* which we will focus on later in this chapter. In *Individualism: An American Way of Life,* he expresses his commitment to the goal of freedom while describing its relationship to, and the importance of individualism.

> In the classic tradition of America, the individual comes first, the establishment of society comes second; the freedom and fellowship of the individual is the goal, the institution of government, religion and affairs are but instruments to attain this goal, . . .[12]

He again examines freedom, this time by focusing on why it is a problem in modern society. In *Freedom in the Modern World,* he states:

> And herein, perhaps, is the ultimate seat of the problem of freedom in the Modern World – in this overwhelming unification and repetition against which everything individual, spontaneous, variant and new is by its very nature condemned to raise a rebellious head.[13]

In *A Study of Liberty,* Kallen continues with the theme of freedom, asserting in effect that science as with the humanities before it can be the guardian of liberty by maintaining a faith in its works and traditions.

> All the sciences and all the arts which this faith engenders, with their signatures in truth or beauty, or laughter or tears, also recognize reason as liberty's most reliable weapon and took in their own stuggle to keep on struggling, their own liberty's pursuit for further liberty.[14]

Democracy Versus The Melting Pot

Horace Kallen, a prodigious writer in many fields, wrote his major work on American ethnicity in a book entitled, *Culture and Democracy in the United States.* This book was published shortly before Fairchild's *The Melting Pot Mistake.* As unlikely as it may seem to those familiar with the popular sentiment expressed by and about these two men, both shared one central point of agreement. Each rejected the symbol of the melting pot as an adequate characterization of the processes at work in American society. Although they are alike in this single respect, their points of disagreement far outweigh their points of intellectual convergence. Their major divergences are of paramount importance for they form the main axes of their theories of American ethnicity. In short, and in simply stated terms, Henry Pratt Fairchild was an assimilationist and Horace Kallen was a pluralist. These, at least, are the ideological classifications rightfully appropriate to the stance taken by each of these men on most social issues. The axis of each of their theories of American ethnicity is a particular conception of human nature and group relations in society. Needless to say, their conceptions in this regard greatly differ. They are conditioned by their background assumptions about the world which in turn guides their perspective organization of facts. The disciplinary orientation of their domain assumptions also exerts an influence on the growth, direction, and outcome of their theories. Whereas Fairchild has approached American ethnicity via anthropology, sociology, and biology, Kallen's major orientation is via psychology and social philosophy.

Kallen begins his major work with the statement that he is engaged in "a study of the psychology of the American peoples". He continues to briefly sketch the main dimensions of this work among which are democracy and culture. Within this major treatise is contained the most comprehensive and articulate formulation of Kallen's theory of American ethnicity. It is entitled, "Democracy Versus the Melting Pot".[15] The central argument in his book revolves around and supports the axiom that democracy is the "indispensable prerequisite to the existence and growth of culture in the United States".[16] Furthermore, any program of social assimilation aimed at homogenization of the population would be inimical to the ideal of democracy and the process of cultural growth.

In developing his argument, Kallen first examines the historical meaning of the Declaration of Independence. He does this in order to clear up some of the seemingly inconsistent meanings and interpreted contradictions in the documents that relate to the ideal of equality. He stresses the function of the document as an instrument of political and economic conflict. He does this by examining the historical context in which it was written. The doctrine of natural rights, which was a central aspect in the Declaration, was formulated to offset the ruling power of those who legitimized their position by the traditional doctrine of divine right. The main function, then, of this doctrine was to strengthen the resistance to traditional claims of superiority espoused and practiced by the English monarchy. This was the political meaning of the Declaration of Independence. This, however, is not what survived. Instead, its verbal and logical meanings are often referred to. Consequently, much of what was stated in the document has been shrugged off as "a list of glittering generalities".[17] This has led to what appears to be a reformation of the document by some "old-stock" Americans who have legitimized their activity under the guise of preserving national unity.

Proponents of this group include the sociologists E. A. Ross and Henry Pratt Fairchild. Kallen refers to an aspect of these two men, their "pride of race", upon which their theories of American ethnicity partly rest.

> Respect for ancestors, pride of race! Time was when these would have been repudiated as the enemies of democracy, the antithesis of the fundamentals of the North American Republic, ... And now they are being invoked in defense of democracy, against the "melting pot", by a sociological protagonist of the "democratic idea". How knowingly purposeful their invocation is cannot be said . . . . This professor, in a word, is no voice crying in a wilderness. He simply utters aloud, and in his own peculiar manner, what is thought and spoken wherever Americans of British ancestry congregate feelingly . . . . he is, in effect, a voice and instrument of theirs. Being so, he could, of course, neither take account of them nor observe them; he could only react in terms of them to the processes of American society that seem to threaten the supremacy of his stock and caste.[18]

Here, Kallen makes evident Ross's domain assumption with respect to race. He demonstrates how these theories of racial superiority have developed out of the fears of some Anglo-Saxon Americans concerning the dilution of their stock. This produced the kind of theory-making used to ward off a threat. The effects of this fear were widespread.

> A widespread hysterical taking of stock began. Immigration, formerly more than welcomed as an economic boom, was now scrutinized as a eugenic menace. The stuff and form of the American being were re-examined, not by visitors from abroad any longer, but by scared lodgers at home. Racial theories were promulgated decanting variously upon the magical superiority of the Nordic stock . . . Fear, because the "inferior" stocks were declared to be increasing so much more rapidly than the "superior," and, like the proverbial camel, crowding the master out of the tent. Vanity, because the "intelligence quotients" were inferred to demonstrate that the "upper" classes are so by original nature and not by institutional accident. In them the excellence of mankind was held to be automatically concentrated.[19]

It occurred to Kallen that a parallel situation, analogous to events taking place at the writing of the Declaration of Independence, was happening in the early part of the twentieth century. Again, those Americans of British ancestry perceived a threat coming from across the Atlantic. However, whereas the threat in 1776 arose from a "superior force", (the British government), the threat of the twentieth century came from an "inferior force", (the immigrants of Southern and Eastern Europe). At both times in history, America was in jeopardy. In 1776, it was necessary to declare all men equal. In 1920, it was necessary to declare all men unequal. Thus the different historical meanings that can be attached to the Declaration of Independence related to a number of factors. One among these was the psychological factor of "like-mindedness" among Americans.

"In 1776," asserts Kallen, "the mass of white men in the colonies were actually free and rather equal".[20] In terms of equality, this didn't mean that there was no great difference in wealth, but there was a prevailing "like-mindedness". Ethnically and culturally, this group of people was homogenous. They derived from common ancestors and they possessed very similar ideals. In speaking of these early settlers in America, Kallen alluded to their reasons for leaving their motherland and the effect it had on them in the new land. Specifically referring to their participation in the War of Independence he reminded those who left places such as Holland for fear of losing their ethnic and cultural identity, that for them America remains a place where they have conserved both their liberty and identity.[21]

The importance of this assertion is lodged in the motives concerning why people left the Old World to come to the New. Their reasons for coming were strong enough that they would leave a home behind and risk a dangerous voyage. It was essential for them to retain their ethnic and cultural identity. Their motives were strong enough that they were carried over and became the basis for a document establishing political liberty for all in the new land. This sense of liberty was recognized by Kallen as something inherent in them. The cause for this valuation of liberty was more than economic. It lay in what he came to refer to as *like-mindedness* and *self-consciousness.*[22]

This assertion denotes the fact that all ethnic groups possess these two attributes which are extremely important not only for group survival but also for the preservation of any type of civilization. This idea found its way into the Declaration of Independence and protected the liberty of early Americans. However, in 1920, this was given a different interpretation, especially as it pertained to new American immigrants.

Focusing increasingly more on the psychological character of groups of Americans, Kallen points to the case of the French and Germans of Louisiana with respect to the way these groups have interacted with British-Americans.

> . . . because of their own like-mindedness and self-consciousness, they have retained a large measure of their individuality and spiritual autonomy to this day, after generations of unrestricted and mobile contact and a century of political union with the dominant British population.[23]

The following assumptions and assertions may be abstracted from this statement. First, it is the nature of ethnic groups in society to possess two attributes, like-mindedness and self-consciousness. Second, over time, ethnic groups retain individuality and spiritual autonomy Third, when people of different ethnic groups come together in the United States, their individuality and spiritual autonomy persist even when contact is between newcomer and host, or dominant and subordinate groups.

At many times in his writings, Horace Kallen has examined the case of particular ethnic groups whether they be Polish, German, Irish, etc. Descriptions of these groups are often followed by an analysis yielding a generalized assertion concerning the particular group. As he examined particular ethnic groups he inevitably focused on the fact that they had a unique culture of their own. It is this factor which made them equal. Without this there could exist no real democracy. By the same token, democracy protects equality. He describes the cultural geography of the United States as having the character of many unique cultural groups dotting the landscape in a pattern which shows very few signs of homogenization. Kallen saw many things around him which made it clear that like-mindedness, ethnic identity, and cultural diversity were definite trends which cut across the nation. For him there was no basis upon which to assert that different ethnic groups were being homogenized even as economic divisions within them began to become more evident.

Kallen knew fairly well the nature of these ethnic communities which dotted the nation. He also knew of the political strategies of the type used by politicians to capture the ethnic vote in various cities. His perspectives had been shaped partly from his life in Boston and New York City and he was not unaware of similar phenomena in other cities of the nation. He also understood the plight of the Southerner. Looking south of the Mason-Dixon Line, he saw a distinct case in which a large amount of homogeneity did exist. The South was not a very powerful political force in the nation at the time. After the Civil War, it had taken a very subordinate position to the North. Kallen characterized this particular section of the South as "the proletarian South". But the South, aside from its great racial divide, was a fairly homogeneous region. Kallen considered the South to be homogeneous largely due to the fact that most of its people were "descendents of native white stock".[24] The fact that they also lived among "nine million negroes", which Kallen explained was perceived as a threat to the native whites, produced an extreme condition of race prejudice. It is interesting to note that Kallen did not consider the plight of the Southern Black in any great detail. He did not attempt to identify any aspect of Black culture. Because he did not see much of a culture evident or try to find any, he was led to conclude that they as a group "standardize the mind of the poor white . . . in speech, manners, and other values of social living."[25] This produced a fear in these poor whites who, in finding themselves in competition, reacted with race prejudice.

One of the things Kallen reacted strongly against was Americanization as a symbol of the social process in which all immigrants in the United State were said to become involved. He viewed this process as a mechanism of the Anglo-conformity pattern in American life. According to Kallen, all immigrants and their offspring underwent Americanization if they remained in one place long enough.

> "Amerianization" appears to imply the fusion of the various bloods, and a transmutation by "the miracle of assimilation" of Jews, Slavs, Poles, Frenchmen, Germans, Hindus, Scandinavians and so on into beings similar in background, tradition, outlook and spirit to the descendants of the British colonists, the "Anglo-Saxon" stock. Broadly speaking, these elements of Americanism are somewhat external, the effect of environment; largely internal, the effect of heredity, social and personal.[26]

This conceptualization of Americanization is not unique to Kallen. The prevalent notion at the time was that it signified the disappearance of external differences and the adoption of many Anglo-American ways. Kallen, however, was one of the first to identify the internal psychological dimensions to be important parts of the process. The accepted notion of Americanization in the early twentieth century largely represented an Anglo-conformity assimilative doctrine, although there were also many strands of the melting pot found within it. Kallen viewed this Americanization movement as merely changing the external conditions of the immigrant. Many of these conditions were economic in nature, i.e., the market mode of American economic individualism. Therefore, if the immigrants participated in this market, assimilation would naturally follow. This was simply one way of viewing Americanization which ignored the internal aspects of heredity and personal history.

Kallen clearly recognized the ideological bias of many writers of native stock who professed and encouraged assimilationist doctrine. He said, "All is not, however, fact, because it is hope; nor is the biography of an individual, particularly of a literary individual, the history of a group".[27] Kallen perceived a certain character within Americanization writers – particularly those that composed the host culture. In fact, he sensed a strain in their writings. Kallen's sensitivity to this type of thing may have been a function of his own background. He, himself, was an immigrant who became a prestigious scholar in America. But, unlike many other immigrants and ethnics of his time, he did not prefer any type of assimilationist doctrine. Referring to many of these individuals such as Riis, Bok, Zangwill, and others, he said:

> . . . they are too self-conscious and self-centered, their "Americanization" appears too much like an achievement, a *tour de force,* too little like a growth. As for Zangwill – at best he is the obverse of Dickens, at worst he is a Jew making a special plea. It is the work of the Americanized writers that is really significant, and in that one senses, underneath the excellent writing, a dualism, and the strain to overcome it.[28]

Kallen did not place himself in this group of writers. He did not have to reconcile this tense dualism. He did not have to overcome it. Nevertheless, as a social reactionist himself, he had much insight into many groups in America that reacted with uneasiness to the invading social circumstances around them. These groups had a vested interest in the political and economic structure of the nation. They were responding to a feeling "of something out of gear."[29] Instead of looking within, they looked outside themselves and sought to transverse a period of economic and political reconstruction. For instance, much attention was being fixed on the growing economic disparity.

In his reference to the growing economic inequalities that existed among social classes in America, he pointed out that it was not the economic disparities that trouble the "Anglo-Saxon" Americans. Rather, it is "the ethnic disparity which has reinforced the economic that troubles him."[32] This had taken place in cities like Gary, Lawrence, Chicago, Pittsburgh are Pawtucket which had become "gigantic camps of foreign industrial mercenaries."[30]

The changing character of the urban workplace became an important concern for the industrialist of the host culture. This concern was well expressed by native sociologists such as E.A. Ross, and H.P. Fairchild. Here, Kallen refers to this concern:

> Because the great mass of the laborers happen to be of continental and not of British ancestry, and because they are late comers, the guilt for this perversion of American public life and social ideals must, of course, accrue to them. There can be only eugenic perfection and political wisdom in the degenerate farming stock of New England, the "poor whites" of the South, the negroes. The anthropological as well as the economic menace to the 100 per cent integrity of the American can come only from the "fusion" of these continental Europeans – Slavs, and Italians and Jews – with the native stock. Professors of sociology, if their race is right, must properly grow anxious over the fate of American institutions in such hands.[31]

Kallen takes a critical stance toward those theorists of race and ethnicity who take a purist position with respect to the American stock. Statements such as this, however, do not reflect any assertions concerning the processes that occur when people of different ethnic groups come together. We can say only that he does not perceive any threat to the national texture when the process occurs. He is indirectly saying that all cultural groups in America, when they come together, will not and do not have to become homogeneous. It is in the spirit of democracy that they remain free to continue to preserve their cultural ways of living and remain equal to other groups in the society.

Horace Kallen's domain assumptions concerning human nature and society manifest themselves particularly when he employs the concept of like-mindedness in his analysis.[32]

First, Kallen notes that the cause of this condition of like-mindedness is a prevailing intrinsic similarity, and not merely the result of a constant set of external conditions. In a sense, what he is saying here is that such intrinsic similarities represent specific sociological conditions of the nature of man and society. These intrinsic similarities are a kind of inherited characteristic which bind a group together. It has its roots in ethnic and cultural unity which has existed over time.

Kallen's conceptualization of cultural pluralism is very much tied to the notion of like-mindedness. The pluralism he speaks of and describes in the United States is not a strict, all-encompassing type. There are similarities that begin to exist between different groups that share similar environments or occupations in the United States. Yet, these similarities are of a superficial type when compared to the inherited type.[33]

> "American" is an adjective of similarity applied to English, Welsh, Scots, Irish, Jews, Germans, Italians, Poles and so on. But the similarity is one of place and institution; acquired, not inherited, and hence not inevitably transmitted.[34]

Translated into ethnic intergroup process assertions, we may abstract the following. First, when people of different ethnic groups come together in similar environments (the U.S.), certain similarities adjectival of "American" are generated. These similarities are external (of place and institution) and not internal (inherited and inevitably transmitted).

All writers of ethnicity deal at one time or another with the pervasive social variable called social class. More often than not, this is measured in socio-economic terms within a system of stratification based on some combination of wealth, power, and prestige. Writers have differed on the relative importance of class and ethnicity within systems of stratification. Some favor class over ethnicity as an all-encompassing, persisting, determining factor of social interaction and social structure. In approaching this issue, Kallen makes the distinction between the many different social classes that exist within each ethnic group. Within this context, he views the different social classes found within each ethnic group as more like-minded than groups of individuals who occupy the same social class but belong to different ethnic groups.[35]

Thus, ethnic status is interpreted as an important element of social interest. Even those of the same class status but different ethnic background will not be as "like-minded" as those of the same ethnic group who are of different class statuses. This assertion is linked to deeper assumptions about human nature.

> At his core, no human being, even in a "state of nature," is a mere mathematical unit of action like the "economic man."[35]

One of Kallen's most important domain assumptions is that Man is a family oriented being in both *space,* (those presently surrounding him), and *time,* (those ancrestrally connected). This is a crucial foundational assumption for Kallen in his argument to support phuralism. One can not erase ancestors from one's mind. They are the elements which give a person strength. They comprise the same elements which give unity to groups. And, this unity is essential for the survival of democracy. these constitute psychological assumptions that are rooted in culture and structured in the identity of each member of the group. This form of cultural identity has both an extrinsic and a more important intrinsic dimension. The latter does not disintegrate, fall away, or become forgotten through space and time. It is a part of the psychology of all human beings. From this point of view, ethnic groups are the main cultural units of American society. Kallen is able to make use of the notion of hyphenated Americans to explain the major social actions and consequences of American life that deal with the interaction of people of different ethnic groups.

> There is ethnic hyphenation in the differences of race, origin, and character among the various peoples who constitute the American citizenry.[37]

From the orientation that all Americans were once immigrants, it follows that they retained a hypenated character. The result is that industrial and social stratification has followed along ethnic lines. Moreover, because the non-British elements of the population were so massive, the resulting effect was what Kallen referred to as the "throwing back of the Brito-American upon his ancestry and ancestral ideals."[38] For in Kallen's mind, even the dominant status culture Brito-American is an ethnic America – a hyphenated American.

In this way, even the early Americans can be viewed as ethnic groups and the historical development of the political and social relations in the U.S. can be explained in this manner. Therefore, as ethnic groups, the first of them to become citizens experienced a process common to all later American ethnic groups. They became thrown back upon their heritage, ancestral background, and ideals. Concerning this type of phenomena, Kallen remarks, "If this is not ethnic nationality returned to consciousness, what is it?"[39]

The central theme of like-mindedness running throughout Kallen's work was composed of a psychological component sometimes denoted as the essence of nationality. Although he never went into any depth concerning this notion, Kallen did refer to some contemporary work done in psychology. But he failed to go much deeper than a scant mention of Sigmund Freud and a few brief paragraphs on the work of the behaviorist Pavlov. Psychology as an academic discipline in the United States was only beginning to develop at that time. Nevertheless, "like-mindedness" was considered a psychological factor by Kallen and he did much to describe the forces working within its domain. He viewed it as the essence of the formation of an American nationality.

It is useful to take note of a logistical point with respect to like-mindedness. Kallen uses it as a constant; it is a typification of a characteristic of social groups, in particular, ethnic groups. He describes the incidence of like-mindedness in terms of the forces acting upon it; some forces have worked to support its existence while others have worked against it. Its logistical point then, concerns the probability that this factor continually operates in a state of dynamic conflict. Why is this important? It is important in relation to the character of the domain assumptions underlying it. Does this concept express harmony or equilibrium or are the forces acting upon it creating a dialectic, or even a perpetual state of conflict? This will become evident as Kallen's theory is presented in the final section of this chapter.

However, in the passage that follows, some of these questions begin to be answered as Kallen focuses more decisively on the actual contact between ethnic groups.[40]

> It is the shock of confrontation with other ethnic groups and the natural feeling of aliency re-enforced by social discrimination and economic exploitation that generate in them an intenser group consciousness, which then militates against Americanization by rendering more important than ever the two factors to which the spiritual expression of the proletarian has been largely confined. These factors are language and religion.[41]

This statement represents one of the most clear and concise expressions of Horace Kallen's theory of American ethnicity. Up to now, he has written separately about such elements as like-mindedness, group consciousness, and Americanization. Here, he brings together a number of factors and describes the processes in which they are involved. We may abstract the following: (1) when people of different ethnic groups come together in the United States, they experience a shock of confrontation. This characterizes the initial encounter between the groups as being far from harmonious; conflict is implicitly operating. (2) When people of different ethnic groups come together in the United States, alienation occurs. This alienation becomes reinforced by (a) social discrimination and (b) economic exploitation. (3) When people of different ethnic groups come together, this alienation and its reinforcing causes generate an intense group consciousness in the group members. In this process, the members of the ethnic group become militant toward Americanization. Finally, (4) the intense group consciousness that is generated becomes a more important factor for the group than religion and language.

The two factors to which the "spiritual expression of the proletarian," referred to above, have been largely confined are language and religion.[42] Religion becomes modified by race, place, and time. It becomes a principal of separation. These two factors play an important role in the unification of the proletarian immigrant groups. They can work strongly against assimilation. According to Kallen, religion and language coordinate each other as conservators of culture. One example of this is the parochial school. It is an institution which acts to conserve the "Natio." This term is the closest expression Kallen has used to denote a feeling of ethnicity. He has referred to it as "traditional social inheritance."[43]

What makes Kallen a theorist of America ethnicity is that he has approached a fundamental issue involved in all theories of American ethnicity. That issue is whether or not a nation can cope with ethnic diversity. Kallen uses a musical metaphor to characterize the true nature of the American nationality. It is protrayed as a large group of different voices singing different tunes at the same time. In short, a dissonance producing situation is evident. The spirit of the land is inarticulate, not a voice but a chorus of many voices each singing a rather different tune. How to get order into this cacophony is the question for all persons who are concerned about justice, the arts, literature, philosophy, science. What must, what can, what *shall* this cacophony become, asks Kallen – a unison or a harmony?[44]

Kallen's Theory of American Ethnicity

Kallen's theory is divided into four phases, each comprised of a set of ethnic intergroup process assertions that resonate with his postulates and domain assumptions. The emphasis in Kallen's theory of American ethnicity is placed upon the immigrant rather than upon the host culture, or in Fairchild's terminology, "the assimilating organism." The process is viewed and constructed from the prespective of the immigrant. This fact makes Kallen's sentiment toward the immigrant very evident. Since Kallen himself was an immigrant, there is much reason to expect not only a change in sentiment but also a very different set of domain assumptions than those set down by Turner or Fairchild.[45]

While the process itself revolves around the interactions between the immigrant and the major institutions of American society, there are no distinctions made between different immigrant groups. The theory is generalized enough that it applies more or less equally to any immigrant group entering the United States. This does not stop Kallen from recognizing the distinct idiosyncracies of the variety of different ethnic groups in the United States. He often begins with a particular description of an ethnic group and moves toward a generalized interpretation of the characteristics and processes common to each. This contrasts with Fairchild's method which was to begin by introducing a generalized theory of human nature and group unity and then move toward a more particular focus.

Since Kallen's theory centered around the changes that the

immigrant group experienced, there was often a reference to the processes which eventually occur "within" the group as a result of the more encompassing intergroup processes.

Kallen viewed the four phases that immigrants passed through as being a course in which they become "automatically Americanized". However, we must take note of the vast difference between this meaning of Americanized, and others, most notably those expressed by Turner and Fairchild. For Turner, becoming Americanized meant essentially to be taking part in the process of frontier building. Hardly any difference existed between being Americanized and being assimilated. Furthermore, no organized, purposeful effort was required in this process. It occurred without any planned intervention.[46] For Fairchild, Americanization referred to "the organization of deliberate purposeful effort ot promote national unification".[47] Moreover, the difference between Americanization and assimilation was that the latter occurred only as a result of the success of the former plus the denunication of national heritage on the part of the immigrant. Therefore, Kallen's conception of Americanization contrasts sharply with Fairchild's and only slightly with Turner's. The latter is in agreement with Kallen concerning the non-deliberate nature of the Americanization process.

Americanization for Kallen signified something much more superficial than other writers on Americanization. All immigrants and their offspring undergo Americanization "if they remain in one place in the country long enough – say six or seven years".[48] The meaning Kallen gives this term is very similar to the meaning of acculturation or cultural assimilation used by the contemporary sociologist of ethnicity, Milton Gordon.[49] Following Kallen:

> "Americanization" appears to signify the adoption of the American variety of English speech, American clothes and manners, the American attitude in politics. "Americanization" signifies, in short, the disappearance of the external differences upon which so much race-prejudice often feeds.[50]

These external differences constitute some of the elements of "Americanization", a term denoting the customs, characteristics or beliefs originating in the United States.[51] These are not key differences for Kallen because they "are somewhat external, the effect of environment", rather than "internal, the effect of heredity, social and peronsal".[52] By the *internal* Kallen is referring to those attributes of an individual that are intrinsic and unalterable. They are matters of heredity and heritage. These attributes tie an individual inextricably to his ethnic group. The group ties are exhibited in the psychological characteristics that group members share in common; namely, like-mindedness and group consciousness. Since these latter two characteristics are such a pervasive part of group life, they can not be separated from culture and therefore must be part of the inalienable rights of Americans. It is at this junction that Kallen supports his argument with the assertion that "democracy presupposes culture".[53] Thus the concept of cultural pluralism was born. As we begin to examine the four phases of Kallen's theory of American ethnicity, the links between, the supports for, and the grounding of his process assertions will become evident.

These four phases may be summarized as follows:

1. Economic eagerness.
2. Attainment of proleterian level of economic independence.
3. Search to find our social level (ancestral throwback).
4. Dissimilation.

1. The first phase may be thought of as an assimilation phase. However, Kallen's meaning of assimilation was very clearly not the same as Fairchild's. It is not nearly as encompassing. In fact, just as Fairchild believes that assimilation must occur for the United States to maintain group and national unity, Kallen would argue that the type of assimilation spoken of by Fairchild is impossible due to the nature of man and society. Kallen also posits a theory of human nature in which certain aspects of heritage are permanent and unalterable thus any amount of purposeful, deliberate, effort to Americanize and assimilate them in the Fairchildian sense would be futile. Basically, what Kallen meant by assimilation was the changing of external conditions to conform to the host society. He even put quotations around the word assimilate in order to convey this meaning.

> In the first phase, they exhibit economic eagerness, the greedy hunger of the unfed. Since external differences are a handicap in the economic struggle, they "assimilate", seeking thus to facilitate the attainment of economic independence.[54]

It is only a superficial assimilation; it is one that allows them to participate in the market mode of American society. They learn to speak English, and dress like Americans, etc., and to this extent they are assimilated. Among Kallen's domain assumptions are that immigrants come to America so that they prosper economically but more importantly, so they may attain independence. Liberty is a highly cherished ideal for Kallen, one that he believes is an inalienable right of all Americans. He also notes that this does not come automatically to the immigrants. Instead, it is won or earned in the economic struggle. A price is paid by the immigrant. He must learn to speak English and 'assimilate'.

Kallen was highly conscious of the role that economic factors played in ethnic intergroup processes in the United States.

> . . . there is a marked tendency in the United States for the industrial and social stratification to follow ethnic lines.[55]

No one during Kallen's time would have had much difficulty noting the economic hierarchy in the United States dominated at the top by British-Americans and at the bottom by the more recent arrivals. There were exceptions, of course, and as time went on and immigrant participation in the market mode of American life expanded and economic divisions became more complex and less definable along ethnic lines. Nevertheless, the economic divisions have never succeeded in abolishing the ethnic ties. Kallen cites examples of this again and again.

> Broadly divided into the sections inhabited by the rich and those inhabited by the poor, this economic division did not abolish, it only crosses the ethnic one. There are rich and poor little Italys, Irelands, Hungarys, Germanys and rich and poor Ghettos.[56]

Again, the reason that ethnic lines do not disappear is because they cannot; they are intrinsic.

> The fact is that similarity of class rests upon no inevitable external condition: while similarity of nationality has usually a considerable intrinsic base. Hence the poor of two different peoples tend to be less like-minded than the poor and the rich of the same peoples.[57]

It becomes very clear that immigrants assimilate for one reason and *only* one reason, and that is to attain economic independence.

This entire first phase concerning the processes that occur when different ethnic groups come together particularly within the market mode of American life resonates with Kallen's deeper assumption about human nature. "No human being, even in a 'state of nature', is a mere mathematical unit like the 'economic man'".[58] Much more important is the common ancestry that people share which runs much deeper than economic lines.

2. Kallen's second phase of his theory of American ethnicity concerned what happens after the immigrant reaches a level of economic independence.

> Once the proletarian level of such independence is reached. the process of assimilation slows down and tends to come to a stop. The immigrant group is still a national group, modified, sometimes improved, by environmental influence, but otherwise a solitary spiritual unit, . . .[59]

Kallen noted that the proletarian level of independence was reached through economic struggle. The processes involved in this struggle are important because it is the antagonism, and conflict between groups in the marketplace that arouse and awaken "group consciousness." This, and "like-mindedness", represented for Kallen the two factors responsible for the cohesion of ethnic groups.

Nowhere does Kallen make any mention of the work of Karl Marx, yet, there is ample evidence to believe that he was aware of and influenced by Marx's work. Many of Marx's texts may not have been translated by 1918, however, Kallen was German by birth and probably could read the texts if available. Having been a part of the New School of Social Research in New York City made it even more likely that Kallen was keenly aware of the works of Marx and other German intellectuals. Upon fleeing Germany, some members of the Frankfurt School did exert an influence at the New School of Social Research.[60] It is Kallen's description of the second phase and, in particular, this next quote that makes one sense a Marxist influence.

> It is the shock of confrontation with other ethnic groups and the natural feeling of aliency reinforced by social

> discrimination and economic exploitation that generate in them an intenser group consciousness, which then militates against Americanization by rendering more important even the . . . factors to which the spiritual expression of the proletarian has been largely confined.[61]

There are several processes occurring here. Between groups there is the shock of confrontation, social discrimination and economic exploitation. The relation between ethnic groups is one of dominance and subordinance. With-ethnic group processes include alienation followed by group consciousness. Underlying both the between and within group processes is the assumption that conflict is a determining element in ethnic relations.

Unlike the previous writers, Turner and Fairchild, Kallen is very comfortable using the term ethnic group. He uses it often to refer to groups of Americans of diverse national origins. He infuses it with a deeper meaning than the term nationality by emphasizing the properties of like-mindedness and group consciousness, and by affirming the unalterable aspects of heredity and heritage.

Kallen never did use the term "ethnicity". Ethnicity is a relatively recent term with a meaning that is still "on the move"[62] However, Kallen did use a term quite similar in some respects to ethnicity. His usage of the word "Natio" appeared in the second phase of this theory, particularly in respect to group consciousness.

> This *Natio,* reaching consciousness first in a reaction against an antagonistic America, then assumes an effect of the competition with "Americanization" spiritual forms other than religious . . . *Natio* is what underlies the vehemence of the *"Americanized"* and the spiritual and political unrest of the Americans. It is among the significant facts of American life today.[63] [Author's italics]

Natio is a salient characteristic of ethnic intergroup processes throughout the next two phases of Kallen's theory.

3. The third phase of Kallen's theory of American ethnicity is also concerned with group consciousness but goes beyond it by exploring the dynamics of ancestry. Ancestry has important implications for assuming the status of citizenship. Referring to the immigrant group's effort to find its way out to its own social level, Kallen says:

> This search brings to light permanent group distinctions, and the immigrant, like the Anglo-Saxon American, is thrown back upon himself and his ancestry.[64]

Take note of the term Anglo-Saxon American. Kallen assumes that all Americans are "hyphenated". Not only are the newer immigrants hypenated, i.e., Italian-Americans, Irish-Americans, Polish-Americans, etc., but older immigrants are also hyphenated, i.e., Anglo-Americans, German-Americans. This is grounded in one of Kallen's assumptions about the nature of man.

> Hyphenation as such is a fact which permeates all levels of life.[65]

The notion of being "thrown back" upon oneself was also used by Turner and Fairchild. Kallen used it to describe what happens as a result of one ethnic group's confrontation with another in its quests for social status in the United States. In the process, group distinctions become more evident and the factors of heritage and ancestry become timeless determinants of group affiliation and differentiation.

> Behind him in time and tremendously in him in quality, are his ancestors; around him in space are his relatives and kin, carrying in common with him the inherited organic set from a remoter common ancestry. In all these he lives and moves and has his being.[66]

These characteristics of heritage and ancestry are so pervasive that they must be given recognition within the political context of group life in the United States. Kallen does this by tying them to the status of citizenship. Since democracy presupposes culture, culture thus becomes identified as the social ideal of Americanism.
of Americanism.

> [Citizenship] puts the problem of the status of the citizen in relation to the ideals of Liberty, Union, and Democracy in a new light. For each man or woman is the intersection of a line of ancestry and a line of social and cultural patterns and institutions, and it is what we are by heredity and early family influence that comes nearest to being inalienable and unalterable.[67]

4. The fourth and final phase of Kallen's theory of American ethnicity identifies and describes a process that is the antithesis of assimilation; that is, dissimilation.

> Then a process of dissimilation begins. The arts, life and ideals of the nationality become central and paramount; ethnic and national differences change in status from disadvantages to distinctions.[68]

This is clearly an explicit expression of cultural pluralism. The entire concept is tied very closely to Kallen's notion of the relationship of democracy to culture. It further implies that democracy involved "not the elimination of difference, but the perfection and conservation of differences".[69] In this respect, Kallen also asserted that this process involved "a give and take between radically different types, and a mutual respect and mutual cooperation based on mutual understanding".[70]

Democracy is the key element in Kallen's theory. The manner in which he defined it and placed it in a relation to other American ideals such as Liberty, Equality, and Union is of critical importance. He went to great pains to make democracy the engine and driving force of his theory. The next two passages are process-orientated assertions that illustrate this point. The first concerns democracy and the second culture.

> Democracy has meant the nullification of contractual relations; it has consisted in the formation, clash, integration, dissolution, and reformation of even more associations wherewith the individual may give his life purpose, import, color, and direction; it has been identical with the manifested growth and diversification of groupings that serve as engines of liability and liberation for the individual. . . .[71]

> Cultural values arise from the confrontation, impact and consequent disintegration and readjustment of different orders with the emergence therefrom of new harmonies carrying unprecedented things in their heart.[72]

The final result of Kallen's theory of American ethnicity is the liberation of nationality. Furthermore, this posed no threat to national unity. On the contrary, It strengthened and developed American culture with more of an emphasis on harmony than on unison. All stands and falls on Kallen's domain assumption.

> Nature is naturally pluralistic . . . . Human institutions have the same character.[73]

Kallen Typology

Concepts: Democracy, Culture, Liberty, Union, Citizenship, Americanism, Americanization, Assimilation, Hyphenation, Natio, Like-Mindedness, Group Consciousness, Ethnic Group, Nationality, Dissimilation, Heredity.

Process Assertions:

(1) Economic Eagerness
 (a) Assimilation, Economic Struggle, Confrontation
 (b) Economic Independence

(2) Attainment of Proletarian Level of Economic Independence
 (a) Assimilation Slows and Stops
 (b) Solitary Spiritual Unit, Group Consciousness

(3) Search for Social Level
 (a) Ancestral Throwback
 (b) Unalterable Heritage, Inalienable Citizenship

(4) Dissimilation
 (a) Ideals of Nationality became Central
 (b) Ethnic Difference become Status Distinction

Postulates:

(1) Democracy Presupposes Culture

(2) Democracy involves the Perfection of Difference

(3) Dissimilation is Antithesis of Assimilation.

Domain Assumptions:

(1) Nature is Naturally Pluralistic

(2) Human Institutions are Naturally Pluralistic

(3) Economic Divisions do not Abolish Ethnic Lines

(4) Ethnicity Supercedes Class

(5) Assimilation occurs Automatically (Acculturation)

(6) Ancestry, Heritage, and Heredity are Unalterable and Inalienable

(7) Confrontationa and Conflict arouse Group Consciousness.

Notes

1. *Who's Who in America,* 1959.
2. Kallen, *Individualism: An American Way of Life,* p. 5
3. Ibid., p. 6.
4. Ibid., p. 7.
5. Ibid.
6. Ibid.
7. Ibid., p. 8.
8. Ibid., p. 9.
9. Ibid., p. 10.
10. Ibid.
11. Ibid., p. 11.
12. Kallen, *Individualism: An American Way of Life,* New York: Liveright, 1933, p. 241.
13. Kallen, *Freedom in the Modern World,* Freeport, New York: Books for Libraries Press, 1927, p. 24.
14. Kallen, *A Study of Liberty,* Westport, Conn.: Glenwood Press, 1950, p. 148.
15. Kallen, "Democracy versus the Melting Pot" (1915).
16. Ibid., p. 11.
17. Ibid., p. 67.
18. Ibid., p. 70.

19. Ibid., p. 25.
20. Ibid., p. 71.
21. Ibid., p. 72.
22. Ibid.
23. Ibid., p. 73.
24. Ibid., p. 78.
25. Ibid.
26. Ibid., p. 79.
27. Ibid., p. 86.
28. Ibid., pp. 86–87.
29. Ibid., p. 86.
30. Ibid., p. 89.
31. Ibid., pp. 90–91.
32. Ibid., p. 92.
33. Ibid.
34. Ibid., p. 92
35. Ibid., p. 93.
36. Ibid., p. 93.
37. Ibid., p. 62.
38. Ibid., p. 98.
39. Ibid., p. 98.
40. Ibid., pp. 101–102.
41. Ibid.
42. Ibid., p. 102.
43. Ibid., p. 103.
44. Ibid., p. 104.
45. See Kallen's biography
46. See, Frederick Jackson Turner, *The Frontier in American History.*
47. See, Henry Pratt Fairchild, *The Melting Pot Mistake,* pp. 156–72.
48. Horace Kallen, *Culture and Democracy in the United States,* p. 79.
49. See Milton Gordon, *Assimilation in American Life.*
50. Kallen, *Culture and Democracy in the United States,* p. 79.
51. Kallen, *Culture and Democracy in the United States,* Chapter entitled "Americanization and Cultural Future," pp. 126–232.
52. Ibid., p. 80.
53. Ibid.
54. Ibid., p. 114.
55. Ibid., p. 98.

56. Ibid., pp. 77–78.
57. Ibid., p. 93.
58. Ibid., p. 93.
59. Ibid., p. 114.
60. See, for instance, Nicholas Mullins, *Theories and Theory Groups in Contemporary American Society,* New York: Harper and Row, 1973.
61. Kallen, *Culture and Democracy in the United States,* pp. 101–02.
62. See, for instance, Glazer and Moynihan, *Ethnicity: Theory and Experience,* Harvard University Press, 1975.
63. Kallen, *Culture and Democracy in the United States,* pp. 103–4.
64. Ibid., p. 114.
65. Ibid., p. 62.
66. Ibid., p. 94.
67. Ibid., p. 60.
68. Ibid., p. 114.
69. Ibid., p. 61.
70. Ibid., p. 61.
71. Ibid., p. 198.
72. Ibid., p. 210.
73. Ibid.

VI Nathan Glazer and Daniel Patrick Moynihan

Nathan Glazer – Biography and Major Works

Nathan Glazer was born on February 25, 1923 in New York City, the son of Louis and Tillie Zacharevich.[1] He received his bachelor of science degree from the City College of New York in 1944, his masters degree from the University of Pennsylvania also in 1944, and his doctor of philosophy degree from Columbia University in 1962. He was married in 1943 to Ruth Slotkin, divorced in 1958, and remarried to Sulochana Raghavan in 1962.

Nathan Glazer was a member of the editorial staff of *Commentary* and of Doubleday Anchor Books in 1954–55. The following year, he was the Walgreen lecturer at the University of Chicago. He was a member of the staff of the Communism in American Life Project, Fund for the Republic, between 1956 and 1957. He was a visiting lecturer at the University of California at Berkeley in 1957–8; instructor at Bennington College, 1958–9; visiting associate professor at Smith College in 1959–60; and fellow at the Joint Center for Urban Studies, Harvard-Massachusetts Institute of Technology in 1960–61. After traveling in Japan between 1961 and 1962, he became an urban sociologist for the HHFA in Washington, D.C. He was also professor of Sociology at the University of California at Berkerley between 1963 and 1969; a visiting professor at the Graduate School of Education at Harvard University in 1968–9; and is presently professor of education and social structure structure at Harvard.

Glazer's early works include the contributions he made to two major works authored by David Reisman, *The Lonely Crowd* (1950) and *Faces in the Crowd* (1952). Glazer also wrote *American Judaism* (1957), *The Social Basis of American Communism* (1961), *Studies in Housing and Minority Groups* (1960), *Remembering the Answers;*

Essays on the American Student Revolt (1970), and *Affirmative Discrimination* (1976). He edited *Cities in Trouble* (1970), *The Poor: A Culture of Poverty or a Poverty of Culture?* (1971), *Ethnicity: Theory and Experience* (with D. Moynihan) (1975), *Bussing: Constructive?* (1976), *The American Commonwealth* (with I. Kristol) (1976), and *The Urban Predicament* (with Gorham) (1976). He co-authored *Beyond the Melting Pot* with Daniel Patrick Moynihan in 1963 and 1970.

Daniel Patrick Moynihan – Biography and Major Works

Daniel Patrick Moynihan was born in Tulsa, Oklahoma on March 16, 1927 to John Henry and Mary Ann (Phipps) Moynihan. He was a student at the City College of New York in 1943; received his bachelor of science degree from Tufts University in 1948; his masters degree from Fletcher School of Law and Diplomacy in 1949; his doctor of philosophy degree from Fletcher School of Law and Diplomacy in 1961, and LL.D. in 1968. He married Elizabeth Theresa Brennan in 1944 and they have three children. He was with the International Rescue Committee in 1954; was successively the Assistant to the Secretary, Assistant Secretary, and Secretary to the Governor of the state of New York 1955–58; a member of the New York State Tenure Commission 1959–60; Director of the New York State Government Research Project at Syracuse University 1959–61; Special assistant to the Secretary of Labor 1961–62 and Assistant Secretary of Labor 1963–65.

Moynihan has held many posts at colleges and universities. The most important was director of the Joint Center for Urban Studies at the Massachusetts Institute of Technology at Harvard, and professor of education and urban politics at the Kennedy School of Government. His positions in government include Secretary of the public affairs committee at the New York State Democratic Convention 1958–60; delegate to the Democratic National Convention in 1960; worked for the Ford White House as ambassador to the United Nations; and at present he is United States Senator from New York State.

Moynihan's major works include *Maximum Feasible Misunderstanding* (1969), *Toward a National Urban Policy* (1970), *The Polities of a Guaranteed Income* (1973), and *A Dangerous Place* (with Suzanne Weaver) (1973). He has edited *On Equality of Educational Opportunity* (with Frederick Mosteller) (1972), *On Understanding Poverty; Perspectives from the Social Sciences* (1969), *Ethnicity: Theory and Experience* (with Nathan Glazer) (1975). He co-authored *Beyond the Melting Pot* with Nathan Glazer in 1963 and 1970.

Beyond the Melting Pot

Glazer and Moynihan's work *Beyond the Melting Pot* was clearly one of the most, if not the most influential book written in the field of American ethnicity since Horace Kallen's *Culture and Democracy in the United States* in 1924. It was the first work to recognize, state, and show conclusively that American ethnic groups were not assimilating as expected. In short, the melting pot did not melt. Furthermore, "ethnicity" is an element in all social equations; it is now a new social form, not merely a survival from a past age.[2] Ethnic identifications have begun to overshadow other identifications such as occupation and class. Their observations concerning the resurgence of ethnicity in the United States have led them to conclude that the American nationality is in a dynamic state.

> But the American nationality is still forming: its processes are mysterious, and the final form, if there is ever to be a final form is as yet unknown.[3]

This work may be viewed as ushering in the second phase of the process of American nationality formation in the twentieth century. The character of American society is rooted firmly in the still fertile ground of ethnicity. Before this time, most of the work studying ethnic groups in the United States was done from an assimilationist perspective. After the time that Kallen and Fairchild published their principal works centering around the idea of the melting pot, many social scientists commenced work on the problem of ethnic groups. However, inevitably, they defined the problem in terms of assimilation.[4]

Glazer and Moynihan, one the son of a working class immigrant, the other the grandson of one, were both keenly aware of the social dimensions of New York City politics especially within the period 1950–1970. This period would be the foreground for their analysis in *Beyond the Melting Pot.* It is from New York City politics that the initial insight for their theory of ethnicity arose.

Most often, the city has been the place where ethnic phenomena in the United States have been studied. This is true for the major theorists in this book with the exception of Frederick Jackson Turner. Turner was keenly aware of, and studied ethnic groups in the United States, even though they may not have constituted the core of this thesis. Rarely making use of the term ethnic, he relied chiefly on such terminology as nationality, culture, immigrant group, aliens, or foreigners. But the character of American society during Turner's time was teetering on a point between rural and urban dominance. Large-scale urbanization had begun but many ethnic groups still ventured West to develop the frontier. With the closing of the frontier came the largest wave of immigrants this country would ever witness until the 1970's and 80's. This became, almost totally, an urban affair. A proletariat comprised of foreigners, mostly seeking to escape political or economic conditions of their homelands, were all lured by the industrial magnet of corporate capitalism. All immigrant and ethnic phenomena were now cast in the dynamic processes of city life. In fact, all American life and societal character was in one way or another influenced by this same process.

Within the period of the coupling of the great immigrations and rapid urbanization, many works pertaining to ethnic groups appeared, especially by the Chicago School of Urbanologists. Ethnic process analysis remained almost totally within the urban context until the large exile from the cities began in about 1950. Ethnic processes in the suburbs were beginning to be examined by Herbert Gans and others.[5] But this was, and still is, largely a tangential symmetric to urban ethnic studies. The city is still the most fertile ground for ethnic studies and it appears than it will be for some time to come. Suburban ethnicity, in most cases, does exist with the outward intensity of urban ethnicity but it is an extension of the city phenomenon; its roots are still there.

The original edition of *Beyond the Melting Pot,* published in 1963, was a view of New York City between 1960 and 1961. Aside from a descriptive and theoretical introduction and conclusion, the center section of the work was a description and analysis of five major ethnic groups which dominated New York City social and political life. The revised edition, published in 1970 made no changes in the middle section of the book, but significant theoretical changes did occur in the introduction and conclusion. Points considered in this study are taken from the later volume.

Glazer and Moynihan begin the second edition of *Beyond the Melting Pot* with a view of New York City in 1970. The view is shaped by an ethno-political perspective. The major theme is that "ethnicity in New York remains important; that it would continue to be important for politics and culture; that from the perspective of New York City; Negroes and Puerto Ricans could be seen as the latest of the series of major ethnic groups that had – oddly enough, two by two, beginning with the Germans and the Irish, going on to the Jews and Italians – come as immigrants to make up the population of the city. These groups embodied the city's basic cultural characteristics, and particularly important among these characteristics was family structure."[6]

The conclusion of the book in 1962 has a final paragraph which states "Religion and race define the next stage in the evolution of the American peoples."[7] But thinking retrospectively, the authors revised this in 1970, saying, "Thus, religion as a major line of division in the city is for the moment in eclipse. Ethnicity and race dominate the city, more than ever seemed possible in 1963."[8]

Also in the final paragraph of the 1962 edition is a statement which found its way, intact, into the 1970 edition. This brief statement typifies the core of Glazer and Moynihan's theory of American ethnicity: "But the American nation is still forming: its processes are mysterious, and its final form, if there is ever to be a final form, is as yet unknown".[9] We are immediately confronted with the aspect of dynamism. Change is imminent. What is more, it is not likely to be curtailed, at least as far as the eye can see. It has no projected final form. The tendency of earlier theories of American ethnicity was to describe the final outcome on the social horizon. Thus the transformation from a static view of American ethnicity to a dynamic one.

One of the first issues to be confronted in this book was a racial one. It was discussed in the context of city life in New York. The issue grew out of the question of why Blacks have not shown the same progression of changes (such as upward mobility) in New York that other groups have. The earlier 1962 edition had presented an optimistic forecast concerning this issue. The authors later conceded that their outlook had been distorted by such things as poor data.

Nevertheless, Glazer and Moynihan choose to view Blacks as an ethnic group in New York City. They assert why:

> Perhaps it made sociological sense in 1963 to treat Negroes as an ethnic group in New York, parallel to other ethnic

> groups, to evaluate their place in the city in contrast to that of immigrant groups, and record how rapidly this position was changing, but it did not make *political* sense. It is even a question, of course, how much sociological sense it made. It made some, we still think. After all, Negroes themselves saw their place in the city in these terms, viewed themselves as fighting to improve their position not in an undifferentiated white society but an ethnically diverse one, and in such a society some groups, for some purposes, were allies. That Negroes were, or were becoming, one group in a society made up of self-conscious groups was the basic assumption of the book – in that sense, it was closer to social reality than some analysts of American society who saw assimilation and integration as already more advanced for most groups in the society than was actually the case.[10]

Glazer and Moynihan spend much time trying to rectify this major issue and comparing their view of it in 1962 as opposed to 1970. They could not accept the idea that Blacks would be eventually fully assimilated into American life with little discrimination or prejudice remaining. One reason for this is that racism was and still is so deeply imbedded within American institutions.[11] The other more important reason is that even white ethnic groups were not conforming to the assimilation model, " . . . the model of America was faulty."[12] White groups, they argued, had not yet assimilated, perhaps they never would. Thus, they saw more reason to treat Blacks in New York City as an ethnic group because certain patterns seemed characteristic for all groups.

> Would not the ethnic pattern prove the model for the incorporation of Negroes into the life of the city, as it had proved for impoverished Irishmen, for Jews and Italians, all of whom when they had arrived, had been considered by some of the best representatives of the American thought of the time as inferior races?[13]

This, of course, was not the only alternative for Blacks in New York City. The other path open was separatism. This constituted another view of how Blacks would adjust to the social structure. The authors' view on this possibility had changed much between editions.

> When we wrote *Beyond the Melting Pot,* the alternatives seemed to lie between assimilation and ethnic group status; they now seem to lie somewhere between ethnic group status and separatism. Earlier assimilation seemed to us the unreal alternative, today it is separatism that holds that status. But unreal unfortunately does not mean impossible. Will makes almost all alternatives possible, even those that are disastrous and that seem sure to guarantee a substantial measure of misery and unhappiness.[14]

Separatism as a model for alleviating the dilemma of Blacks and the problem of a black-white confrontation was unacceptable as far as Glazer and Moynihan were concerned. They did not see it as an alternative of any value. They feared that lines of separation such as this would only become battle lines later. "The demand for a rigid line between the races is now raised again, more strongly from the black side, this time".[15] Moreover, they refused to abandon their ethnic categorical scheme. "We believe that the ethnic pattern offers the best chance for a humane and positive adaption to group diversity, offering the individual the choice to live as he wishes, rather than forcing him into a pattern of a single 'Americanized' society or into the compartments of a rigidly separated society".[16]

As in the previous theories of American ethnicity, a reactionary response to a very old movement – Americanization can be seen. Both Fairchild and Kallen, while never totally rejecting the Americanization concept, nevertheless disagreed with the goals and activites of the organizers of the movement. No such organized and identifiable movement existed during Glazer's and Moynihan's writing. Their reference to Americanization is one denoting the general processes of assimilation in the U.S. Furthermore, they reject Americanization along with separtism as an alternative to the ethnic pattern.

Glazer and Moynihan have categorized the processes that occur when people of different ethnic groups come together as the "ethnic pattern." They have also rejected separatism as an alternative. It should be made clear that this doctrine of separatism to which they refer is not the same as the doctrine of cultural pluralism as a way of achieving harmony in America. Glazer and Moynihan view separatism as a means of producing a rigid division that would inevitably split the nation.

They believe that there should be efforts to incorporate Blacks into the society. "All the work of incorporating Negroes, as a group and as individuals, into a common society – economically, culturally, socially, politically, – must be pushed as hard as possible".[17] Regardless of their recommendations on this issue, they point out that the lines of division are still firmly drawn and divisive.

One of the most noted social phenomena of the 1960's and early 70's was the so-called "resurgence of ethnicity". It was a social pattern with an extremely high visibility. Its significance was in the fact that by all indications of earlier writers of American ethnicity, "ethnic consciousness" or "ethnicity" was supposed to have disappeared by the 1960's and 1970's. By the third and fourth generation, descendants of immigrants were expected to be assimilated. Glazer and Moynihan noted that the significance of ethnicity had not diminished between 1960 and 1970.

> The long-expected and predicted decline of ethnicity, the fuller acculturation and the assimilation of the white ethnic groups, seems once again delayed – as it was by World War II, and the cold war.[18]

Having stated that ethnicity still persists, Glazer and Moynihan were pressed to explain why it did so. They were sure it had persisted because they were witness to it in New York City. They could describe it and interpret it; they now had to explain it, or at least attempt to. They did so in this way:

> . . . ethnic groups, owing to their distinctive historical experiences, their cultures and skills, the times of their arrival and the economic situation they met, developed distinctive economic, political, and cultural patterns. As old cultures fell away – and it did rapidly enough – a new one, shaped by the distinctive experiences of life in America, was formed and a new identity was created. Italian-Americans might share precious little with Italians in Italy, but in America they were a distinctive group that maintained itself, was identifiable, and gave something to those who were identified with it, just as it also gave burdens that those in the group had to bear.[19]

This is an historical explanation of a functional nature as to why ethnicity persists. It helps to bind groups together. It helps them to develop identifiable political and economic patterns within the larger society. Ethnic identity is the emergent phenomenon in the process of adaptation to American life. In brief, the inference seems to be that ethnicity is functional for groups within the American social structure.

There is also a second reason given for the resurgence of ethnicity. This relates directly to a domain assumption concerning the nature of man and society.

> Beyond the accidents of history, one suspects, is the reality that human groups endure, that they provide some satisfaction to their members, and that the adoption of a totally new ethnic identity, by dropping whatever one is to become simply American, is inhibited by strong elements in the social structure of the United States . . . One is a New Englander, or a Southerner, or a Mid-westerner, and all these things mean something too concrete for the ethnic to adopt completely, while excluding his ethnic identity.[20]

First, ethnic identity is explained as existing because it serves a function. Yet, this leaves open the question of whether or not it would exist if it didn't serve a social function. From this perspective, one could do a functionalist analysis complete with specifications of latent and manifest functions. Second, ethnic identity does not assimilate easily into the American identity because it is inhibited by a strong element in the social structure of the United States. This suggests a power theory orientation. There is an implicit reference that relations of dominance and subordinance exist.

Glazer and Moynihan suggest three hypotheses with respect to the changing position of ethnic identity in recent years.[21] When they say 'changing position,' they more or less mean resurgence. First, ethnic identities have become more important in the process of self-definition. They have overshadowed occupational and particularly working class identities (as Horace Kallen stated earlier). The latter have lost status and respect while the former have gained it. Second, international events have changed and there as an enormous decline in tendency to submerge sympathetic attitudes toward ancestral homelands. Ethnic identities are more secure. Third, religion has also declined as a form of group identity. In terms of ethnic intergroup process assertions, it seems to be the view of Glazer and Moynihan that the most significant thing to happen when people of different ethnic groups come together in the United States, is that they begin to form an "ethnic identity." Furthermore, the interaction between groups seems to accent this identity. Beyond this point it is difficult to infer whether this proposition is grounded in the assumption that an ethnic identity structure, like all social structures, arises because it serves a function; or that ethnic identity is inherent in human nature and it becomes used in the struggle between status cultures in a society over access to power and resources.

The question has often been raised – Did ethnic identity arise as a reaction of whites to Black activision? Was it really a resurgence of racism? Glazer and Moynihan disagree with this type of reasoning and illustrate it by using the concept called "positive discrimination".

> It may be granted that there is some legitimacy to what we call positive discrimination, which can be defined simply as the effort to bring together people of distinctive backgrounds or interests or potential interests for some socially valued end. "Religion" is such an end. "Ethnicity" can be considered such an end. But what about "race"? "Race," we all agree, has been rejected as such an end. Thus, we do not want to see "white" institutions maintained or established in this country. For the purpose of "white," as most of us see it, is not to defend or maintain a "white" culture of religion but to exclude blacks. By the same token, is not the maintenance and creation of black institutions illegitimate? We do not think so, because whatever some black militants may think, "black" defines not a race but a cultural group, in our terms, an ethnicity.[23]

Thus their designation of Blacks as an ethnic group permits them to legitimize any institution established to bring people of distinctive backgrounds together. However, the question still remains regarding ethnicity and racism. They continue:

> Indeed, much of the answer to the question we have posed – ethnicity or racism? – is a matter of definition and self-definition, and much of the future of race relations in the city and country depends on what designations and definitions we use.[24]

The melting pot, according to Glazer and Moynihan, did not happen.[25] This has become particularly evident when one views the third and fourth generation of immigrants; they did not blend into a standard uniform type. This is the point at which their theory of American ethnicity takes off. A more explicit formulation of the theory now begins to emerge. It includes many aspects of the processes that occurred between the arrival of large groups of immigrants on the shores of the United States, through the transformations that occurred as they adapted to their new social context. The representations of these processes are the most important elements to consider. In terms of migration theory and more recent social scientific theories of ethnicity, such as the work of E.K. Francis and R.A. Schermerhorn, these processes are viewed in a variety of different ways – all focusing on the notion of "intergroup relations". Therefore, in sketching and summarizing Glazer's and Moynihan's work, it may be useful to employ a variety of the teminology used in the contemporary work in ethnic intergroup relations.

Glazer and Moynihan have a view of the different processes that occurred between the arrival of immigrants to the United States and the present status of their descendant ethnic groups. These differences are measured in a number of ways, one of which is in terms of group cohesion and identity. Of all the processes that have been referred to and said to occur during this time, assimilation is, of course, the most popularly espoused. The main point which Glazer and Moynihan make concerning this process as it relates to the differences between immigrants and their descendants, is that it is the "powerful assimilatory influences of American society" that make the divergence between immigrants and their descendants occur. Although this is very straightforward and clear, the point should not be missed that from their point of view, assimilatory influences always make people assimilate. The emphasis is on "influence" as passive or active. In short, they seem to miss the point that assimilatory influences can have the unintended effect of reversing the assimilation process.

The descendants of immigrants to the United States, in the process of adaptation to social life, are labeled as "ethnic". Labels such as this denote certain meanings. The label has meaning for both the person labeled ethnic and for the person doing the labeling. A useful way of understanding the dynamics of this process is to refer to the works of such people as Jonathan Suma (1978) and George Devereux

(1975) who employ the delineation between ethnic personality and ethnic identity.[26] The latter has designated ethnic personality as "an inductive generalization from behavioral data," and ethnic identity as the product of a "self-mystique" and an "ascribed mystique." These definitions leave many things unaccounted for, however, one does not have to accept the definitions in order to understand the importance of the labeling process within the context of ethnic intergroup relations. Labeling is itself a process that occurs when people of different groups come together. Furthermore, it exerts an influence on all subsequent ethnic intergroup processes. Labeling involves a process of definition, a way of organizing social realities, a way of creating diversity, a way of drawing battle lines, a way of including and excluding, of legitimizing the self and invalidating the other, a way of designating interests and so forth.

Which of the above is most evident will depend on the assumptions one holds about the nature of man and society. When Glazer and Moynihan assert that ethnic groups label each other, they do not make clear any related domain assumption. Again, inference can only be made. Most of their assumptions concerning the nature of man and society up to this point have been of a political nature. Beyond this, they have remained very descriptive. In fact, it may be possible to state that the entire work is founded on a few related assumptions concerning human nature. Most of the work arises out of the broad metaphor that "Man is a political animal". This may have been a notion about man and society which the authors had before they began this study, or, it may have been created as they gathered their data and made their observations.

This 'leading assumption', that man is a political animal, is one upon which all others will hinge. It can be viewed as the tip of a hierarchical structure in a formalized theory in which the leading assumption consumes the sub-layers of propositions and concepts. None of the five theorists considered in this study explicitly spell out their theories in a formalized manner. Neither was it their intention to do so. The reasons for not doing so vary. First, their works were highly ideological. They often wanted to build a case or espouse an argument regarding the legitimation of certain social arrangements. Second, their writings were directed to a more general audience rather than a group of social scientists, thus they had to be more informal in their approach. Third, the historic period in which the first three theorists participated was one in which instances of generally formalized theoretical activity was the exception rather than the rule. Most theory was implicit in such works which were often highly descriptive and interpretive.

Glazer and Moynihan, in trying to describe, interpret, and explain just what was happening in the United States with respect to its present development, not only dismissed the melting pot, but they refused to swing the pendulum to another extreme, that represented by cultural pluralism.[27] For them, a new Ireland, or new Germany in America was not the least bit likely.

In their definition of ethnic group, they make it clear that "the group is not a purely biological phenomenon".[28] They would probably have a very difficult time coming to terms with Henry Pratt Fairchild's often biologically grounded conception of racial and national groups. From their more recent writings however, they do express an interest in primordialist and socio-biological perspectives on ethnicity, although they sense its inability to help explain the composition of groups.

> Were we to follow the history of the term plasm alone – if we could – we should find that many in the group really came from other groups, and that many who should be in the group are in other groups.[29]

Rather than a biologically determined conception of ethnic group, these express a strong interest in the voluntary nature of ethnic groups. The implication is that to a degree, one may choose an ethnicity. This has been noted on studies of ethnic identity in the southwestern United States where Native-Americans have been know to take on a Mexican-American's identity in cases where it would influence job acquisition. The reverse might also be true. Other cases of *passing* have been noted throughout the history of ethnic groups, however Glazer and Moynihan find that the degree of passing often depends on the particular ethnic heritage of the mixed background individual.

> The Irish-named offspring of German or Jewish or Italian mothers often find that willynilly they have become Irish. It is even harder for the Jewish-named offspring of mixed marriages to escape from the Jewish group; neither Jews nor non-Jews will let them rest in ambiguity.[30]

The important thing seems to be that people of mixed background choose a particular ethnic identity rather than a mixture of the others. The reasons are again political.

> Parts of the group are cut off, other elements join the group as allies. Under certain circumstances, strange as it may appear, it is desirable to be able to take on a group name, even of a low order, if it can be made to fit, and if it gives one certain advantages.[31]

The following assertion may be abstracted. When people of different ethnic groups come together, some individuals will choose the group name that gives one certain advantages. In these terms, ethnicity is voluntary. Moreover, the degree of voluntary attachment that one has with a particular ethnic group is often a matter of interest. "The ethnic groups in New York are also interest groups. This is perhaps the single most important fact about ethnic groups in New York City".[32] This is exemplified by the manner in which New York City Jews are bound together by their interest in the garment industry, or Italians as homeowners in Staten Island.

In addition to being linked together by common interests, ethnic groups are also bound together by "family and fellowfeeling", and social organization. This next statement contains a domain assumption related to this.

> There is a satisfaction in being with those who are like oneself. The ethnic group is something of an extended family or tribe. And aside from ties of feeling and interest, there are concrete ties of organization. Certain types of immigrant social organization have declined, but others have been as indigenous in remolding and recreating themselves as the group itself.[33]

First, it is suggested that it is human nature to want to be with those who are like oneself, and secondly, ethnic groups are bound together by ties of organization. It is here that one begins to realize that the emphasis is upon what pulls the ethnic group together rather than on what pulls it apart. The forces that draw the ethnic group apart do not necessarily mean that assimilation will follow, although it is often thought of in these terms. Moreover, if an ethnic group is a social form,it must have the same general tendencies as other social forms, one of which is disunity.

Glazer and Moynihan have considered the potential, past, present, and future, of American society to assimilate groups. In the past, the Old American type – the Anglo – did assimilate their cousins who were close to them physically and culturally; these were the Scottish-Irish and Dutch. These groups did, of course, have more time to assimilate but as Glazer and Moynihan argue, if one is not close to the White Anglo-Saxon Protestant core value model, time alone will not do it.

In order to assimilate, one must have something *to which* one can assimilate. It follows that how much and how fast one assimilates will be a function of the assimilative distance between groups; host and newcomer, dominant and subordinate, etc. It will also depend on things like the desire of the group to assimilate, the desire of the target group to have a group assimilate to itself, the amount of power and resources available to both groups, institutional arrangements, etc.. In the case in which there is no one model to which one can assimilate, but rather an approximation between groups, (i.e., the Melting Pot), certain adjustments must be made to these factors. Glazer and Moynihan talk about this ability of America to assimilate groups.

> Conceivably the fact that one's origins can become only a memory suggests the general direction for ethnic groups in the United States – toward assimilation and absorption into a homogenous American mass. And yet, as we suggested earlier, it is hard to see in the New York of the 1960's just how this comes about. Time alone does not dissolve the groups if they are not close to the Anglo-Saxon center. Color marks off a group, regardless of time; and perhaps most significantly, the "majority" group, to which assimilation should occur, has taken on the color of an ethnic group, too. To what does one assimilate in modern America? The "American" in abstract does not exist, though some sections of the country, such as the Far West, come closer to realizing him than does New York City. There are test cases of such assimilation in the past. The old Scotch-Irish group, an important ethnic group of the early nineteenth century, is now for the most part simply old American, "old Dutch families have become part of the upper class of New York. But these test cases merely

> reveal to us how partial was the power of the old American type to assimilate – it assimilated its ethnic cousins.[34]

Here, they have defined the central problem in assimilating groups in America, namely the absence of any "American in the abstract" to which one can assimilate. Without a common model, the process has no hope for success.

Glazer and Moynihan's work illustrates that the theories of American ethnicity, like most other social theories, have an ideological component. The ideological component may be reflected in the reactionary quality of the work or in its domain assumption. Some theorists make this explicity obvious while others leave it for the reader to discover. In the case of Glazer and Moynihan, they have stated that their work is "inevitably filled with judgments, yet the critical judgment – an overall evaluation of the meaning of American heterogeneity – we have tried to avoid because we do not know how to make it."[35] The meaning of American heterogeneity can be translated as the meaning of American ethnicity. For this they admit they have no answer, although their work is a conscious effort to come to terms with it.

Glazer's and Moynihan's Theory of American Ethnicity

Like other theorists of American ethnicity, the context in which Glazer and Moynihan wrote their theory had a significant influence on it. The theory emerged from a descriptive study of the social and political dynamics of ethnic groups living in New York City between 1960 and 1970. Of the five theorists, they were the only ones to confine themselves to such a particular environment. Therefore, their theory moves from the particular to more generalized statements. Their perspective can be categorized as socio-political since they view group interest as a key factor in holding ethnic groups together. Their underlying orientation is upon the question of what forces hold ethnic groups together rather than what forces pull them apart. With respect to the structure of intergroup relations, the particular context of their work is one in which relations vary between dominant-subordinate, dominant-dominant, and subordinate-subordinate. A major difference between their work and the previous three theorists concerns the recentness of immigrations, and the ethnic and racial background of the groups involved. The previous three theorists largely confined their work to white immigrant groups of European origin. For example, each makes scant mention of Blacks, no mention of Asians, and only Frederick Jackson Turner gave any significant consideration to the plight of native American Indians. Glazer and Moynihan, on the other hand, although confining themselves to a smaller geographical area, cover a much broader spectrum of racial and ethnic differences. In particular they are concerned with the within and between group interaction of Black-Americans, Puerto Rican-Americans, Italian-Americans, Irish-Americans, and Jewish-Americans. With respect to these last three groups of European origin, the focus is on the second and third generation ethnic generation rather than solely on the immigrant generation.

The theory itself attempts to reflect the perspective of these ethnic groups in New York City, the ways in which they live, work, and survive as a group within a largely ethnically determined social and politcal environment. It is only peripherally a theory of assimilation. As with each of the previous theorists, this term assimilation takes on a new meaning. While for Turner, Fairchild, and Kallen, there did exist a dominant "American type", even though this turned out in reality to be the Anglo or British-American, Glazer and Moynihan pose the question – "To what does one assimilate in America?" – to which they respond – "The 'American' in abstract does not exist".[37] Glazer and Moynihan refer to the pattern that occurs when people of different ethnic groups come together as the "ethnic pattern".

This "ethnic pattern" represents the heart of their theory and the place from which the major process assertions will be drawn. Unlike the previous three theories in which there were four or five major stages, processes, or phases, this one has only two. They are:

1. Old cultures fall away
2. New cultures and identities are created.

These two processes occur to each ethnic group within the larger context of ethnic intergroup relations. Whether this is labeled assimilation or Americanization becomes increasingly less important, for, as we examine the process itself, new meanings begin to emerge and old meanings for these terms begin to waiver.

The first phase of the ethnic pattern occurs as groups of immigrants and ethnics come into contact with other groups of immigrants and ethnics. This is a dynamic process in the sense that it is always going on. Just as it happened with first generation immigrant-Americans, it is now occurring with third and fourth generation white ethnics, all generations of Black and Hispanic-Americans, and to any new immigrants or old ethnic Americans. The implication is that this process is, and always will occur in the United States, *in conjunction with* the second phase. In short, old cultures are falling away and new cultures and identities are constantly being created. The catalyzing force between these two dynamic terms is the action in which ethnic groups, in their contact with American life, develop distinctive economic, political, and cultural patterns. The character and quality of these patterns depends upon such factors as the distinct historical experience of the group, their culture and skills, their time of arrival in the United States, and their economic situation.[38]

Old cultures do fall away. But the result is not a melting pot, nor is it cultural pluralism. Glazer and Moynihan place great stress on both of these points. With the melting pot in mind, they assert:

> The notion that the intense and unprecedented mixture of ethnic and religious groups in American life was soon to blend into a homogeneous end product has outlived its usefulness, and also its credibility.[39]

With cultural pluralism in mind they assert:

> It is true that language and culture are very largely lost in the first and second generations, and this makes the dream of "cultural pluralism" . . . as unlikely as the hope of a melting pot.[40]

The second major process assertion is comprehensive enough to subsume the first. The element that has been added to give shape to the dynamic transformation is ethnic "identification."

> . . . as the groups were transformed by influences in American society, stripped of their original attributes, they were recreated as something new, but still as identifiable groups. Consequently, persons think of themselves as members of that group, with that name; they are thought of by others as members of that group, with that name; and most significantly, they are linked to other members of that group by new attributes that the original immigrants would

> never have recognized as identifying their group, but which nevertheless serve to mark them off, by more than simply name and association in the third generation and even beyond.[41]

This transformation occurs by something identified by Glazer and Moynihan as "the powerful assimilating influence of American society".[42] This assimilation is measured in the changes that the ethnic group passes through over time while interacting with other groups in American society. This interaction may occur in many arenas; however, Glazer and Moynihan are thinking most of the economic arenas of the marketplace and the political arenas of urban politics. These are powerful assimilating influences; however, the end product is not homogeneous. It is still diverse. Each ethnic group maintains an identity. It is a changing identity, but one nonetheless. Thus, Italian-Americans of the third generation, for instance, are still an identifiable group, yet, they are very different from Italian-American immigrants of the first generation, and still different from Italians in Italy.

The way in which ethnic-Americans "assimilate," and by this we mean change and become recreated, yet maintain an identity as a group is one of the most important and unique aspects of the Glazer and Moynihan theory. Group identification becomes reinforced and group identity persists. "There may be more reasons than accident that explain why ethnicity and ethnic identity continue to persist."[42] One of the reasons is, that the ethnic group is a kind of extended family or tribe and there is a satisfaction in being with those who are like oneself. Another reason is that ties of feeling and interest shared by ethnic group members become concrete ties of organization. But these reasons alone are not enough to keep ethnic identifications salient. Another important factor concerns the elements of social structure in the United States. These elements of social structure are strong enough to inhibit the dropping of one's ethnic identity to become "simply an American".

> It is inhibited by a *subtle system of identifying* [Author's italics] which ranges from brutal discrimination and prejudice to merely naming. It is inhibited by the unavailability of a simple American identity.[44]

One may, however, choose one's ethnic identity. People of mixed background, for instance, choose a particular ethnic identity rather than a mixture of others. There may be certain limitations put on this by race that may inhibit choosing certain "ethnicities".

> It is better in Oakland, California, to be a Mexican than an Indian, and so some of the few Indians call themselves, at certain times, for certain occasions, "Mexicans" . . . West Indian Negroes achieve important political positions as representatives of Negroes; Spaniards and Latin Americans become the representatives of Puerto Ricans; German Jews rose to Congress from districts dominated by East European Jews.[45]

Glazer and Moynihan stress the voluntary aspect of ethnicity. It is a reflection of the domain assumptions of these theorists. Both theorists, especially Daniel Moynihan, are active politically in state and national governmental affairs. An individual working in such a milieu or occupying a political position in government is very likely to over-emphasize the political dimension of man at the expense of the psychological, cultural, spiritual, etc. To this extent, the metaphor, 'man is a political animal' begins to reign supreme, yielding a view of ethnicity as an interest-bound, symbolic and voluntary entity, which becomes perpetuated by "ethnic interest serving institutions".[46]

> Social and political institutions do not merely respond to ethnic interests; a great number of institutions exist for the specific purpose of serving ethnic interests. This in turn tends to perpetuate them . . . it recognizes them, and rewards them, and to that extent encourages them.[47]

As far as Glazer and Moynihan are concerned, this may very well be one of the causes for the American pattern of subnationalities. They know very well, however, that the answers are much more complex. At this point, they are only prepared to say generally that there is "some central tendency in the national ethos which structures people . . ."[48]

> The tendency is fixed deep in American life generally; the specific pattern of ethnic differentiation, however, in every generation is created by specific events.[49]

These events are, of course, too numerous and complex for Glazer and Moynihan to explore in any detail except to generalize that they are of a political, economic, and cultural character. The process running through and guiding these events is the "ethnic pattern." This is Glazer's and Moynihan's effort to explain the basic character of the processes that occur when people of different ethnic groups come together in the United States. They also affirm this pattern as one that is ". . . American, more American than the assimilationist".[50] In this sense they mean that it reflects those positive values of American life that contribute to a humanistic society.

> We believe that the ethnic pattern offers the best chance for a humane and positive adaption to group diversity, offering the individual a chance to live as he wishes, rather than forcing him into a pattern of a single "Americanized" society or into the compartments of a rigidly separated society.[51]

The two most important conclusions that emerge from Glazer's and Moynihan's work are first, that "The ethnic group in American society became not a survival from the past age of mass immigration but a new social form".[52] Second, with respect to the character of American society, they are led to conclude that "The American nationality is still forming: its processes are mysterious, and the final form, if there is ever to be a final form is as yet unknown".[53] This view of American culture as still emerging is grounded partially in assumptions concerning the reality that human groups endure and, that time alone does not dissolve ethnic groups.[54]

Glazer and Moynihan Typology

Concepts: Ethnic Group, Ethnicity, Ethnic Pattern, Ethnic Identification, Ethnic Consciousness, Ethnic Differentiation, Ethnic Group Status, Integration, Assimilation, Americanized, Immigrant.

Process Assertions: (1) Old Cultures Fall Away
(a) Ethnic groups develop distinctive economic, political, and cultural patterns, owing to

- distinct historical experience
- culture and skills
- time of arrival
- economic situation

(b) Ethnic Group become transformed by the influence of American Society

- stripped of original attributes

(2) New Cultures and Identities are Created

(a) by elements of American social structure

(b) by unavailability of a simply American identity

Postulates:

(1) Human Groups Endure

(2) Ethnic Group is a New Social Form

(3) Ethnic Group is an Extended Family or Tribe

(4) Man is a Political Animal

(5) There is a Satisfaction in Being with Those Like Oneself.

Domain Assumptions:

(1) Critical Tendency in the National Ethos to Structure Groups

(2) Ethnicity is Voluntary

(3) The American in the Abstract does not exist

(4) Time Alone does not dissolve Ethnic Groups

(5) Group Conflicts resolve as Ethnic Groups are recreated and Identities change

(6) What holds Groups Together rather than What pulls Them Apart?

Notes

1. *Who's Who in America.*
2. See Glazer and Moynihan (eds.) *Ethnicity: Theory and Experience,* "Introduction," Cambridge: Harvard University Press, 1975, pp. 1–28.
3. Glazer and Moynihan, *Beyond the Melting Pot* (Cambridge: MIT Press, 1970), p. 315.
4. For example, see Robert E. Park, MacKenzie, Borgardus, and Miller (Chicago School of Urbanologists).
5. See Herbert Gans, *The Levittowners,* and *The Urban Villagers.*
6. Glazer and Moynihan, *Beyond the Melting Pot,* pp. vii-viii.
7. Ibid., 1962 edition.
8. Ibid., 1970 edition, p. viii.
9. Ibid., p. 315.
10. Ibid., p. xiii.
11. Ibid., p. xxii.
12. Ibid.
13. Ibid.
14. Ibid., p. xxiii.
15. Ibid., p. xxiv.
16. Ibid.
17. Ibid.
18. Ibid., p. xxxiii.
19. Ibid.
20. Ibid.
21. Ibid., p. xxxv.
22. Ibid., p. xxxvii.
23. Ibid., p. xxxix.
24. Ibid., p. xl.
25. Ibid., p. xlvii.
26. Jonathan Do Sarna, "From Immigrants to Ethnics: Toward a New Theory of Ethnicization." in *Ethnicity* 5, 370–378, (1978); and George Devereux, "Ethnic Identity: Its Logical Functions and its Dysfunctions," in *Ethnic Identity,* edited by DeVos and Romanucci-Ross, pp. 42–70, Palo Alto, Ca.: Mayfield, 1975.
27. Glazer and Moynihan, *Beyond the Melting Pot,* p. 13.
28. Ibid., p. 16.

29. See the Introduction to Glazer and Moynihan's Ethnicity: *Theory and Experience*, 1975.
30. Glazer and Moynihan, *Beyond the Melting Pot,* p.16.
31. Ibid., p. 17.
32. Ibid.
33. Ibid., p. 18.
34. Ibid., p. 20.
35. Ibid., p. 21.
36. Glazer and Moynihan, *Beyond the Melting Pot,* p. 21.
37. On Ethnicization, see, for instance, Jonathan D. Sarna, "From Immigrants to Ethnics: Toward a New Theory of Ethnicization," *Ethnicity* 5, pp. 370–378, 1978.
38. Glazer and Moynihan, *Beyond the Melting Pot,* p. xxxiii.
39. Ibid., p. xlvii.
40. Ibid., p. 13.
41. Ibid.
42. Ibid.
43. Ibid., p. xxxiii.
44. Ibid.
45. Ibid., p. 17.
46 Ibid., pp.310–311.
47. Ibid.
48. Ibid., pp.290–91.
49. Ibid.
50. Ibid. p. xxii.
51. Ibid.
52. Ibid., p. 16.
53. Ibid., p. 315.
54. Ibid., p. 20 and p. xxxiii.

VII Francis Xavier Femminella

Biography

Francis X. Femminella was born in Brooklyn, New York on June 19, 1929 to Lawrence John and Catherine Luongo Femminella.[1] He was a descendant of Italian immigrants from Sicily. As a child, he attended a Catholic elementary school in the ethnically mixed section of Ridgewood, Brooklyn. He often recalled the ethnic diversity of the families who inhabited the large apartment dwelling where he lived. There were families of German, Chinese, Irish, Polish, and Italian descent living there. It was a place he most appropriately referred to as a "house of nations". After he graduated from high school, he attended St. Paul's Abbey and Iona College. Throughout his college career, Femminella was active in many organizations. He was a staff member of Casita Maria Settlement House in 1950–52; a social investigator for the New York Department of Welfare in 1952–54; and a research design specialist and casework supervisor for the Angel Guardian Home in Brooklyn, New York between 1956 and 1961. During this time, he received his A.M. degree in sociology from Fordham University in 1959, and his M.S.S. degree in psychiatric social work also from Fordham in 1960. In 1961 he became an assistant professor of anthropology and sociology at Adelphi College. In 1968, he received his Ph.D. at New York University in sociology and anthropology. He was appointed to the National Advisory Council on Ethnic Heritage Studies in 1975; he was elected vice chairman in 1976, and appointed chairman in 1977. He married Concetta Cianciotto in 1952 and they have two children. At present, he continues to teach and conduct research at the State University of New York at Albany, where he remains active in local politics and ethnic affairs.

Major Influences

Femminella's major influence at Fordham University was Father Joseph P. Fitzpatrick who wrote on ethnicity and on delinquency, and Frank A. Santopolo, a reasearch methodologist. During his time at Fordham and at New York University, Femminella occupied himself with the works of Timasheff, Sorokin, C.W.Mills and the 19th Century classical writers in sociology; Leslie White, V. Gordon Childe, and Louis S.B. Leakey in anthropology; Freud and Erikson in psychology; and Teggart, Mumford, Bloch and Vico in history. His professors at New York University who constituted an influential configuration of scholars included Harvey Zorbaugh, Frederick Kerlinger, Dan Dodson, Mozell Hill and Marvin Bressler. His colleagues included Victor Gioscia, Anthony Romeo, John Kavanagh and Martin Adler.

Major Works

The major theme of ethnicity runs throughout the work of Femminella. He has applied the disciplines of sociology, psychology, and anthropology to this theme. His work has been a vital part of the advancement of the study of American ethnicity in general, and of the Italian American experience in particular. His major works include *Ethnicity and Ego Identity* (1968) and "The Immigrant and the Urban Melting Pot," (1973). He has also edited *Power and Class: The Italian American Experience Today* (1973). Among the many articles he has published are "The Impact of Italian Migration on American Catholicism" (1961), "The Italian-American Family: Ethnicity and Family Life" (1970), "Italian American Family Life Styles" (1976), and "Ethnicity and Community Analysis" (1971). He has also been a keynote speaker reading a paper entitled "Ethnic Heritage and Citizenship" at the White House in 1976. He spoke on other topics including "Societal Ramifications of Ethnicity in the Suburbs" (1979). His "Education and Ethnicity" (1980), was recently published by the United States Commission on Civil Rights.

The Immigrant and the Urban Melting Pot

One of the first postulates set down in this book is that – "no nation, and in particular, the United States, gets just people out of immigration; it acquires an "immigrant culture".[2] On the basis of this postulate a number of comments can be made, some more speculative than others, about this theory of American ethnicity, its assertions concerning the processes that occur when people of different ethnic groups come together, and its domain assumption about man and society. In short, a few important initial statements can be made about the structure and infrastructure of his theory.

First, American culture is more or less an immigrant culture. It is therefore impossible to explain American culture without the immigrant and an understanding of his role in the formation of that culture. Implicit in this definition of culture, then, must be provision for heterogeneity since the immigrants in the United States are a diverse group. Each group migrated from a different geographical area and brought with it a unique culture which developed in that area over time. The phase "immigrant culture" also implies that immigrants do have a culture and that they can bring it with them from one place to another. Care has to be taken, however, that it is not also implied that American culture is a "foreign" culture; that is, it is composed of the cultures of other nations and lands. The existence of an immigrant culture does not necessarily mean that the culture of an immigrant in the United States is exactly the same as the culture which he left behind. Femminella does not share the latter notion. He views the immigrant's culture and the culture of his homeland to be different in at least two years. First, there is a basic value difference involved. The immigrant's values reflect his movement from one land to another while his countrymen in the homeland possess a value which keeps them from moving. In this way, the immigrants are very different kinds of people from their countrymen. Second, arrival of the immigrant on the shores of a new land produces an effect upon the culture that the immigrant carries within him. Through critical contact with the host culture, a new set of adaptive capacities become part of the immigrant's culture.

Focusing on the phrase "immigrant culture" something can also be inferred about Femminella's theory concerning the domain assumptions. One may begin to infer that Femminella's perspective on culture is more orientated to the *gemeinschaft* view of society, rather than to a *gesellschaft* view of society. This observation seems even more plausible if note is taken of the four words that immediately follow the phrase "immigrant culture". They are: "which is a distinctive quality". This phrase resonates a positive sentiment and might possibly be lodged in the biography of the theorist (immigrant parents or grandparents).

Referring to the phrase "immigrant culture", Femminella asserts that "what this means and how it happens is a theme we shall develop by exploring the fascinating interconnections between a number of ideas. Ideas concerning immigrants, concerning cities, concerning intergroup process".[3] Femminella's approach contains three elements which have a logical relationship to the concept "immigrant culture". Although Femminella could have used a different set of elements in his approach, I believe these three elements reflect something important to the theorist. The first element 'immigration' hinges directly on the phrase "immigrant culture", while the second two hinge on the "melting pot". The melting pot was an urban notion; intergroup processes reflect this along with the theorist's sociological orientation.

As Femminella continues to construct an approach to the subject, he, while referring to the idea of melting pot, points out "the multiplicity of statuses and functions which certain salient ideas have".[4] Since this idea, melting pot, is central to his piece, (as it has been for the last four theoristis), Femminella conducts a brief analysis of it. He identifies three statuses of the idea, namely, "ideology", "social theory", and "utopian wish image". Γhe first represents a belief and a hope, and, it is a symbol for allaying fears"; the second "is a description and explanation of social events and processes"; and the third is "a historical fiction, one of those myths, whose function was to stabilize the social order".[5] Building upon this idea, he asserts:

> As we shall see, too often, the social theories which explained certain events have followed and fit too perfectly the social and political ideologies of the day. When this occurs, we cannot help but suspect that these ideological projections have fostered, if not conscious falsification, then at least unconscious self-deception. The projection of these values and beliefs have had not only scientific but political and social consequences as well.[6]

This statement represents the perspective by which Femminella will evaluate all the theories of American ethnicity. It expresses the fact that ideas have power in society.[7] Conceptions which attempt to interpret the social processes which occurred when immigrants came together in the cities of the United States had a very large influence on what did happen. As these conceptions developed into total theories, they had an effect on social policy and political consequences.

What makes this important for Femminella is the idea that how we *define* a phenomenon will have serious implications for how we act. "We act on the basis of our subjective understanding of a situation".[8] Femminella uses the classic remarks by W.I. Thomas and Robert Merton (the self-fulfilling prophecy) to illustrate this point.[9] His central purpose here is to affirm that ideas have multiple statuses and functions. This is a secondary theme in his work, for he also examines ideas that have had a tendency to be viewed in a variety of different ways.

Having set down a postulate, and identified an approach, Femminella further develops his approach by examining two of the three above mentioned ideas, "immigrants" and "cities". His analysis of these terms follows a pattern just previously set down. For Femminella, ideas serve basically three types of statuses and functions. The melting pot is an excellent example with which to view this pattern of approach. Although the status of the term "melting pot" is much different from the status of the terms "immigrants" and "cities", a similar pattern of analysis is used. These terms evoke ideological images which generate a set of emotional and cooperative feelings.

Femminella points to examples of tendencies to use "migration" in an ideologically colored way, or as part of a circular reasoning process, both of which are "largely apart from empirical historical referents."[10] To correct these tendencies, he asserts "men have from prehistoric times migrated over long distances presumably to better their life chances, and they settled in large number in areas where their life chances were enhanced or where they were forced to stay. Finally, we might want to add that certain of these settlements developed into cities".[11] One gets the impression here that Femminella is dismissing the ideologically colored images and injecting a value-neutral assertion concerning immigration and cities. However, the fact that he prefaced the assertion with the words "For our purposes . . ." testifies to his acknowledgement of the value-laden character of social scientific work.

Examining this assertion from the angle of the model presented in chapter two, it is basically a sociological generalization. The statement is a modification of one made by the historians Teggard and adapted by Femminella. Contained in it are the postulates that man is a migratory animal by nature, and man is self-interested in bettering his life chances.

With the use of Peterson's typology, Femminella goes on to characterize the immigration movements to the United States. He labeled the 19th and 20th century immigrations as "Free and Mass", and while the earlier one was "conservative", the latter was "innovating".

In analyzing migration characteristics, he asserts, "Industrialism, urbanization, and immigration became tied to one another; and the United States became a very changed world".[12] This tri-thematic type of assertion, in effect, says that these three processes had an understandably large impact on the United States. The significant point here is the position of the word "immigration". Immigration is tied in with the other terms industrialism and urbanization. It is not uncommon in most contexts that these two terms overshadow immigration. The commonly lesser status attributed to immigation as a major process having a profound impact on American society and culture is critically questioned and changed by Femminella. He equalizes the status of the three terms.

Femminella tries to entertain the range of social processes involved in these larger themes. He interprets the interconnection between the three factors of economy. ecology, and demography as having been "grossly misunderstood" and "largely ideological".[13] Concerning these three processes, he believes that the problems generated by one become confused with the problems generated by another; this occurring both in the mind of the nativist and also the immigrant. He believes that the nature of these problems has not changed so drastically from earlier times. Furthermore, he believes that the characteristics of the crisis of modern times would be listed as follows: "social and personal disorder, feelings of alienation and anomie, and, violent conflict between individuals and nations".[14]

In naming the characteristics of the crisis of modern times, certain questions arise. First, why does Femminella focus on the crisis, instead of the more positive aspects that have come out of the above three processes? Second, in choosing these three salient characteristics of the crisis of modern times, he has made somewhat of an arbitrary decision. Although this may represent a consensual view among social societists, nevertheless, it does reflect the domain assumptions of Femminella. In particular, these three problems of man and society have run throughout the twentieth century. Another two questions may be raised even though it does not appear that Femminella will answer them. First, are these social problems self-correcting or will they have to be solved by intentional human intervention? Second, is it possible to infer from this whether society is precarious or fundamentally stable?

The next statement is important because it cites important elements that will be useful for later analysis and comparison.

> Our image of "early times" and of traditional societies is an image of orderliness, of feeling a sense of belonging and knowing one's place, and of cooperation among men. The "halo effect", which induces us to remember the agreeable or positive aspects of an experience or historical event, tricks us into forgeting the repugnant or negative aspects which, in the case of changing notions of community, refers to the inflexible dimensions of stability.[15]

Take note of the attention given to the contradictory notion of orderliness and stability. The "halo effect" basically translates as a backward-looking activity toward an image of orderliness. The assumptions read as (1) if men in a situation of social crisis look back into the past, they will perceive order and cooperation; and (2) when a social crisis arises, men will look toward the past; and (3) finally, in the case of community, they look back and perceive stability.

Another assumption embedded in the statement is that man prefers stability over disorder. While Femminella attributes this order seeking backward-looking behavior to the psychological nature of man, he argues this by pointing to things that men forget about the past, such as a rigid social structure, the press of over-conformity upon one's values and behavior, and the violent treatment of deviants. With respect to this point the says:

> . . . from the point of view of many social theorists, it is out of the dialectics of these positive and negative conditions that man's culture evolves. Put in another way, out of man's wish to have order without inexorability, out of his need to be both a part of and simultaneously apart from others, and out of his desire to be both ruled

> and free, there arises a tension, and this tension is synthesized in new and changing social forms.[16]

It is critical to note the value placed on the tension between contradictory conditions, between the ruled and the free, between thesis and antithesis. This Hegelian notion is important for out of the synthesis between these conditions a new social form arises.

There is a clue here to Femminella's definition of culture. Two parameters may be added. First, culture has an evolutionary character to it, and second, culture is a product of a dialectic. Regarding the evolutionary character of culture, it is difficult at this point to say anything more specific about it. The emphasis is on the process of culture rather than the structure of it. This is found in much of Femminella's work.

The second part of this statement makes some rather explicit claims concerning human nature. First, men have wishes, needs, and desires. These three words have very different psychological meanings. While wishes and desires are closely related to each other, "need" signifies something different. Needs are often seen as presupposing wants. That is, while the human organism cannot function properly if its needs remain unsatisfied, it can function if its wishes and desires are not fulfilled. There is quite a bit of psychological readjustment and redefinition that can go on over the meaning of these terms, but the critical point here is whether Femminella considers this important or not. It might be well to speculate that he might accept an interchangeability between these terms within the context of this sentence.

It is safe to work on the assumtpion that the selection of words was not for stylish reasons but for a specific purposeful meaning. Three assumptions of a psychological nature are evident, (1) It is the nature of man to wish for order without inexorability; (2) It is the nature of man to need to be both a part of and apart from others; and (3) It is the nature of man to desire to be both ruled and free. Together, these three assumptions yield a set of primary domain assumptions: Man is a tension-plagued animal; Man's psychological needs are responsible for creating this tension. Man is a tension reducing animal, and man is a tension synthesizing animal. There is also a primary domain assumption that can be inferred from the last segment of this statement: Social forms are created and/or changed out of man's tension synthesizing nature.

Femminella introduces another set of interconnected notions. Again they are comprised of three elements, "the evolution of culture, the attainment of freedom, and the growth of cities". It would be interesting to speculate about this tendency to introduce social elements in sets of three. The first inclination would be to tie it in some way to the dialectic. Another way, however, of regarding these sets of interconnected notions is by considering them as couched in Christian infrastructure – the symbol of the trinity.

The relationship between this particular set of elements can be traced throughout the history of civilization. From the classical Philosophers of Greece to the contemporary social scientists of the United States, many have used this trilogy to describe and interpret all forms of social and cultural change. Before the Industrial Revolution, the city was taken by many to be the image of society itself. During the eighteenth and nineteenth century, the city was viewed initially as a "good" place, later on as an "evil" place, and finally, as neither virture nor vice. During the twentieth century, social theorists developed a broad view of urbanism. Non-economic as well as economic variables were considered critically important to the social structure of the city. Social conditions such as heterogeneity, forms of alienation, and human irrationality were identified as aspects of urban culture. Cities were also viewed as integrated social forms.[17]

In the United States particularly, cities played a central role in all forms of social development. The immigration movement of the early twentieth century made a major impact on urban life. Description and analysis of United States cities before World War I were largely made by reformers of various types. The purpose of their writing was often to contribute to the support of various forms of legislation directed at social change. After World War I, new social scientific orientations began to emerge, such as Robert E. Park's ecological approach. The development and adoption of concepts such as competition, dominance, accommodation, and invasion and succession, became used to explain urban social phenomena. This new type of sociological thinking interpreted the city as "a vital product of human nature".[18] It was believed that by studying the city, one could learn about human nature and the evolution of culture.[19]

Femminella asserts that the notions about human nature and culture in the United States were "infused with 'American', more properly – 'United Statesian' ideology".[20] The themes running throughout included a stress on equality, freedom, individualism, practicality, success, and concern for the opinion of others".[21] These elements were not only found in the work of the disciples of Park, but also in the earlier writing by Creveceour, de Tocqueville, Martineau, and Bryce on the subject of dominant American traits.[22]

One of the central themes in the work of Femminella is that the image of culture, cities, and immigrants has, in some ways, been ideologically colored. Furthermore, these images have influenced not only the social theories but political consequences as well. Concerning the writers in America on this subject, it appears that the traits they have used to describe Americans are also infused with ideology – United Statesian ideology. Femminella, in addressing this situation, poses the thought that:

> . . . if we accept the anthropological truism that cultures are integrated, then we must explóre the apparent contradiction in placing high value on both conformity with concern for others, on the one hand, and non-conformity and individuality, on the other; between, on the one hand, equality for all with racial heterogeneity – the "melting pot", and, on the other hand, disdain and distrust of foreigners with feelings of superiority over them, and national conceit.[23]

Here, he is pointing to the fact that there is a contradiction in the characteristic traits that people in the United States were traditionally thought to possess and have coexisted as part of a larger process that is occurring in the United States.

> The coexistence of these conflicting values and ideas in the United Statesian culture system can be accounted for by virture of their origins in the intergroup processes of evolving human nature including the processes of cooperation, competition, conflict, accommodation and assimilation. These important paradoxes are supported by a kind of logic which emanates out of the ideologies of the group. Thus, there is no contradiciton in a group's "strain for consistency" with its consequent imposition of uniformities, and its stress on personal competition for economic advantage.[24]

This statement is important because it includes many assertions concerning intergroup processes. It also ties these processes inextricably to the evolution of human nature. Femminella affirms the Parkian processes of cooperation, competition, conflict, accommodation, and assimilation as occurring when people of different ethnic groups come together in the United States. This all occurs under the assumption that there is a background condition of conflicting values and ideas. Femminella views this social phenomenon in the United States as being colored by conflict, contradiction, and paradox. The paradoxes are supported by the logic of ideologies. The paradox as it relates to the immigrants is described.

> Immigrants residing in the cities of the United States are strangers in their host society and they are easily identified as foreign. These foreigners must learn the meaning and the manners of our society, at first for sheer survival, then after some initial success they are impelled, seemingly by some inner human dynamic in order to participate in the great American dream. In practice, this meant they entered into the life of the city – and especially the action of the market – learning to compete. Once this happened, the "race relations cycle" was begun.[25]

The ethnic intergroup process assertions can be coded as follows: (1) Newcomer ethnic group is identified by the host culture as a foreigner. The former then assumes the status of stranger in that society; (2) For survival, the newcomer ethnic learns and abides by the norms of the dominant host ethnic culture; (3) After some success in the new environment, the newcomer ethnic is impelled by some "inner human dynamic" to participate in the "great American dream". This inner human dynamic may very well be translated as a hope to be successful, a faith in the new land, or simply a psychic motivation caused by the hope of economic success. The "great American dream" is familiar and is reflected in the ideological rhetoric of the time; (4) The newcomer ethnic, upon participation in the economic market-place of the host society, learns to compete. Femminella affirms this process as part of the beginning of the Parkian 'race relations cycle'. If the newcomer retains his cultural ways, the competition becomes racial, impersonal, and conflictual. On the other hand, if the newcomer ethnic group member surrenders his cultural ways, good relations follow and assimilation grows.

Many writers have embraced the notion that the cities are the melting pots of races and cultures. (This is not to infer that assimilation does not occur in rural areas.) Assimilation symbolized by the melting pot may be of many different types. It is only necessary to consult the conceptions of Turner, Fairchild, Creveceour, and Zangwill to make this point clear. There are, however, two very prominent concepts of assimilation that early twentieth century social scientists used. One was Robert E. Park's definition of assimilation, while the other was Henry Pratt Fairchild's meaning. Park's conception of assimilation referred to that social process whereby people of different races and cultures are drawn into "the ever narrow circle of common life".[26] In interpreting Park, Femminella further states:

> It referred to the erasing of external differences, the development of superficial uniformities particularly in manners and fashion but also in language which enables newcomers to participate in the new life, in a "practical working arrangement", so that like-mindedness in individual opinions, sentiments and beliefs may eventually accrue.[27]

It is interesting to note the use of the term like-mindedness. Kallen had used this term as a characterization of the trait all ethnic groups possess. In Park's usage, it becomes a characterization for the larger social group which includes ethnic groups within it. The other meaning of assimilation comes from Henry Pratt Fairchild who wrote, "The process by which a nationality preserves its unity while admitting representations of outside nationalities is properly termed assimilation".[28]

Femminella analyzes the difference between these two terms in the following way. First, the direction of the change involved in assimilation is different. For Park, assimilation is a two-way process. Not only does the newcomer assimilate by adapting to the conditions of the market in order to participate and survive, but the host ethnic also adapts the social structure of the market place so that the newcomer is able to participate. Fairchild, on the other hand, takes an almost opposite viewpoint. For him, it is the newcomer who must be completely transformed into the "type of the receiving nationality". The receiving nationality does not change at all in order to maintain national unity. These two notions of assimilation do in some ways bear a relationship to Milton Gordon's set of definitions of assimilation; *cultural assimilation and structural assimilation.*[29]

The melting pot, then, for Femminella denotes the assimilation of people; however, there are two important points raised by definition. The first is the direction of the change, and the second is the distinction between cultural and structural assimilation. The profound influence of the melting pot idea on the city in the United States is analyzed by Femminella in its socio-cultural context. His reason for doing this reflects his awareness that all ideas are socially constructed. "Melting pot", he says, "relates to the peopling of the country and the development of a culture".[30] From the birth of the nation, the union of the people of the United States was legally defined. The early colonists established themselves as a united group. The United States, from early times, had an open immigration policy. Since colonial times, 45 million immigrants have entered. About as early as the first large immigration, the melting pot notion was developed to characterize the immigrants interaction with the host society. Creveceour, in the late eighteenth century used it to describe the processes that had occurred between northern Europeans in rural America. Although Creveceour described a type of assimilation, the records of the period indicate that there were many instances of "sufficient aggressivity" demonstrated against assimilation.[31] Moreover, there were records of abusive treatment of Germans and Scottish-Irish immigrants as they resisted becoming Anglicized. This type of resistance in the past and the more recent instances of the same, led Femminella to conclude:

> That the melting pot was not understood, or rather was interpreted differently at different times according to prevailing ideologies is seen in the arguments for and against free immigration which began early in our history and still go on today.[32]

Even in early America as immigrants entered the new nation, assimilation did not proceed as rapidly as people wished. Immigrant societies for mutual protection were formed for the preserving of old country ways. Femminella points out "For the Anglo-American, whether consciously or not, the melting pot had a very distinct meaning; it meant the dissolution of all non-English ways".[33]

By the end of the nineteenth century, the United States was

going through a period of great economic change. Forces such as "mass industrialism, paralyzing depressions, and so forth, were having a major impact on the nation".[34] With the dawn of the twentieth century, newcomers flooded the shores and cities of the nation. This time, the immigrants were very different. They were no longer northern and western European, a people with similar racial and religious characteristics of the host society. Rather, the new immigrants were from southern and eastern Europe. The anti-newcomer sentiment that had existed was supplemented with anti-Catholic and anti-Semetic sentiments. About this time, Israel Zangwill produced his play entitled *The Melting Pot* (1909). In it he portrayed the city as "a seething cauldron into which have been poured people from all the nations and all the races of mankind, and out of which comes a new unified super-being, the 'American'".[35]

The melting pot ideas of Creveceour and Zangwill were both similar in the double sense that they predicted a total assimilation, and, they predicted changes in both the immigrant and the host society. There were, however, major differences. For Creveceour, the people were fairly homogeneous to begin with. They immigrated for various reasons, and had a particular response to the social and cultural conditions of the host society. Finally, the result of the process of assimilation was a "rural, Protestant, Anglo-American". For Zangwill, the people were very heterogeneous, their immigration could be characterized as a mass, rural migration, and they "sought to become a vital working part of the strange culture they encountered and to share in the American dream of freedom and prosperity".[36] Finally, the product of the assimilation process for Zangwill would be an urban superman. In contrast to both Creveceour and Zangwill, Femminella gives his appraisal of the character of this process.

> The immigrants came to the cities of the United States; and they made the cities of the United States; and the cities made them United Statesians. As we review the recent studies of these groups we find that they have not "melted". These Germans, Italians, Irish, Jews, Poles, Africans, Japanese and others have in so many ways not become Anglo-American, and indeed, they seem not to want to be Anglo-Americans. They want to be German-Americans, Italian-Americans, Irish-Americans, Jewish-Americans,

> Polish-Americans, African-Americans, Japanese-Americans and so on.[37]

The process assertion here is that when people of different ethnic groups come together in the United States, they do not fully assimilate into the host society. Moreover, they do not want to. They want to become part of the nation, yet, they do not want to relinquish their ethnicity. The embedded domain assumption is that people of ethnic groups do not want to totally assimilate. From this, it may be inferred that it is the nature of man to retain a segment of his ethnicity even while engaging in the social process of assimilation. Two important questions grow out of the above conception of the ethnic intergroup process in the United States: (1) How is the process to be explained? and (2) What does it signify about American culture?

In answering these questions, it becomes useful for Femminella to take account of the theories of assimilation. These he believes, follow very closely the ideologies respecting immigration. Initially, it was thought that all immigrants would assimilate within two or three generations. When it became apparent this was not happening, the Zangwill melting pot notion began to serve an explanatory purpose. However, the establishment of organizations such as the Ku Klux Klan and the revival of nativism after World War I took the position that the melting pot idea was a mistake. The view of the host society then became supportive of restricting immigration and educating ethnicity out of the immigrants. The Americanization movement grew and many called upon the immigrant to renounce his natural ancestry. By the 1930's it became apparent that the cities were not becoming mono-cultural centers but rather they more accurately reflected the nation of nations conflict. Horace Kallen's concept of cultural pluralism then became popular. In this notion, democracy presupposes culture. That is, groups have the right to retain their cultural identity and remain separate from each other. Based upon these theories of assimilation, Femminella judges the situation as follows:

> They as groups, have learned to communicate in English, become citizens, acquire the values of success and upward mobility, and so on. In a word, they have moved in the direction of the Anglo-American.[38]

We can begin to see the borders of Femminella's theory of ethnicity. There exists a certain degree of tension in this idea that, yes, ethnic groups have shown some degree of assimilation, but no, they have not (and will not be) totally assimilated. Theories previous to this have usually taken one side or another on this issue. *Straight line assimilation* has been largely unquestioned. Femminella's viewpoint places the newcomer and host at opposite poles. They approach each other on a continuum but never intersect. For this reason, there is always a tension that exists. Equilibrium is never reached, nor is it a desired state. A point of intersection, although always focused upon by both groups, is never reached. A group may move in the direction of another but never merge. This is similar to the idea of walking toward a wall by continually cutting the distance in half. One never reaches the wall.

The host society is greatly affected by this state of tension that exists between itself and the newcomer. Its intergroup relations with the newcomer draws it into patterns of accommodation.

> White, Anglo-Saxon, Protestants, however, are now seen not as the model to which all other groups must necessarily conform but rather as the most successful fellow-United Statesian group with whom one must deal. What this means is that WASP-Americans are entering, consciously or unconsciously, willingly or unwillingly into accommodation patterns with the ethnic communities around them; and particularly in the cities, have recognized that structural pluralism is a salient aspect of the United States culture.[39]

The abstracted ethnic process assertion can be translated as – when a dominant and subordinate ethnic group come together in the United States, over time, the dominant group no longer becomes an object of assimilation for the subordinate ethnic group. Rather, these groups enter into accommodation patterns with each other. Moreover, the assimilation that occurs is past of a bi-directional process, that is, while the subordinate ethnic group has assimilated to a degree conducive to participation in the market economy, it becomes thrown back upon itself and its heritage.

Femminella attributed particular values to immigrants which he later tested empirically.[40] In doing this he developed the notion of "ethnic ideological themes." These refer to those motifs and principal features (of which an individual may or may not have awareness) of one's ideals and aspirations and the specific pattern of variation (i.e., rank ordering) of value orientations of individuals who are members of an ethnic group. These themes are located in that aspect of the individual's personality known as the ego-identity. The Eriksonian notion of ego-identity is the basis for this concept. Together, the concepts of ego-identity (K. Mannheim), and themes (H.A. Murray) are used to generate the notion of ethnic ideological themes. These themes have been tested empirically within groups of Italian-Americans (Femminella, 1968) German-Americans (Stall, 1981), and Black-Americans (Calhoun, 1976). Each of these studies reached the same conclusion, namely that (1) despite the disappearance of immigrant communities and the emergence of new generations in the United States, some intra-psychic form of ethnic identification and affiliation continues; (2) This "ethnicity" is centered in that aspect of an individual's personality identified as the "ego identity"; and, (3) Social relations engendered by this "ethnicity" constitute a new social formation: a now-spatial ethnic community.[41] Similar research on this subject is presently being conducted with Chinese-Americans and Iranian-Americans.

Francis X. Femminella's Theory of American Ethnicity

Femminella's theory may be viewed as a series of process assertions constituting essentially four stages taken by ethnic intergroup relations in the United States. As before, these process assertions can be identified along with the key concepts that comprise them and an attempt will be made to locate their grounding in a set of postulates and domain assumptions.

Unlike the other theories presented, this one is unqiue in the sense of the perspective from which it views ethnic intergroup processes. The previous theories that have acknowledged the nature of the power relationship between immigrant newcomer and host ethnic group (as being one of subordinate-superordinate), and have taken the perspective of *either* one of those groups in constructing their theory, but never *both.* That is, they have written a theory concerning the processes that occur when people of different ethnic groups come together; however, it has been done from the view of either the dominant Anglo-American group, as in the case of Turner and Fair-child, or from the view of the subordinate immigrant newcomer or ethnic descendant, as in the case of Kallen and Glazer and Moynihan. For the most part, these theories did not go very far outside of one perspective, but rather, consciously or unconsciously, based themselves largely on the experience of one of these groups. The effort, I believe, is conscious rather than unconscious. The apparent strain in bringing these two views together is evident in the literature. Understandably, there is a great gap to be filled between the divergent ways these two groups view the world in general and their status position within the society in which they live in particular. An attempted convergence of views comes up against the problem of finding a scarcity of common ground. It becomes a complex task of synthesizing contradictions. However, Femminella does accomplish this rather well resulting in a theory that has one major difference from those before it. It is not a theory of ethnic separation. Rather, it is a theory of ethnic integration.

This activity of identifying divergent concepts and contradictory ideas, bringing them together, and posing them against each other in such a way as to create a tension that can only be alleviated through a process of dynamic synthesis, is a central aspect of Femminella's intellectual style. We can see this done again and again as two or three ideas are brought together. They also become integrated, not assimilated or left separated. The style is reflected in the theory it yields.

Certainly any theory that posits itself within the cleavages and contradictions of the social world will normally find itself immersed in the web of conflict that inhabits such life spaces. Whereas other theories of American ethnicity have wallowed in the organicism of homeostasis and equilibrium, this one, on the contrary, tumbles in a torrent of division and disruption. In short, although all theorists of American ethnicity have taken note of the process of conflict in ethnic intergroup relations, Femminella is the first to make it a point of orientation.

Just as the previous theorists of American ethnicity have built upon, discarding some parts while retaining others, and have utilized in some ways, the theories preceding their own, Femminella does the same. For instance, each theorist has used, consciously or unconsciously, the melting pot as a catapult of sorts to launch their analytical scheme. Femminella has used the melting pot as a point of departure but he has also elaborated upon a critical dimension of the "emerging culture theory." In the theory that Femminella presents – the impact-integration theory – he focuses on the conflict that is generated when ethnic groups come together. This becomes a most important element in the theory because of the confrontation and collision between groups that follow. Whereas Glazer and Moynihan have observed and recorded this conflict between ethnic groups, they leave off without fully elaborating on the processes which follow, except to say that each ethnic group goes through changes that make it very different from the original immigrant group yet still identifiable as an ethnic group. The development of their theory is limited by their grounding in assumptions about the political and interest-bound nature of individuals and ethnic groups. Femminella draws upon sociology, psychology, and anthropology to ground his theory of human nature in broader assumptions of culture and personality. The result is a theory of American ethnicity that assesses the penetrating aspects of social conflict as they change not only the individual, the ethnic group, but also the society in which they live. It is a theory with a focus on the processes that all ethnic groups, whether dominant, subordinate, host, or newcomer, go through. It is a theory which emerged out of an urban context, but it applies to a suburban context as well. It is a theory which moves from the general to the particular and swings back to the general. Finally, it is a theory that is aware of, and acknowledges, its relationships to ideologies and utopian views, an acknowledgement that other theories of American ethnicity have not made.

The four phases of Femminella's theory can be summarized as follows:

1. Boundary Crisis.
2. Conflict.
3. Impact – Integration.
4. Community.

1. The first phase of Femminella's theory of American ethnicity concerns the processes that occur between the dominant host ethnic group and the immigrant newcomers on their arrival in the United States. This first phase largely describes the reaction of the core of the dominant ethnic group of the host society to the newly arriving immigrant. Take note that the theory is generalized to a level applicable to any society.

> The core of the dominant ethnic group of a society reacts territorially to the immigration of a large number of newcomers. It observes the different, sometimes mutually

> exclusive, cultural systems of the migrants, and perceives them, ideologically as adversaries. This "boundary crisis" may be heightened if there is competition for limited rewards, otherwise absorption may be facilitated. Territorial defensiveness takes various forms and goes on in many ways. There are, for example, a whole set of behaviors for emphasizing priority, and there are the many ways, with varying degrees of subtlety, of pressing one's own appropriateness to the country. "We belong to the land; and the land is ours!" Deprecating the newcomers, and negating their attempts at "making something of themselves," the core group generates its polar opposite – the estranged intruder.[42]

There are a number of sub-processes to be subsumed within the general process called "boundary crisis". There is the 'territorial reaction' followed by the perception of the migrants as 'adversaries'. The 'territorial defensiveness' also becomes followed by the 'pressing of one's own appropriateness'. The most important result is that of the core group generating its polar opposite – the estranged intruder. A major factor which becomes evident in this process concerns the reference to the dominant ethnic group. Femminella is the only theorist of American ethnicity, who in dealing with the power relationship between ethnic groups. distinguished between the dominant ethnic group and the "core" of the dominant ethnic group. He displays the same domain assumption as Kallen did, as evidenced in their references to all groups, even the host group, as ethnics. The assumption is that all Americans are descended from the immigrants.

There are a number of postulates and domain assumptions which tie this group of process assertions together. The first group concerns the nature of man and relates to the immigrant group.

> . . . men have from prehistoric times migrated over long distances presumably to better their life chances; and they settled in large numbers in areas where their life chances were enhanced or where they were forced to stay.[43]

The two postulates which follow are: (1) man is a migratory animal, and (2) man is self-interested in bettering his life chances. A third postulate which emerges from the first phase of Femminella's theory and which ties in with these two is: (3) man is a territorial animal. These three help to form a basis for the first phase, however, the most critical grounding comes from the domain assumptions concerning the psychological nature of man. There is an implication about the character of the perception of the individual that is a function of territoriality. Viewing another as a stranger is an action which each individual psyche experiences. It produces a set of sentiments about the immigrant intruder that result in a painful dissonance between the two groups involved. Finally, the activity in which the core group generates its polar opposite – the estranged intruder, is tied to another of Femminella's assumptions about the nature of man and society. The question of why one can generate a total *opposite* finds an answer in the dialectical character of human nature to which Hegel referred. It is the contradiction of opposites (thesis and antithesis) that is a part of the continual resolution (synthesis) of ideas and human affairs.[44] This notion is crucial because it carries through all four phases of the impact-integration theory. It provides an underlying point of orientation which also illuminates Femminella's emphasis on *process* rather than structure.

2. The second phase of the impact-integration theory changes the focus slightly from the reaction of the core of the dominant ethnic group to the action, interaction, and reaction of both the dominant and subordinate (immigrant) ethnics. This stage occurs in the context in which the immigrant has learned the ways of survival and having become impelled by some "inner human dynamic" to participate in the American dream, he learns to compete in the market.[45] It is in the American marketplace that much of the conflict between groups occurs.

> In the conflict that ensues the price demanded of the immigrant to legitimize his presence is social, economic, and cultural subordination and submission. But healthy men who have grown stronger by their choice to migrate, do not submit easily. For them, freedom is too attractive a treasure to surrender, the empirical evidence seems to indicate that no ethnic group in the United States, has ever totally submitted.[46]

The three processe encompassed within this phase are: conflict between groups, demanded subordination by the dominant group, and a resistance to submission by the subordinate group. It is in this phase, that the impact-integration theory truly becomes a theory of American ethnicity. This becomes so because of the general historical processes that have accompanied immigration in the United States, the central role immigration has played in the development of this country, and the core values of the American culture, which, as Femminella assumes at the outset, is an "immigrant culture."

An immigrant coming to the United States also becomes aware of the great contradiction he experiences between the demand for him to submit and the value of freedom which he associates with American society. The conflict generated out of such a contradiction is resolved only through a dynamic synthesis, one which is described in the second two phases of his impact-integration theory.

3. The third stage of Femminella's theory of American ethnicity is most appropriately 'the impact-integration' phase.

> . . . for it is out of this impacting that new syntheses evolve. The conflict is resolved in a cultural integration that changes not only the persons involved, nor even also their groups, but the whole society itself.[47]

Here again, the Hegelian dialectic provides a framework with which to understand this process. The four main parts of the process are conflict resolution, cultural integration, change in the ethnic groups, and change in the entire society. There is a dynamic concept to this process. Once the conflict is resolved and cultural integration takes place, the resulting changes, to groups and the society as a whole, set the entire process in motion again. For as ethnic groups change, they must reintegrate themselves and since every time people of different ethnic groups come together and it changes them, they must be constantly reintegrating themselves. They do this rather than assimilate totally. Thus ethnicity is a "new social form", one that does not disappear. While Glazer and Moynihan have recognized the existence of this new social form, Femminella has attempted to explain it as a synthesis of the positive and negative forces of man's culture.

> . . . it is out of the dialectics of these positive and negative conditions that man's culture evolves. Put in another way, out of man's wish to have order without inexorability, out of his need to be both a part of and simultaneously

> apart from others, and out of his desire to be both ruled and free, there arises a tension, and this tension is synthesized in new and changing social forms.[48]

There are a number of postulates and domain assumptions to be found here. Among the postulates are (1) culture is evolutionary (culture evolves), and (2) man's culture arises out of the dialectics of positive and negative conditions. Among the domain assumptions are (1) man is a tension plagued animal; (2) man is a tension reducing animal; (3) man is a tension synthesizing animal; and (4) new social forms are created and/or changed by man's tension synthesizing nature.

By far the most challenging aspect of this theory concerns the notion of integration. How is it that ethnic groups in the United States can retain a culture, not become assimilated, yet become integrated with other ethnic groups? How can this occur in the midst of the varied and pervasive ideologies that support the melting pot as the symbol for the end product of the character of American society and culture? Again, Femminella draws upon theories of human nature to answer these questions.

> . . . if we accept the anthropological truism that cultures are integrated, then we must explore the apparent contradiction in placing high value on both conformity with concern for others, on the one hand, and non-conformity and individuality, on the other; between on the one hand, equality for all with racial heterogeneity – the "melting pot," and, on the other hand, disdain and distrust of foreigners with feelings of superiority over them and national conceit. . . the coexistence of these conflicting values and ideas in the United Statesian cultural system can be accounted for by virtue of their origins in the *intergroup processes of evolving human nature* including the processes of cooperation, competition, conflict, accommodation and assimilation. These important paradoxes are supported by a kind of logic which emanates out of the ideologies of the group. Thus, there is no strain in a group's "strain for consistency" with its consequent imposition of uniformities, and its stress on personal competition for economic advantage.[49]

Another important aspect of the third phase of the impact-integration theory is its relation to two aspects of the melting pot theory of assimilation, namely, the direction of assimilation and whether it is cultural or structural. As quickly as Femminella acknowledges that a certain degree of assimilation has taken place, he just as swiftly notes that it has not been total.

> That ethnic groups in the cities of the United States have shown some degree of assimilation is as obvious from what has been said as the fact that they have not been totally assimilated.[50]

This statement is grounded in the domain assumption that the *immigrants do not want to assimilate totally*. "They *want to be* German-Americans, Italian-Americans, Irish-Americans, Jewish-Americans, Polish-Americans, African-Americans, Japanese-Americans, and so on."[51]

Concerning the direction of assimilation, Femminella rejects the linear one-way conception.

> Assimilation then must be seen as having two directions – toward the core culture and then back to the ethnic subculture.[52]

This occurs because white Anglo-Saxon Protestants are not seen as the model to which all groups must necessarily conform, but rather the most successful American ethnic group with whom one must deal. In this context assimilation becomes more cultural than structural.

4. The final phase of Femminella's theory of American ethnicity concerns the persistence of ethnicity and the patterns of residence of ethnics in the American community.

> One sees this best in the cities, where ethnic colonies persist. But it can be seen, too, in the suburbs where voluntary segregation along ethnic lines as well as social class lines has developed. What's more important is that it exists where it cannot be seen, at least not with the naked eye. Impacting also changes the people in the society; the migrants are changed most of all, but so are the earlier residents.[53]

This phase implies a number of processes occurring. First, ethnic communities persist. This is meant in a spatial as well as a non-spatial sense. Second, voluntary segregation develops in cities and suburbs. And third, ideological reorientation in all groups occurs.

Using a perspective of social conflict that is grounded in assumptions about the nature and process of assimilation in the United States, Femminella has generated a new theory to explain the processes that occur when people of different ethnic groups come together. By forcing a reconsideration of the straight line theories of assimilation, he has been able to solve the problem of unification that all theorists of American ethnicity since Turner have tried to do. By utilizing the notion of the dialectic, he has been able to develop a new set of ideas to understand the dynamics of ethnicity and American culture:

> The dialectical integration of native resident and newcomer is of the form . . . that a synthesis occurs which unites but does not homogenize the groups.[54]

Femminella Typology

Concepts: Immigrant, Culture, Social Theory, Ideology, Utopian Wish Image, United Statesian Culture, Foreigners, Host Society, Assimilation, Boundary Crisis, Estranged Intruder, Cultural Integration, Ego-Identities, Ethnic Ideological Themes.

Process Assertions:

(1) Boundary Crisis
  - (a) Territorial Defensiveness
  - (b) Adversary Perception
  - (c) Generate Polar Opposite-Estranged Intruder

(2) Conflict for Limited Rewards
  - (a) Market Competition
  - (b) Demand for Subordination and Submission for Legitimate Presence
  - (c) Resistance to Submission

(3) Impact-Integration
   (a) Conflict Resolution
   (b) Cultural Integration
   (c) Change in Groups and Whole Society

(4) Persistence of Ethnicity
   (a) Ethnic Communities (Spatial and Non-Spatial)
   (b) Voluntary Segregation

Postulates:

(1) Social theories follow Social and Political Ideologies

(2) Man is a Migratory Animal

(3) Man is Self-interested in Bettering his life Chances

(4) Man's Culture Arises out of the Dialectics of Positive and Negative Conditions

(5) Culture is Evolutionary

(6) Assimilation has two Directions

(7) Man is a Territorial Animal.

Domain Assumptions:

(1) Notions about Human Nature and Culture in the U.S. are infused with United Statesian Assimilation

(2) The Immigrants do not want to Totally Assimilate

(3) Equilibrium is not always a Desired State

(4) Ethnic Intergroup Processes Change the Total Society

(5) The United States has an Immigrant Culture

(6) Man is a Tension Plagued Animal, Tension Reducing Animal, and Tension Synthesizing Animal

(7) Social Forms are Created out of Man's Tension Synthesizing Nature.

Notes

1. *Who's Who in the East.*
2. Francis X. Femminella, "The Immigrant and the Urban Melting Pot", in M. Urofsky (Ed.). New York: Double-Day Publishing Pot", in M. Urofsky (Ed.) *Perspectives on Urban America.* Also in David Ward (ed.), *Perspectives on America's Past.* Oxford University Press. 1979 New York: Double Day Publishing Co., 1973, p. 44. (pages of reference listed for this article correspond to original mimeo.)
3. Femminella op. cit., p. 44.
4. Ibid.
5. Ibid.
6. Ibid., p. 45, footnote 1.
7. See, for example, Karl Mannheim, *Ideology and Utopia,* New York: Harvest Books, Harcourt Brace, 1936.
8. Femminella, "The Immigrant and the Melting Pot", original mimeo, p. 2.
9. See, for example, Robert K. Merton, *Social Theory and Social Structure,* Illinois: Free Press, 1949, p. 179.
10. Femminella, op. cit., p. 3.
11. Ibid.
12. Ibid., p. 4.
13. Ibid.
14. Ibid., p. 5.
15. Ibid.
16. Ibid.,
17. Ibid., pp. 6–8.
18. Ibid.
19. Ibid.
20. Ibid.
21. Ibid., p. 8
22. Ibid.
23. Ibid., p. 9.
24. Ibid., pp. 9–10.
25. Ibid., p. 10.
26. Robert E. Park, *Race and Culture,* Glencoe, Ill.: The Free Press, 1950, p. 150.
27. Femminella, "The Immigrant and the Melting Pot", p. 11.

28. Henry Pratt Fairchild, *The Melting Pot Mistake,* Boston: Little, Brown, 1926, p. 136.
29. See Milton Gordon, *Assimilation in American Life,* 1964.
30. Femminella, "The Immigrant and the Melting Pot", p. 14.
31. Ibid., p. 16.
32. Ibid., p. 17.
33. Ibid., pp. 17–18.
34. Ibid.
35. Israel Zangwill, *The Melting Pot,* p. 109.
36. Femminella, ibid., p. 22.
37. Ibid., p. 23.
38. Ibid., p. 26.
39. Ibid., p. 36.
40. See Femminella, *Ethnicity and Ego Identity.* Ph. D. Dissertation New York University, 1968 (69–3169 University Microfilm, Ann Arbor, Mich.)
41. See Femminella, "Ethnic Dimensions of Citizenship" (mimeographed). Also Peter Stoll's *Ethnicity and Ego-Identity: A Study of German-Americans.* Doctoral Dissertation State University of New York at Albany 1981.
42. Femminella, "The Immigrant and the Melting Pot", p. 28.
43. Ibid., p. 3.
44. See the work of Hegel.
45. Femminella, "The Immigrant and the Melting Pot", p. 10.
46. Ibid., p. 29.
47. Ibid., p. 29.
48. Ibid., p. 5.
49. Ibid., p. 8.
50. Ibid., p. 26.
51. Ibid., p. 23.
52. Ibid., p. 26.
53. Ibid., p. 29.
54. Femminella, "Societal Ramifications of Ethnicity in the Suburbs", op. cit.

PART THREE

FOLLOWING THE PATH OF AMERICAN ETHNICITY THEORY

VIII Counterposing Typologies: Evolutionary Patterns in Ethnicity Theory

In this chapter, two methods of comparison are used. While the first attempts to develop a scheme to view certain elements of the theories presented in previous chapters, the second method works at integrating the elements of the typologies presented thus far in the book's Chapters III to VII. There is an important logistical point to keep aware of when doing either type of comparison. This point concerns the issue discussed in Chapter I about the ideological nature of the theories of American ethnicity. Each theorist has an ideological set of perspectives which, he, whether he likes it or not, brings to bear on his theory of American ethnicity. Each theorist is observing, describing, and interpreting events in an attempt to come up with an explanation of what is happening within the character of American society as it anchors itself in ethnicity. However, each theorist's view of that society is shaped by his position in its social matrix. The social basis of his knowledge about that society may be based on his social class, ethnicity, intersections with particular institutional structures, etc. Because of these factors, his ideology will legitimize certain societal arrangements. Although, in constructing his theory, he will attempt to adhere to the scientific canon of objectivity, he will in effect be perpetuating a view of society. Often times, this does not occur intentionally. It inevitably happens as the ideology of each theorist intersects with his attempts at theory construction. This can occur in a number of ways. The way suggested in this book is that each ideology generates a set of domain assumptions about man and society that become infused into each theory at the sub-structural level. An understanding of this will be useful as the comparison is carried out.

Within the first suggested method an attempt is made to structure a comparison of the process assertions. First a brief examination is made of the basic nature of the dynamic process of social interaction in general, and of ethnic intergroup action in particular. Second, having examined the basic components of the process that occurs when people of different ethnic groups come together, a typology of American ethnic intergroup response will be constructed. Third, within this typological framework, the necessary comparisons between the theories can be made. A similar format will be followed later in which the underlying assumptions of these theories will be compared. In this case, the differences in the basic assumptions of the theories of American ethnicity will be examined, and, speculation concerning the relationship between these and the process assertions will be made. This will occur in the second half of this chapter as the elements of the selected theories of American ethnicity are compared to each other by positing them against the essential structure of the two major theoretical models of sociological theory; functionalism and conflict theory.

Comparative Mode A
Ethnic Intergroup Response Typologies

The core element of the comparative analysis of process assertions will be comprised of the form and substance of the social interaction itself as it occurs between ethnic groups. The nature of social interaction can be viewed in general by adopting the perspective of situational theory.[1] In this case, when two groups come together (i.e., ethnic groups), what is occurring, in effect, is the face-to-face interaction of two individual members of these groups. At least, this is one way to view it. This type of analysis is grounded in a micro-level perspective, however, the extended implications of this type of analysis can lead to a series of macro-level assertions concerning social interaction.[2] In terms of action theory and situational theory, any interaction between two individuals includes at least two things, the contextual nature of the event including the ideas, motives, and resources each individual brings to bear on the substance of the situation, and also the process character of the event including the definition, construction, and negotiation of the form of social reality.

Since the domain in this book consists of the processes that occur when people of different ethnic groups come together, ethnicity becomes elevated to the key variable in this analysis of social interaction. The implication of this elevation for the total character of the social interaction begins to emerge. Ethnic intergroup action now becomes viewed in terms of the activity of status designation – a part of both the contextual and process nature of social interaction. Status designation, as it occurs in ethnic intergroup relations, becomes part of a larger process called ethnic status structuralization.[3] Status designation includes the implicit or explicit imposition of the parameters of a power relationship that will exist between individuals of different groups, in this case – of ethnic groups. The central parameters of this ethnic status designation are those of dominance and subordinance or subordination. Although this status designation is usually established even before individuals of different ethnic groups come together, it is an aggregation of the actual face-to-face interaction that institutionalizes the ethnic status system in a society.

It is within this aspect of ethnic intergroup action – status designation – that certain responses will occur which will have a lasting effect on the nature of the social interaction between ethnic groups. Both the dominant ethnic status culture and the subordinate ethnic status culture have available to them a response to the other's status designations. The aggregate of this response will in turn shape more specifically the ethnic intergroup relations that will follow. Two simple typologies of American ethnic response will aid our analysis.

Typology of American Ethnic Response to Status Designation

A. Dominant Ethnic Status Culture[4]

1. Acceptance – behavioral response ranging from actual welcome to tolerance and accommodation
2. Indifference – behavioral response ranging from simple lack of concern to disregard and neglect
3. Rejection – behavioral response ranging from abuse and exploitation to exclusion, and even murder.

B. Subordinate Ethnic Status Culture[5]

1. Acceptance – a set of behavioral responses including *acquiescence* (i.e., necessary for survival as in the Southern caste system) *cultural amnesia* (i.e., a willingness to lose their ethnic identity) *eagerness and intensity to assimilate* (including a degrading perception of their own culture).

2. Resistance – a set of behavioral responses including *refusal* to accept status designation; *non-violent techniques* – boycotts, strikes, legal action, political activity, mass protest, etc. *violent techniques heightened sense of ethnic identity* – resurgence of ethnicity.
3. Avoidance – a set of behavioral responses including *neither acceptance nor resistance* of status designation *setting themselves apart from dominant ethnic group* – shields the subordinate group from prejudice and discrimination and enables them to preserve their own culture and social institutions with a minimum of outside interference; *separation* – the most extreme form of avoidance; little if any interaction with the dominant ethnic group; *dissimilation* – avoidance of the pressures of assimilation.

Using these ethnic response typologies as a focal point, the five theories of American ethnicity can now be compared. As each theory is taken in turn, note will be taken of (a) the status designation that each theorist explicity or implicity recognizes between ethnic groups, (b) the response of the dominant ethnic status culture that each theorist describes, interprets, forecasts, ideologizes, theorizes, etc., whatever the case may be, (c) the response of the subordinate ethnic status culture that each theorist describes, interprets, forecasts, ideologizes, theorizes, etc., whatever the case may be. There is sure to be a certain amount of overlapping as far as these three criteria are concerned. Particular theorists, for instance, may have described more than one response pattern by a subordinate ethnic status group. Note will be taken of this. However, general ethnic response patterns that best typify the work of each theorist are being looked for. On the basis of the material presented in Chapters III-VII, the following conclusions about each theory can be drawn.

Frederick Jackson Turner did take note of the status designations between ethnic groups. Within his descriptions of American ethnic groups, we find chronicles of the plight of the Germans of Pennsylvania and Wisconsin, the Puritans of New England, the Scottish-Irish of the Mid-West, the native British and Dutch of New York, the Blacks and poor Whites of the South, the Indians of the frontier, and the newer immigrants of Irish and Italian ancestry of Boston and New York. The distinction between the status of different ethnic groups that appear in his writings are sometimes descriptive and at other times interpretive. For instance, he describes the power relationships that existed between the French and Indians, between the southern Blacks and native whites, and between the Pennsylvania Germans and native Dutch and English. However, he also interprets the status designation between the native Americans of the older immigration, and the newer immigrants of southern and eastern Europe. He does this by the use of the adjective "alien," a term which he did not apply to the earlier immigrants of the nineteenth century. At other times, Turner implied an equal status designation between ethnic groups. However, this occurred as he described intergroup relations on the fringes of the frontier. Turner's use of the term composite nationality seems to suggest that a fusion between different ethnic groups was and would occur via the frontier. Nevertheless, the character of this composite nationality would in the end result be a type closely marked by Anglo-Saxon and northwestern European style. This was the case because the aggregate of frontier people was largely of that group, while immigrants of "other" backgrounds made their lives in the cities. Thus, for Turner, the cities were a very different place than the frontier. The term composite nationality was not used to describe or interpret the ethnic intergroup processes of the city.

Again, when speaking about the response of the dominant ethnic status culture to the matrix of ethnic intergroup power relations, Turner's view must be dichotomized between his frontier writing and his later urban-focused writing. On the frontier, the key word for Turner is "cooperation." It was the cooperation between all groups that built the frontier. This occurred regardless of the status designation. Turner described this phenomenon between groups as he referred to frontier building, and, he interpreted this activity as part of the total character of ethnic intergroup relations in the United States. From this point of view then, it can be concluded that the dominant ethnic status culture response is typified as *acceptance.* In the cities, however, it becomes a wholly different story. Turner describes the dichotomized relationships between capital and labor. At that time this relationship was clearly one between the dominant ethnic group and the subordinate newcomers who provided the manpower for the means of production. In this case, Turner has described the exploitation that occurred by capital toward labor. Moreover, at other times he described, both in urban and rural areas, the territoriality of groups and their resistance toward each other. From this, we can typify the response of the dominant ethnic group as one of *rejection.*

When speaking about the response of the subordinate ethnic culture, note must again be taken of the dichotomy between the frontier and post-frontier eras, and also the difference between the situations of various ethnic groups. For the most part, both on the frontier and in the emerging urban areas of the nation, Turner described the immigrant response to their status in the new nation as *acceptance.* The immigrants' eagerness and willingness to assimilate was described from their eagerness and willingness to cooperate with each other in frontier building. However, Turner's description of the response of the immigrants cannot be categorized as totally accepting their subordinate status with a motive and desire to assimilate. There were many times when Turner noted the *resistance* of the Germans, for instance, to assimilate to the dominant ways in Pennsylvania. He also described the "persistence of inherited morale" of the Irish, Italian, and German immigrants.

It appears that Frederick Jackson Turner's typification of the response of dominant ethnic and subordinate ethnic groups, through his descriptions and interpretations of ethnic intergroup processes in the United States, does not fall neatly into the categories of the suggested typology. The reasons for this may be twofold. First, there is a signficant difference between his frontier writing of the nineteenth century and urban writings of the twentieth century. Second, and probably more important, is the fact that his descriptions often contradicted his interpretation of the character of American society. That is, while on the one hand, his interpretation of the character of American society often noted the cooperative aspects of democracy and nation-building – typifying mutual responses of *acceptance,* his descriptions, on the other hand, took note of the resistance, of the subordinate ethnic groups and the exploitation by the dominant ethnic group, all of which typified responses of *resistance* and *rejection,* respectively.

Henry Pratt Fairchild's theory of American ethnicity more closely fits the parameters of the typology than does Turner's. The status designation between ethnic groups was made very clear by Fairchild. The native and assimilated Anglo-Saxon Americans were the dominant status groups and all others were subordinate. The important point that Fairchild tries to communicate is that subordinance has no connection with inferiority of race and nationality, but rather a subordinate status of the newcomer is necessary to maintain national unity. Using Fairchild's metabolic analogy of digestion, the assimilatory organism, (the American organism), is the dominant ethnic group and the assimilable and non-assimilable substances are the subordinate ethnic newcomers. Fairchild, in *The Melting Pot Mistake,* seldom mentioned groups in particular, as Turner had; therefore, only these two categories yielded by his interpretation are left.

Fairchild interprets the response of the dominant ethnic status culture as being consonant with his view of the character of American society, which is the duty of Americans to assimilate the foreigners to their own type. They *must* do this for the unity of the nation is at stake. If they want to maintain their superior status as a nation in the world and, if they want to prevent the destruction of their nationality, Americanization of the immigrant then becomes the responsiblity of every citizen. The response of the dominant ethnic group then is *acceptance.* However, Fairchild makes it explicitly clear through his support for immigration restriction policies that he favors exclusion of the immigrants, some in greater quantities than others. Exclusion is part of a set of behaviors typified by a *rejection* response. Fairchild takes this rejection response position on two conditions. First, it is a response toward those immigrants of foreign race and nationality who want to come to the United States – those he refers to as "the New Menace." Second, he recognizes the appropriateness of the rejection response for those immigrants who are living in the United States, but either cannot or will not assimilate.

Concerning Fairchild's interpretation there is no question of the response that the subordinate ethnic group *should* take. Since he does not rely on descriptions of the actual response that they did take, as in the case of Turner, he totally relies on his ideological interpretation. Their response, therefore, should be one of unquestionable *acceptance.* According to Fairchild, the newcomer must possess a willingness to lose their ethnic identity and acquiesce into the ways of the dominant status culture. They must demonstrate their eagerness to assimilate, and although he would see cultural amnesia as a good thing for this group, he would go as far as espousing that they should have a degrading perception of their birth culture.

It appears that Fairchild's theory of American ethnicity falls more closely to an acceptance response by both the dominant and subordinate ethnic groups. However, his dominant group interpretation will have to be dichotomized according to the factor of assimilation.

Horace Kallen's theory of American ethnicity, like Turner's, must also be viewed in both descriptive and interpretive terms, that is, as theoretical and ideological. For example, while he acknowledges in a descriptive manner the status designation between dominant and subordinate ethnic groups in the country, he believes they should all be viewed equally as hyphenated Americans. He often takes note of the Anglo superiority myth and the social doctrines which not only recognize the dominant status of that group but also legitimize it. His many descriptions of the ethnic status system of the United States attest to the clear existence of status designations of dominance and subordinance. From his descriptions of this, he is led to conclude that the economic divisions that cut across ethnic lines are not strong enough to split ethnic group consciousness.

In accordance with Kallen's doctrine of cultural pluralism, the response of the dominant ethnic group should be one of *acceptance,* for in this way, they would be acting in accordance with the principles of democracy. As the dominant ethnic status culture accommodates itself to the presence of the subordinate ethnic status culture, a condition of liberty and equality can be said to prevail in the nation. The union that is fostered among ethnic groups of the nation creates a national harmony of ideals and interests. Heterogeneity remains the texture of the national character, yet it is fully *accepted* by the dominant group. This view differs significantly from the actual descriptions which Kallen provided with respect to the response of the dominant ethnic status group. He has described the fear and anxiety of the dominant ethnic group and their efforts to relieve themselves of these feelings. He recounts the efforts of the national movement,. the Know-Nothing Party, and the Ku Klux Klan to act with tyranny toward the immigrant. This type of response could only be described as *rejection.* Concerning the actual response of the dominant ethnic group toward his doctrine of cultural pluralism, he leaves off by saying:

> But the question is, do the dominant classes in America want such a society? The alternative is before them. Can they choose wisely? Or will vanity blind them and fear

> constrain them, turning the promise of freedom into the fact of tyranny, and once more vindicating the ancient habit of man and aborting the hope of the world?[6]

According to Kallen's doctrine of cultural pluralism, the response of the ethnic newcomer to his subordinate status, a status which forces him to assimilate to the ways of the dominant status culture, should be *avoidance.* That is, they neither accept, nor actively resist their status designation, but instead set themselves apart from the dominant ethnic group. In this way they will shield their ethnic group from prejudice and discrimination and enable them to preserve their own culture and social institutions with a minimum of outside interference. Kallen never actually advocates separation, the most extreme form of avoidance, although many groups who profess this position have in fact aligned themselves with this doctrine of cultural pluralism. Another response which Kallen attributes to the ethnic newcomer is dissimilation, a process in which, "the arts, life and ideals of the nationality become central and paramount; ethnic and national differences change from disadvantages to distinctions."[7] This response is part of the process which Kallen interprets as occurring to all immigrants. It is the third phase of his set of process assertions. When he does describe the actual situation of ethnic newcomers in the United States, such as in the case of the Germans, Irish, Scandinavians, and Jews, there is ample evidence in his description of a response in which each group preserves its culture and social institutions.[8]

Nathan Glazer and Daniel Patrick Moynihan, both of whom are very politically conscious, have viewed the status designations of the ethnic composition in New York City as one of dominance and subordination. It could be best categorized this way because they have shown the many ways of demarcation both politically and economically, between the ethnic groups they were dealing with. Although they did deal predominantly with the Blacks, Puerto Ricans, Jews, Italians, and Irish, there is much indication of the presence of the German, the old Dutch and Anglo-Saxon families in New York City, and the smaller groups such as the Chinese, Czechs, and Poles.

The major power demarcations in New York City are divided in three blocks among the Jews, the Catholics, and the Blacks and Puerto Ricans. As they have often noted, the power relations in the city of New York are very complex. However, they make it clear that the dominant ethnic status groups are the Jews, Irish, and Italians, while the subordinate groups are the Blacks and Puerto Ricans. If the status designations are viewed in this manner, a problem encountered is that of passing over the aspect of ethnic intergroup relations that occurs between groups within the two major status designations. That is, we tend to gloss over the ethnic intergroup responses between Irish and Italians, or between Puerto Ricans and Blacks. There is no way to avoid this; the nature of *Beyond the Melting Pot* is very different from the other works we have dealt with in this book. It is highly descriptive, and it confines itself to inter-ethnic relations in the New York City of the 1960's, a time when ethnic relations in the U.S. were evolving into a highly complex scheme. Nevertheless, it does attempt to interpret the major patterns that are occurring between ethnic groups and generalize these patterns to apply to all major urban areas in the United States. As is the case with the previous three theorists, there is a noticeable split between theory and ideology.

Assuming that the dominant ethnic status culture in New York City comprises the Jews, Irish, and the Italians, the description of their response to the subordinate ethnic groups are found to be very mixed depending on the issues surrounding particular events, the relation of one event to another, the particular ethnic group within the dominant block that is making the response, and the political ideology of that segment of this group. This is the complex nature of New York City's social, political, and economic relations that Glazer and Moynihan are attempting to clarify. In this context, the responses which they describe range from acceptance to indifference to rejection. It is much easier to decipher their ideological posture toward questions of the type that should be made by the dominant ethnic group. To this extent they believe it should be *acceptance.* It becomes again a much more intricate issue when trying to categorize the type of acceptance that they propose. This can be drawn out from their policy suggestions.

Glazer and Moynihan have described the response of the subordinate ethnic status groups to their position in the power matrix. In the first edition of *Beyond the Melting Pot,* they described the response of the Blacks as being somewhere between assimilation and ethnic group status. By the second edition, they described it to be somewhere between ethnic group status and separation. The political activity, legal action, mass protest, and violent demonstrations of the

1960's typified a response of *resistance* by Black groups in the United States to their status designation. The next state after this type of resistance is one of separation – typified by *avoidance* – a response which Glazer and Moynihan express as being disastrous and sure to guarantee a substantial measure of misery and unhappiness. The response which Glazer and Moynihan believe offers the best alternative for Black and Puerto Rican groups is the ethnic pattern. The work of incorporating these groups into a common society – economically, culturally, socially, politically – must be pushed as hard as possible. Thus the desired response by both dominant and subordinate groups is one of *acceptance.*

The recognition of the status designation among ethnic groups in the United States played a major role in Femminella's theory of American ethnicity. It is the structural relationship between the host ethnic group and the immigrant newcomer, *and* between the newly integrated ethnic and the immigrant newcomer, that is the central focus of his analysis of ethnic intergroup relations in the United States. Structural aspects are very important, for in this theory, the social conflict that occurs between ethnic groups is interpreted as social and economic, rather than cultural. Previous theories of ethnicity have stressed the primacy of culture in the conflict between ethnic groups, which was at the expense of factors concerning social structure. One of the processes which both groups – dominant and subordinate – have in common, according to this theory, is assimilation. Both assimilate to the emerging culture of the United States. That is, assimilation is described as a two-way process, toward the core culture and also toward the ethnic sub-culture.

Femminella bases his interpretation of ethnic intergroup response on the historical data that is available about the experiences of each ethnic group in the United States. He describes the reaction of the dominant ethnic status culture by utilizing a conflict perspective. He specifically makes use of the notion of the dialectic. The response toward the subordinate ethnic newcomer is described as *rejection.* Included in this response are a set of processes such as territorial defensiveness, spurning of the newcomer, and engendering of a dialectical opposite – the "estranged intruder." Beyond this, Femminella describes the process by which the power elite encourages status anxiety between the newly integrated ethnic and the newcomer. This is done by regulated tokenism and prudent co-option. Both of these actions encourage racial and ethnic conflict.

The response of the subordinate ethnic newcomer to his status designation in the nation can be best typified according to Femminella as being largely one of *acceptance* and partly one of *resistance.* The subordinate ethnic newcomers, because of their status positions in the new nation, and, due to the response they receive from the dominant ethnic group, remain close to one another. They do this for defensive purposes and for succor. At the same time, they work vary hard to emulate the success of the native. Their thinking is that by doing acting in this manner, they will thereby be accepted. As a group, they end up working very hard for less money and in the process, they become rejected by those whose jobs they took, or as the case may be, they were given. Thus, the conflict between subordinate ethnic groups becomes perpetuated. At times they resist: "no immigrant has ever totally submitted."

Groups have collided socially and culturally in the United States, and the conflict has gone on over generations. Out of the heat of the conflict, a new fusion has resulted. It is an impact integration, a result very different from that described in any of the previous four theories. The final synthesis is one that unites but does not homogenize.

Comparative Mode B
Ethnic Intergroup Process Assertions

Another way to compare our theories of American ethnicity is to pose them against the two theoretical models of sociological theory, functionalism and conflict theory. This is done by pairing off a series of statements about the nature of the assertions and assumptions of functionalism and conflict theory and then by examining the nature of the assertions and assumptions of each theorist of American ethnicity. Each pair of statements, one concerning functionalism and the other concerning conflict theory, will emphasize social elements and issues such as culture, social structure, power, institutions, inequality, change, holism, and conflict. The basic orientation toward society of each theorist will also be posited. Before beginning, it is important to point out that these two theoretical models are not absolutes which exist totally outside each other. Social theories rarely conform to the parameters of either one or the other. Most of the theories of American ethnicity contain certain elements of both models. Therefore, it is more useful and proper to view them as opposites on a continuum rather than as totally enclosed, self-sustaining systems. Nevertheless, although social theories do contain certain elements of each model, they usually have a major orientation deriving from either functionalism or conflict theory.

The following set of ten comparative elements will serve as a guide for analysis. Within the discussion of the five American ethnicity theorists, the specific Roman numeral of the appropriate comparative element will be attached as it pertains to our analysis.

Ten Comparative Elements of Sociological Inquiry[9]

I. The functionalist model emphasizes those aspects of society that are harmonious.
The conflict model emphasizes those disruptive aspects of society.

II. Functionalism focuses on stability and continuity. Conflict focuses on what produces change and alteration.

III. Functionalists view society as a social system with various needs of its own which must be met if the needs and desires of its members are to be met.
Conflict theorists tend to view society as the setting within which various struggles take place.

IV. When studying social interaction (ethnic intergroup relations) – Functionalists ask – what function it serves?
Conflict theorists ask – for whom is it functional?

V. Functionalists place much importance on maintaining the status quo.
Conflict theorists place much emphasis on social change.

VI. The functionalists analyze power by looking at how it is diffused throughout society.
The conflict theorists tend to focus on the groups that control the big decisions.

VII. For the functionalists, the whole of society is thought to be understood by examining the parts.
The conflict theorists look for very large social units and attempt to explain the parts as a reflection of the characteristics of the whole.

VIII. Functionalists emphasize the mutuality of interests among different groups in society.
The conflict theorists emphasize the inherent conflict of interests

among different groups in society.

IX. Functionalists emphasize the primacy of culture.
Conflict theorists emphasize the primacy of social structure.

X. Functionalists see culture as shaping social structure.
Conflict theorists see social structure as shaping culture.

Frederick Jackson Turner

In examining the major assertions concerning the processes that occur when people of different ethnic groups come together, it can be found that Turner has emphasized both the harmonious and disruptive aspects of this societal process. However, on examining these assertions as exemplifying a process – a series of stages – that occurs between ethnic groups, *and,* when viewing this process against the background of Turner's postulates and domain assumptions, it becomes clear that the major emphasis of this theory is on the aspects of society that are harmonious, stable, and well organized.

There is a progression found within Turner's process assertions that begins as he notes the conditions of diversity and heterogeneity that exist among the American population. The differences of social ideals and social interests possessed by the various ethnic groups composing American society are described along with the nature of the encounter that occurs between these groups. That encounter is typified as conflictual; it is an event characterized by such reactions as territoriality and resistance. From all historical evidence, this was in fact the case. What becomes important to note at this point is the manner in which Turner deals with this conflict. From this point in his progression of process assertions, he minimizes that aspect of conflict which he so vividly described. This occurs as he brings his postulates and domain assumptions to bear on his interpretation of the rest of the process of ethnic intergroup relations. Society is organic and it is evolutionary. Differentiation of its parts assures a developmental evolution of advance and progress. At the same time Turner introduces the core values of competion and individualism into the process that now begins to emphasize "mutual education," and "a giving and taking" between groups. A certain amount of ideological content and metaphorical expression follows as the notions of crucible, fusion, and composite nationality become essential elements of the process. It is through democracy and cooperation and other forms of conjunction of mutual interest that the end product – order and unity – are achieved (VIII). The assimilation of newcomers that occurs via frontier building is "straight line" assimilation with the result being a composite nationality of Americans.

There is unity and consensus of belief and motive because the needs of frontier America must be met; in this way the needs of its individual members can be met (III). Rather than viewing the frontier as a place where various struggles were taking place, Turner characterizes it as a place where Americans of different backgrounds cooperated with one another to serve the nation, not individual groups in the nation (IV). The power of the nation was diffused throughout the political institutions and the frontiersman could exert his individualism to establish local government founded on the principles of democracy (VI). The whole of the nation is to be understood by examining its parts – the sections (VII). Sectionalism, like functionalism, suggests that the whole of society is to be understood by examining the role which the parts play in maintaining the system.

The parts of Turner's theory of American ethnicity form a series of developmental stages in which disruptive aspects of ethnic societal processes become gradually minimized. They finally give way to a state of order, stability, continuity, and harmony. Underlying the entire process is a set of postulates and assumptions deriving from the doctrines of organicism and evolutionism; both of which have guided Turner's interpretation of ethnic intergroup relations.

Henry Pratt Fairchild

More than any other theorist examined in this study, Fairchild has placed an extraordinary amount of emphasis on the harmonious aspects of society. He, like Turner, anchors his theory in organicism and evolutionism, but unlike Turner, Fairchild omits the actual delineation of the interaction of newcomer and host except to describe the racial and national characteristics of these groups. The closest he comes to discussing interaction is through his speculative analysis of the effect of the "mixing of different peoples" on group unity in the United States. The organic analogy, and a theory of human nature derived from biological, sociological, and anthropological principles, provide Fairchild with the elements he needs to emphasize the centrality of group unity, stability and order. His modification of the organic analogy yields a metabolic analogy that he likens to ethnic intergroup processes in the United States; one he calls social assimilation. This is a strict, one-way, straight line assimilation in which only the newcomer changes, while the host group maintains its distinct quality in order to preserve national harmony and equilibrium (I, II). Each process assertion is clearly directed at the goal of national unity. This is not to suggest that Fairchild does not emphasize the disruptive aspects of society. He believes there is a dangerously disruptive aspect – the new menace; these are the immigrants of southern and eastern Europe. However, his emphasis in taking note of this menace is for the purpose of stressing the importance of maintaining the status quo – the Nordic and Aryan races (V). Change in this dominant group would not be in the interest of the organism – the United States. This organism is a social system with various needs of its own that must be met if the needs and desires of its members are to be met (III). Among these needs are racial and national purity, a condition accomplished by the exclusion of foreigners.

Fairchild's ideology helps him to choose those assumptions about nature that will build and support his analysis of racial and national mixing. A powerful domain assumption that he brings to bear in his analysis is that men are exactly like plants and animals with respect to the dynamics of breeding and reproducing. As with functionalism, Turner's orientation to understanding the whole society is by examing the parts; it is an organic analysis (VII). Finally, looking at the way in which Fairchild deals with culture and social structure, it is not surprising that his emphasis is on the primacy of culture (IX). His extensive exposition of the complexities of nationality bear this out. The problem of immigration he interprets largely to be one of the mixing of nationalities and the effect it will have on the social structure of the nation. He warns about the effect of culture on the shaping of social structure (X).

Fairchild's theory of American ethnicity places much stress on the question of what holds societies together. His metabolic analogy applied to ethnic intergroup relations legitimizes the existence of the Americanization movement, and immigration quotas aimed at the restriction of immigrants to the United States. Moreover, he suggests that these two structures serve important functions in American society. His emphasis is more toward the functions it serves for society rather than for whom in society it best functions.

Horace Kallen

Horace Kallen's theory of American ethnicity puts forward the notion that the United States can achieve social harmony through diversity. Unlike the theories of Turner and Fairchild, this one asserts that differences in the ethnic composition of the country do not have to be abolished by a type of metabolic social assimilation or by fusion in a crucible. Nevertheless, the end product of Kallen's ethnic intergroup process is a harmony and unification that minimizes and occurs without unbiquitous social conflict (I). Unity through stability has been the theme of these last three theories. In Kallen's case it is also through continuity.

Kallen's theory places an emphasis on preserving the ethnic distinctions among groups in the United States. He explains these distinctions to be a function of inheritance and heredity. The focus is clearly placed on the continuity of these two factors in society (II). This continuity becomes actualized within the individuals of each ethnic group; it comprises the psychological state Kallen refers to as like-mindedness. This condition of like-mindedness and its counterpart, group consciousness, are two factors which can be seen as emphasizing the consensual nature of societies; that societies are held together by the consensus among its members. Kallen's notion that all ethnic groups in the United States are hyphenated Americans, that they each are free according to the principles of liberty in this country to practice their own unique culture, (and that which makes all groups equal is their right to culture, a right safeguarded by democracy), all emphasize the mutuality of interests among these different groups in society (VIII). The disruptive aspects of society, particularly the reality of economic struggle between ethnic groups, is asserted by Kallen as part of the process of ethnic relations. However, just as Turner described certain conflictual elements as part of a larger set of ethnic intergroup processes, Kallen does the same. He describes economic struggles as occurring only in the first phase by which an immigrant newcomer becomes Americanized. His next three phases are marked by a development toward status consciousness and distinction. Another similarity between Fairchild, Turner, and Kallen is that for each, the whole of society is thought to be understood by examining its parts; in Turner's case it was the section; in Fairchild's case it was the races and nationalities; and in Kallen's case, it is culture (VIII).

Concerning the primacy of and the relation between culture and social structure, Kallen's position seems to lie somewhere in between a functionalist and social conflict perspective. While he does stress the primacy of culture, he does not totally ignore social structure. He has succinctly described the economic exploitation of the immigrant newcomer by the dominant Anglo-American. His awareness of the structure of the relations of production in the urban areas of America is clearly evident. So, for Kallen, social structure is an important element of consideration, yet, whether it supercedes his emphasis on the primacy of culture is questionable. The doctrine of cultural pluralism is the central component in Kallen's theory and this would surely have immense repercussions for the social structure of the United States. The extent of these repercussions, however, is not analyzed by Kallen. The most important thing is that of the right of groups to retain and perfect the differences between them. This will contribute to the development of culture in the United States. Among his domain assumptions are that human nature and human institutions are naturally pluralistic. More important, economic divisions do not abolish ethnic lines, and, ethnicity supercedes class as a factor in most societal relations. Thus, there does seem to be an emphasis on the primacy of culture with the suggestion that the developing culture of the United States will shape its social structure more than the reverse.

Glazer and Moynihan

Of the theories we have so far examined, this one leans more toward the conflict model than the previous three, although in essence it is in many ways still an equilibrium theory. The emerging culture theory of Glazer and Moynihan, like other versions of the emerging culture theory, appeared as social scientists began refining their notions about assimilation in the United States.[63] This group of social scientists, Glazer and Moynihan included, were aware of the work of the previous three theorists examined in this book. They attempted to move aside from the ideological content of these theories and particularly examine the explanatory content. They looked at what was happening in America and saw aspects of the melting pot, cultural pluralism, and Anglo-conformity all occurring simultaneously. Newcomers were conforming to the Anglo ways, e.g., speaking English. There were continuities of different cultural forms in cultural pluralism. Finally,

Americans were indeed a new group with a mixture of traits, i.e., melting pot. The new notion that the emerging culture theorists, Glazer and Moynihan developed is that with every new wave of immigrants beyond the "population threshold," the culture of the United States emerged a little different. Its values were altered and its norms were transformed. The view is of a dynamic United States constantly in flux (II). This view of change reflects very closely the conflict model. There is also an alignment with the conflict model in Glazer's and Moynihan's position that cultural mutations occur as structural adjustments take place; social structure is viewed as shaping culture (X, IX). This is the first of the theories to take this position. The assertion that ethnicity is a new social form and that there is a critical tendency in the national ethos to structure groups, reaffirms this.

Up to this point, many of the elements of Glazer's and Moynihan's theory of American ethnicity have been aligned with the conflict theory model. There are, however, some major exceptions. This theory is also an equilibrium theory in the way it deals with the key process of ethnic intergroup conflict. One of their domain assumptions is that group conflicts resolve as ethnic groups are recreated and identities change. There is a tendency to de-emphasize the disruptive aspects and to search for an interpretation that emphasizes the harmonious (I). In line with this, Glazer and Moynihan have spent a significant amount of time trying to answer the question – what holds ethnic groups and societies together? The question of what pulls them apart receives less emphasis.

There are other ways that their theory can be seen as a conflict theory. For instance, it emphasizes the inherent conflict of interest among different groups in society rather than the mutuality of interests (VIII). Ethnic groups in New York City are a conglomeration of different interest groups, each vying for power with the others. In the analysis of this situation in New York City, the focus is more on the groups that control the big decisions than on the idea that power is widely diffused (VI). There are relations of dominance and subordination between Jews, Italians, Irish, Blacks, and Puerto Ricans within various societal arenas. Within each arena, whether it be political, social, or economic, there are various struggles taking place. This perspective also reflects a conflict model stance (III).

It becomes clear that Glazer and Moynihan exhibit a posture

more in line with conflict theory than that of any of the previous theorists examined. The only strong leanings toward functionalism that are exhibited by Glazer and Moynihan are, first, their handling of conflict – dealing with it as functional for institutional relations rather than as functional for a particular group; second, the fact that this theory falls short of aligning itself with the conflict model in its interpretation of assimilation. Although it goes beyond the previous theories by noting the actual persistence of ethnicity and ethnic identity over three generations, it stops at the suggestion of a non-linear pattern of assimilation and does not explore the implications of the reality of such a process. That is, while the theory makes it clear that newcomer ethnics have not over time become totally assimilated, they fail to describe what this has meant for the character of ethnic intergroup relations except by saying that American culture is an emerging culture. The nature of the connection of patterns of dominance and subordination to this process of an emerging culture is not explored.

Francis Xavier Femminella

Femminella's theory of impact-integration picks up on the void left by the emerging culture theory. The emerging culture theory had forced a reconsideration of the straight-line idea of assimilation. It described the persistence of ethnic identity over three generations and was led to interpret the character of American society as an emerging culture constantly changing and in flux. Femminella has followed up on the implicit suggestion in this analysis that assimilation is actually a two-way process. For ethnic identity persists in all groups, and if cultural mutations occur as a result of the structural adjustments which take place in American society, then no group, even the dominant ethnic status culture, can avoid some type of assimilation into the ever emerging culture of the United States. The way in which Femminella generates his theory of impact-integration is by adopting a social conflict perspective. Thus, the impact-integration theory is very firmly aligned with the conflict mode, more so than any of the four other theories.

Femminella develops his theory by focusing on the conflict aspect of ethnic intergroup relations in the United States. By looking at the response of the host ethnic group to the immigrant newcomer, a new explanation unfolds. For Turner, that response was acceptance through the key process of cooperation. For Robert E. Park the response was acceptance through the key process of competition. For Femminella the history of the relations of host ethnics and immigrant newcomers in this country is characterized by the rejection response of the host culture. The key processes include abuse, degradation, exploitation, and exclusion (I).

Femminella continues to utilize a conflict perspective by adopting the notion of the dialectic to explain what happens when host and newcomer "collide." The emphasis is clearly placed on the disruptive aspects of societal events (I). The response pattern of these groups toward each other stresses the inherent conflict of interest among the different ethnic groups in American society (VIII). The response pattern of the dominant host group includes territorial defensiveness, spurning of the newcomer, and engendering of their dialectical opposite – the "estranged intruder." The response pattern of the newcomer includes remaining close to one another for defense and succor, working hard to emulate the success of the native host group – thereby to be accepted, working hard for less money – and thereby being rejected by those whose jobs they took. Here, Femminella has focused on a process by which the host group perpetuates intergroup conflict through manipulation of the occupational structure, a type of intergroup conflict that is functional for the maintenance of power by the power elite (IV, VI).

Femminella describes the conflict that occurs between ethnic groups as persisting over generations, not dissipating as suggested by the theories of Turner and Kallen. The conflict does become resolved at times, yet it is a pervasive aspect of ethnic relations occurring anew as each preceding conflict is resolved (II). Ethnic groups in American society collide socially and culturally. Out of the heat of the conflict of this collision, a new fusion results. This fusion is not of the melting pot type, nor the emerging culture type; it is not assimilation, it is integration – an impacted integration. The synthesis that results unites but does not homogenize. The synthesis is a temporary state, for the entire process is dynamic and occurs again and again as new interactions form. Fused together, the nation remains a diversity. Its people are mono-cultural and multi-ethnic; they live in a cultural democracy. Heterogeneity is their right.

A major aspect of intergroup ethnic relations stressed by Femminella is that it is not a conflict of culture, but rather an economic conflict (IX, X). The primacy of social structure in ethnic relations is highly emphasized. He describes the status anxiety that is encouraged by the power elite between newly integrated ethnics and the recently arrived ethnic newcomer. The methods used by the power elite to encourage race and ethnic conflict include regulated tokenism and prudent co-option. The result – institutional racism – helps to maintain the American class system.

Assumptions in this theory which resonate well with the conflict model are that assimilation has two directions – toward the host society and toward the culture of the newcomer; that immigrants never wanted to totally assimilate – nor could they, because of an ego-identity that was formed by many ethnic related processes; that notions about human nature and culture in the United States are infused with United Statesian ideology; and that man is a tension-plagued, tension-synthesizing animal, a nature out of which social forms are constantly being recreated.

Summary

This book has identified five major theories of American ethnicity and has analyzed them, both individually and comparatively, based upon two elements – process assertions and domain assumptions. Speculation concerning the relationship between domain assumptions, theory, ideology, and the dual orientation of contemporary macro sociological theory was systematically discussed. A broad overview of the theories of American ethnicity was presented in which five organizing models were posited to facilitate categorization of these theories. A methodology was then constructed to help achieve the objective. Five theorists of American ethnicity were chosen, one from each of the models presented in Chapter II. Each theorist's biography, major influences, and major works were briefly described. The central work comprising each theory of American ethnicity was examined in detail and each theory of American ethnicity, abstracted from major works, was exposed in concise form and followed by an indentification and analysis of the process assertions and the domain assumptions. The comparative analysis was then performed in order to identify and analyze the difference in process assertions and domain assumptions between the theories and to speculate concerning the relationship between these two elements within each of the theories.

The comparative analysis was accomplished in two ways: first, by constructing "an ethnic intergroup response typology," and using it as a basis for comparison; and, second, by positing ten sets of propositions that differentiate between the dual orientation of contemporary macro sociological theory and utilizing them as a basis for comparison in order to check the alignment of the theories of American ethnicity with the functionalist and conflict models.

The results of the analysis seem to suggest that:

1. The theories of Frederick Jackson Turner, Henry Pratt Fairchild, and Horace Kallen are more closely aligned, in terms of their process assertions and domain assumptions, with the major orientation of sociological functionalism than they are with sociological conflict theory.
2. The theory of Nathan Glazer and Daniel Patrick Moynihan is closely aligned with the conflict model because of its theoretical emphasis on change, the primacy of social structure, intergroup conflicts of interest, and power struggles. Yet, this theory exhibits a posture that leans toward functionalism because of its conception of the assimilation process, its emphasis on group harmony, and its preoccupation with the question of what holds societies together.
3. The theory of Francis Xavier Femminella is more closely aligned with the theoretical orientation of sociological conflict theory than any of the previous four theories of American ethnicity.
4. The relationship between the process assertions and domain assumptions in each of the theories is one of "resonance." That is, there is an intensification of the meaning of the process assertions when they are conjoined with a set of domain assumptions that emphasize elements of the same sociological orientation. This has been the case throughout.

The four conclusions have been presupposed by the notion that each theory of American ethnicity has certain points of alignment with both functionalism and conflict theory, and moreover that each theory has a major overall orientation to one *or* the other. It has also been possible to speculate concerning the relationship between domain assumptions, theory, and ideology in the theories of American ethnicity. To this extent it is possible to suggest that:

1. All theories of American ethnicity have an ideological component.

2. This ideological component is, in part, responsible for generating the domain assumptions that become infused into the development of the theory at the sub-structural level.
3. The locating of the domain assumptions may also be done by inferring them from the process assertions.

Notes

1. See, for instance, Paul Meadows, "Situational Theory: Perspective Construction of Social Reality", a paper read at the American Sociological Convention, Montreal, 1974.
2. See, for instance, Randall Collins, *Conflict Sociology: Toward an Explanatory Science* (1975) in which he describes the essentiality of and the way in which sociological analysis on both micro-level and macro-level can and must be integrated.
3. See, for instance, Paul Meadows, "Insiders and Outsiders, Toward a Theory of Overseas Cultural Groups", *Social Forces* 46, 1 (September) 61–70.
4. Francis X. Femminella, "Societal Ramifications of Ethnicity in the Suburbs", 1979.
5. George Ritzer, *Sociology: Experiencing a Changing Society,* Boston: Allyn Bacon, 1979, p. 338–340.
6. Horace Kallen, *Culture and Democracy in the United States,* p. 125.
7. Ibid., pp. 114–115.
8. See, for instance, Kallen, pp. 108–114.
9. William Chambliss, *Sociological Readings in the Conflict Perspective.* Reading, Massachusetts: Addison-Wesley, 1973, pp. 4–5.

IX Toward a Theory of Critical Pluralism

A book of this size naturally leads into many related areas of thought and consideration, some new and some not so new. While new questions and issues have been generated by this work, still others remain as part of the intellectual domain of the sociology of American ethnicity. Concerning the latter, this book has at the very least, moved in the direction where new answers may be found. At most, it has opened new ways of viewing transformation patterns of the central concepts and ideas in the study of American ethnicity.

Any major study in the sociology of American ethnicity must remain aware of a series of questions. Why do some groups, in part or in whole, seem to disappear? Is it possible that many ethnic groups have fully assimilated? Why have some assimilated more than others? What specific factors contribute to holding ethnic groups together or pulling them apart? Finally, what form will American ethnicity take on in the future?

The subject of identity is a critical concern in the study of American ethnicity. It is here that one runs into the problems of reconciling the pluralism of American society with the formation of the unified identities of its members. Multiple pluralisms create multiple identities. In this context, one must ask – Do ethnic identities muddle other identities (e.g., class, power, religion, etc.)? What are the dynamics involved in forming a unified identity in the context of multiple pluralisms? Was religion and the triple melting pot dismissed too early as an important aspect of identity? A related question is – Why have some of our authors chosen to ignore a whole range of issues, while others have not?

This last question leads directly into the problem concerning the time and space coordinates of each theorist. Historical context cannot be ignored and even though it is outside the scope of this study to do an in-depth analysis of this area, a brief consideration of the evolution of the ideas concerning American ethnicity can be useful. In this regard, one must ask what patterns and processes seem to have emerged over time not only in the social reality of American society with regard to ethnicity, but also in the transformation of ideas reflected in these historical processes. Is there any significant pattern that should be seized upon here? Moreover, if culture and social structure are used as coordinating points, does this help to shed light on any process?

The above series of inquiries comprise some of the elements of the intellectual domain of the sociology of American ethnicity, and they also include some of the thoughts generated from a book such as this. It is possible to group these concerns into three categories of analysis. They are (a) historical context, (b) multiple pluralisms, and, (c) future forms of American ethnicity. Each can be taken in turn.

The theories produced by each theorist were formulated in the midst of many socio-cultural forces. Some of these had a significant influence on the shaping of these theories. For instance, each perceived the problem of social order very differently. This fact in turn has influenced the social theory that was generated, the way social order was perceived and the values placed on different types within historical contexts. Also, ethnicity as some specific pluralism in American society has always been positioned among many other sets of pluralisms. Moreover, these sets of multiple pluralisms have at time vyed for hegemony over each other. Out of the political and economic struggles that have occurred, certain types of structural alignments between pluralisms have often became reflected in emergent social theories. Much overlapping takes place, the end result often being that one pluralism will subsume the others. In terms of American culture, it seems as if ethnicity has taken over this position. Its persistence over time, its shifting struggle with other pluralisms, its dominant position in American community life, and its increasingly central role in international affairs all attest to this fact.

When the historical pattern of ideas is traced, there is a significant pattern that should be picked up. Through the theories of Turner, Fairchild, Kallen, Glazer and Moynihan, and Femminella, emerges an historical dialectic. There is a movement from a pole of assimilation in the writings and times of Turner and Fairchild to a pole of pluralism in the writings of Kallen and Glazer and Moynihan. The resulting synthesis which grows out of this dialectical process is a form of thought exemplified in the work of Femminella, namely "critical pluralism."

This dialectical process can also be found by taking note of the historical shift from the primacy of culture to the primacy of social structure in explaining social phenomena and events. This classical dichotomy between culture and social structure is sometimes best understood through the contrasting perspectives of Parsons and Marx on this subject. In this respect Parsons supports the notion that it is culture which shapes the social system via the process of institutionalization. Marx, on the other hand, sees culture as a type of "after the fact" creation designed to support existing social structures. A similar shift is evident in the historical unfolding of the theories of American ethnicity. This was made clear in Chapter VIII. Critical pluralism, as presented by Femminella, emphasizes the primacy of social structure over culture. However, it goes further. It helps us to move beyond this point by providing a better understanding of the primacy problem between culture and social structure. By adopting the use of the concept of dominant ethnic status culture and subordinate ethnic status culture, it is possible to pinpoint the following ideas. Culture does shape social structure, however, in this case it is the dominant ethnic status culture to which we are referring. Conversely, social structure (as formed by the dominant ethnic status culture) does shape culture; in this case referring to the subordinate ethnic status culture. A useful framework is provided here for analyzing not only ethnic status cultures in American society, but also the situation of multiple pluralism that is so common within American society and culture. In this respect, more research can provide useful information.

Critical pluralism recognizes the assimilative, pluralistic, and integrative patterns that have been and still are characteristic of American society. It finds, within each American, remnants of all three processes. It is at this point that the study of the central sociological problem of American society itself comes to focus on identity. Americans have been consistently preoccupied with attempting to define themselves, and critical pluralism's emphasis on identity has opened up new areas and provided an alternative way of viewing the character of American society. The multiple identities that Americans possess and grapple with every day present them with a unique dilemma. Ethnicity occupies a key position in this dilemma of identity structure. One is forced to consider the probability that the non-disappearance of aspects of ethnicity may well be rooted in deeper psychological processes of which identity is a part. From this point it would become important to try to explain why certain dimensions of identity take precedence over others at particular times and places. Again, these are the paths which new research must follow. Ethnicity is a dynamic element. It changes as part of the total change in the character structure and of the accompanying social structure. It does, however, remain a constant in both these areas. It is difficult to describe the form that American ethnicity will take in the future except to say that it is an indispensable element in the complex equation of American culture and social structure. No American community has yet been fully explained without it.

Bibliography

Adamic, Louis. *My America.* New York: Harper and Row, 1938.

Aron, Raymond. *Main Currents in Sociological Thought.* 2 vols. New York: Basic Books, 1965.

Aronson, Dan R. "Ethnicity as a Culture System," in Frances Henry (ed.), *Ethnicity in the Americas.* Mouton Publishers: The Hague, Paris. 1976.

Banks, James A. *Multiethnic Education: Practices and Promises.* Bloomington, Indiana: Phi Delta Kappa Educational Foundation, 1977.

——. "Multiethnic Education Across Cultures: United States, Mexico, Puerto Rico, France, and Great Britain," in *Social Education* 42 (March 1978): 177–185.

——. "Ethnicity and Schooling: Implications for Dissemination." 1978. Unpublished.

——. "Ethnicity in Contemporary American Society: Toward the Development of a Typology," in *Ethnicity* V5, 238–251.

Bahr, Howard M., Bruce A. Chadwick, and Joseph H. Stauss. *American Ethnicity.* Lexington, Mass.: Heath, 1979

Barth, Frederick. *Ethnic Groups and Boundaries: The Social Organization of Cultural Difference.* Boston: Little, Brown and Co., 1969.

Bell, Daniel. "Ethnicity and Social Change." In *Ethnicity: Theory and Experience.* Edited by N. Glazer and D.P. Moynihan. Cambridge: Harvard University, 1975.

Bennett, James D. *Frederick Jackson Turner.* Boston: Tyayne, 1975.

Berkson, Issac B. *Theories of Assimilation.* New York: Columbia University, 1920.

Bernstein, Richard J. *The Restructuring of Social and Political Theory.* New York: Harcourt, Brace and Javonovitch, 1976.

Blalock, Hubert M. *Toward A Theory of Minority Group Relations.* New York: John Wiley and Sons, 1967.

——. and Paul H Wilken. *Intergroup Processes: A Micro-Macro Perspective.*

Calhouln Stan. *Ethnicity and Ego-Identity, A Study of Afro-Americans.* Dissentation proposal State University of New York at Albany, 1976.

Chambliss, William. *Sociological Readings in the Conflict Perspective.* Reading, Mass.: Addison-Wesley, 1973.

Church, Robert, *Education in the United States, An Interpretative History.* New York: Free Press, 1976.

Collins, Randall. "Two Approaches to Comparative Politics." In *State and Society: A Reader in Comparative Political Sociology.* Edited by R. Bendix, et. al., Boston: Little, Brown and Co., 1968.

——. *Conflict Sociology: Toward an Explanatory Science.* New York: Academic Press, 1975.

Comte, Auguste. *A General View of Positivism.* Translated by John H. Bridges. New York: Spieler, 1975.

Coser, Lewis. *The Functions of Social Conflict.* New York: Free Press, 1965.

Cubberly, Ellwood P. *Changing Conceptions of Education.* Boston: Houghton and Mifflin, 1909.

Curti, Merle. "Frederick Jackson Turner." In *Wisconsin Witness to Frederick Jackson Turner.* Compiled by O. Lawrence Burnette. Madison, 1961.

Davie, Maurice R. *World Immigration.* New York: Houghton Mifflin Co., 1936.

Davis, Allen F. and Haller, Mark H. *Peoples of Philadelphia: A History of Ethnic Groups and Lower Class Life,* 1790–1940. Temple University Press, 1973.

Dahrendorf, Ralf. "Toward a Theory of Social Conflict." *Journal of Peace and Conflict Resolution.* XI, 1958.

Devereux, George. "Ethnic Identity: Its Logical Functions and Dysfunctions." In *Ethnic Identity.* Edited by De Vos and Romanucci-Ross. Palo Alto, CA: Mayfield, 1975.

Drachsler, Julius. *Democracy and Assimilation: The Blending of Immigrant Heritages in America.* New York: Macmillan, 1920.

Durkeim, Emile. *The Rules of Sociological Method.* New York: Free Press, 1964.

Eisenstadt, S. N. *The Forms of Sociology: Paradigms and Crises.* New York: Wiley, 1976.

Fairchild, Henry Pratt. *Greek Immigration to the United States.* New York: Yale University Press, 1911.

——. *Immigration: A World Movement and its American Significance.* New York, 1913.

——. *Outline of Applied Sociology.* New York: Macmillan, 1916.
——. *The Melting Pot Mistake.* Boston: Little, Brown and Co., 1926.
——. *Immigrant Backrounds* (editor). New York: John Wiley and Sons, 1927.
——. *The Foundations of Social Life.* New York: John Wiley and Sons, 1927.
——. *General Sociology.* New York: John Wiley and Sons, 1934.
——. *People: The Quantity and Quality of Population.* New York: Henry Holt & Co., 1939.
——. *Race and Nationality as Factors in American Life.* New York: Arnold Press, 1947.
——. *The Prodigal Century.* New York: Philosophical Library, 1950.
——. *Versus: Reflections of a Sociologist.* New York: Philosophical Library, 1950.
Femminella, Francis X. (ed.) *Power and Class: The Italian American Experience Today.* Papers presented at the Annual Conference of the American-Italian Historical Association, New York, 1973.
——. "The Impact of Italian Migration and American Catholicism. *American Catholic Sociological Review* (Fall 1961): 233–241.
——. "The Italian-American Family: Ethnicity and Family Life." *Marriage and the Family.* M. Rarash and Alice Sourby (eds.) New York: Random House, 1970.
——. "Ethnicity and Power: Analysis of Communities." *Proceedings of the Equal Education Institute Conference.* Hartford, Conn.: University of Hartford, 1971.
——. and Joseph A. Scimecca. "Italian-Americans and Radical Politics. *American-Italian Historical Association Conference.* New York City October, 1971. Published 1973; also in Femminella, *Power and Class.*
——. "The Immigrant and the Urban Melting Pot." *Perspectives on Urban American.* M. Urofsky (ed.). New York: Doubleday Publishing Co., 1973.
——. and Jill S. Quadango. "Italian American Family Lifestyles." *Ethnic Families in America: Patterns and Variations.* Charles H. Mindel and Robert W. Haberstein (eds.) New York: Elsevier Co., 1976.

——. "Ethnic Heritage and Citizenship." Donald W. Robinson (ed.). *Selected Readings in Citizen Education.* Kansas City, MO.: U.S. Office of Education and Council of Chief State School Officers, 1976.

——. "Societal Ramifications of Ethnicity in the Suburbs," in S. La Gumina, *Ethnicity and Suburbia: The Long Island Experience.* Garden City, N.Y.: Nassau Community College, 1980.

——. "Education and Ethnicity" in *Euro-Ethnic Americans in the United States: Opportunities and Challenges,* The United States Commission on Civil Rights, Chicago, Ill., 1980.

——. With Peter Stoll. *The Immigrants Journey in America: A television series script.* Albany, N.Y., S.U.N.Y. at Albany, Educational Communications Center, 1981.

Fitzpatrick, Joseph P. *Puerto-Rican Americans.* Prentice Hall: Englewood Cliffs, New Jersey. 1971.

Francis, E.K. *Interethnic Relations.* New York: Elsevier, 1976.

Gans, Herbert. *The Urban Villagers. New York: The Free Press, 1962.*

——. *The Levittowness.* New York: The Free Press, 1967.

Geschwender, James A. *Racial Stratification in America,* Dubuque, IA: William C. Brown Company, 1978.

Glazer, Nathan. *Beyond the Melting Pot,* with Daniel P. Moynihan. Cambridge: MIT Press, 1970.

——. *Remembering the Answers: Essays on the American Student Revolt.* New York: Basic Books, 1970.

——. *The Poor: A Culture of Poverty or a Poverty of Culture.* Philadelphia: Temple University, 1971.

——. *Affirmative Discrimination: Ethnic Inequality and Public Policy.* New York: Basic Books, 1975.

——. *Ethnicity: Theory and Experience.* with Daniel Moynihan. Cambridge: Harvard University Press, 1975.

——. *Cities in Trouble,* (edited). Chicago: Quadrangle Books, 1970.

——. *The Social Basis of American Communism.* New York: Harcourt Brace, 1961.

Gordon, Milton. *Assimilation in American Life.* New York: Oxford University Press, 1964.

——. "Theory of Racial and Ethnic Group Relations." In *Ethnicity: Theory and Experience.* Edited by Nathan Glazer and Daniel Moynihan.

——. *Human Nature, Class, and Ethnicity.* New York: Oxford University Press, 1978.

Gouldner, Alvin. *The Coming Crisis of Western Sociology.* New York: Avon, 1970.

Grant, Madison. *The Passing of the Great Race.* New York: Scribner, 1916.

Greeley, Andrew *Ethnicity in the United States.* New York: John Wiley, 1974.

Greer, Colin. *The Great School Legend.* New York: Basic Books, 1972.

Handin, Oscar. *The Uprooted.* Boston: Little. Brown, 1951.

Hansen, Marcus Lee. *The Immigrant in American History.* Cambridge: Harvard Press, 1940.

Hegel, Georg Wihelm Fredrich. *The Philosophy of History.* Translated by J. Sebree. New York: Dover Publications, 1956.

Herberg, Will. *Catholic-Protestant-Jew.* New York: Doubleday, 1955.

Hill, Howard C. "The Americanization Movement." *American Journal of Sociology 24 (May 1919).*

Henry, Frances. *Ethnicity in the Americas,* Mouton Publishers: The Hague, Paris. 1976.

Holloman, Regina and Arutiunov Senghei A., *Perspectives on Ethnicity.* Mouton Publishers: The Hague, Paris. 1978.

Hraba, Joseph. *American Ethnicity,* Itasca, IL: F. E. Feacock, 1979.

Isijaw, Wsevolvd. "Definitions of Ethnicity." *Ethnicity* 1, 111–124 (1974).

Jacobs, Wilbur R. *Frederick Jackson Turner's Legacy.* San Marino, CA: Huntington Library, 1965.

——. *The Historical World of Frederick Jackson Turner.* New Haven: Yale University Press, 1968.

Johnston, Barry and William Mihalo, and William C. Yoels. "On Empirically Assessing Competing Models of Ethnicity." 1978. Unpublished.

Kallen, Horace. *Culture and Democracy in the United States,* 1924. New York: Arno Press (1970).

——. *Education, The Machine and The Worker.* New York: New Republic, Inc., 1925.

——. *Individualism: An American Way of Life.* New York: Liveright, 1933.

——. *Education versus Indoctrination in the Schools.* Chicago: University of Chicago, 1934.

——. *Art and Freedom,* 1942. New York: Greenwood Press (1969).

——. *The Education of Free Men: An Essay Toward A Philosophy*

of Education for Americans. New York: Farrar Strauss, 1944.
——. *Patterns of Progress.* Freeport, New York: Books for Library Press, 1950.
——. *Culture Pluralism and the American Idea.* Philadelphia: University of Pennsylvania, 1956.
——. *Utopians at Bay.* New York: Theodor Herzl Foundation, 1958.
——. *A Study of Liberty.* Yellow Springs, Ohio: Antioch Press, 1959.
——. *American Philosophy Today and Tomorrow* (edited). Freeport, N.Y.: Books for Libraries Press, 1968.
——. *Freedom in the Modern World* (ed.). Freeport, N.Y.: Books for Libraries Press, 1969.
——. *Creativity Imagination, Logic: Meditation for the Eleventh Hour.* New York: Gorden and Breach, 1973.
Karabel, Jerome and A. H. Halsey. *Power and Ideology in Education.* New York: Oxford University Press, 1979.
Kennedy, Ruby Jo Reeves. "Single or Triple Melting Pot? Intermarriage Trends in New Haven." *American Journal of Sociology* (1944): 55–59.
Lieberson, Stanley. *A Piece of the Pie: Blacks and White Immigrants Since 1960.* University of California Press.
Litt, Edgar. *Beyond Pluralism: Ethnic Politics in America.* Glenview, Ill.: Scott, Foresman and Co., 1970.
Luhman, Reid and Stuart Gilman *Race and Ethnic Relations: The Social and Political Experience of Minority Groups.* Belmont, CA: Wadsworth, 1980.
Mannheim, Karl. *Ideology and Utopia.* London: Routlege and Kegan Paul, 1929.
McKinney, John C. *Constructive Typology and Social Theory.* New York: Meredith Publishing Co., 1966.
Marx, Karl. *The German Ideology,* with Frederich Engels. Translated by C. J. Arthur, 1979. New York: International Publications, 1945.
——. *The Grundrisse. Edited and translated by David McLellan.* New York: Harper & Row, 1971.
McClean, Timothy. *A Study of Irish-Americans in New York State.* Dissertation proposal, State University of New York at Albany, 1978.

Meadows, Paul, "Ethnicity and Human Relations" in *Southwestern Social Science Quarterly. V37 N4 (1957): 341–346.*

——. "Insiders and Outsiders: Toward a Theory of Overseas Cultural Groups" in *Social Forces.* V46 N1 (1967): 67–71.

——. "Encounters of an Ethnic Kind." 1973.

——. "Ethnic Encounters and Race Relations: A Comparative Typological Approach." 1973.

——. "Situational Theory: Perspective Constructions of Social Reality." 1974. Prepared for American Sociological Association Convention.

——. Immigration Theory: A Review of Thematic Strategies" in *The New Immigration* edited by Roy Bryce-Laporte. New York: Transaction Press, 1978.

Merton, Robert K. *Social Theory and Social Structure.* Illinois: Free Press, 1949.

——. *On Theoretical Sociology. New York: Free Press, 1967.*

Moore, Joan W. *Mexican Americans,* Prentice Hall: Englewood Cliffs, New Jersey 1970.

Moynihan, Daniel Patrick. *Beyond the Melting Pot,* with Nathan Glazer. Cambridge. Mass.: MIT Press, 1963.

——. *On Understanding Poverty: Perspectives from the Social Sciences.* New York: Basic Books, 1969.

——. *Toward a National Urban Policy.* New York: Basic Books, 1970.

——. *On Equal Opportunity,* edited with F. Mosteller. New York: Random House, 1972.

——. *Coping: Essays on the Practice of Government.* New York: Random House, 1973.

——. *Ethnicity: Theory nd Experience,* edited with Nathan Glazer. Cambridge, Mass.: Harvard University Press, 1975.

——. *A Dangerous Place,* with Suzanne Weaver. Boston: Little, Brown Co., 1978.

Mullins, Nicholas. *Theories and Theory Groups in Contemporary American Sociology.* New York: Harper & Row, 1973.

Nisbet, Robert. *The Sociological Tradition.* New York: Basic Books, 1966.

Novak, Michael. *The Rise of the Unmeltable Ethnics.* New York: Macmillan, 1972.

Paisley, W. J. "Studying Style as Deviation From Encoding Norms," in *The Analysis of Communication Content: Developments in Scientific Theories and Computer Techniques,* by G. Gerbner, O. R. Holsti, K. Krippendorff, W. J. Paisley, and P. J. Stone (edited). New York: Wiley, 1970.

Parenti, Michael. "Ethnic Politics and The Persistence of Ethnic Identification," in *American Political Science Review* 61 (September 1967): 717-726.

——. *Power and The Powerless.* New York: St. Martin's Press, 1978.

Park, Robert E. *Race and Culture.* Glencoe, Indiana: The Free Press, 1950.

Parelius, A. P. and R. J. *The Sociology of Education.* Englewood Cliffs, N.J.: Prentice-Hall, 1978.

Parsons, Talcott. *The Structure of Social Action.* 2 vol. New York: Free Press, 1968.

——. "Some Theoretical Considerations on the Nature and Trends of Ethnicity," in *Ethnicity: Theory and Experience.* by Nathan Glazer and Daniel Moynihan (editors), 1975.

——. *The Evolution of Societies.* New York: Englewood Cliffs, N.J.: Prentice-Hall, 1977.

Petersen, William. *Japanese Americans: Oppression and Success.* New York: Random House. 1971.

Peterson, William. "A General Typology of Migration." *American Sociological Review* 23:3 (June 1958).

Pettigrew, Thomas F. "Ethnicity in American Life," in *Ethnic Groups in the City,* edited by Otto Feinstein. D. C. Heath and Co., 1971.

Polenbery, Riachard. *One Nation Divisible: Class, Race and Ethnicity in the United States since 1938.* New York: Viking Press. 1980.

Rex, John. "The Plural Society in Sociological Theory. *British Journal of Sociology,* X. pp. 144–124.

Rose, Peter I. *Nation of Nations: The Ethnic Experience and The Raical Crisis.* New York: Rondam House House. 1972.

Sarna, Jonathan D. "From Immigrants to Ethnics: Toward a New Theory of Ethnicization," in *Ethnicity* 5:370–378 (1978).

Schermerhorn, Richard A. *Comparative Ethnic Relations: A Framework For Theory and Research.* New York: Random House, 1970.

Shibutani, Tomatso and Kian Kwan. *Ethnic Stratification.* New York: Macmillan, 1965.

Sjostrom, Barbara. *A study of Puerto-Rican Americans.* Dissertation proposal State University of New York at Albany, 1981.

Sowell, Thomas. *American Ethnic Groups.* (editor) The Urban Institute, 1978.

Spencer, Herbert. *Social Statics.* London: John Chapman, 1851.

Strasser, Hermann. *The Normative Structure of Sociological Theory.* London: Routledge and Kegan Paul, 1976.

Stoll, Peter. *Ethnicity and Ego-Identity: A study of German-Americans.* Doctoral Dissertation, State University of New York at Albany, 1981.

Parrillo, Vincent N. *Strangers to These Shores: Race and Ethnic Relations in the United States,* Houghton Mifflin, 1980.

Steinberg, Stephen *The Ethnic Myth: Race, Ethnicity, and Class in America,* Atheneum. 1981

Turner, Frederick Jackson. *The Character and Influence of Indian Trade in Wisconsin; a Study of the Trading Post as an Institution,* 1891. New York: B. Franklin, (reprint 1970).

——. *The Rise of the New West 1819–1829.* New York: Harper, 1906.

——. *The Frontier in American History.* New York: Holt and Co., 1920.

——. *The Significance of Sections in American History.* New York: Holt and Co., 1932.

——. *The United States 1830–1850: A Nation and Its Sections.* New York: H. Holt and Co., 1935.

——. *The Early Writings of Frederick Jackson Turner,* with an introduction by Filmer Mood. Freeport, N.Y.: Books for Libraries Press, 1969.

Turner, Jonathan. *The Structure of Sociological Theory,* Homewood, Ill.: The Dorsey Press, 1974.

Vincent, Joan. "The Structuring of Ethnicity," in *Human Organization.* Vol. 33, No. 4, pp. 375–379.

Wax, Murray. *Indian Americans,* Prentice-Hall: Englewood Cliffs, New Jersey. 1971.

Weber, Max. "'Objectivity' in Social Science and Social Policy," in *The Methodology of The Social Sciences.* Translated by Edward Shils and Henry Finch, 1949. New York: Free Press, 1904.

——. *The Theory of Social and Economic Organization.* New York: Oxford University Press, 1947.

——. "The Ethnic Group," in *Theories of Society*. Vol. 1 Talcott Parsons, editor. Glencoe, Ill.: The Free Press, 1961.

Williams. Robin M. *Mutual Accomadation: Ethnic Conflicts and Cooperation.* University of Minnesota Press. 1977.

Wirth, Louis. *The Ghetto.* Chicago: University of Chicago Press, 1928.

Zangwill, Israel. *The Melting Pot.* New York: Macmillan 1909 and 1917.

Zeitlin, Irving M. *Ideology and The Development of Sociological Theory.* Englewood Cliffs, N.J.: Prentice-Hall, 1968.

Index